The Serpent in the Cup

The
SERPENT in the CUP

TEMPERANCE IN AMERICAN LITERATURE

EDITED BY

David S. Reynolds AND Debra J. Rosenthal

University of Massachusetts Press
AMHERST

Copyright © 1997 by
THE UNIVERSITY OF MASSACHUSETTS PRESS
Printed in the United States of America
LC 96-53230
isbn 1-55849-081-7 (cloth); 082-5 (pbk.)
Designed by Steve Dyer
Set in Minion
Printed and bound by Braun-Brumfield, Inc.

LIBRARY OF CONGRESS CATALOGING-IN-PUBLICATION DATA
The serpent in the cup : temperance in American literature / edited by
David S. Reynolds and Debra J. Rosenthal.
p.   cm.
Includes bibliograpical references and index.
ISBN 1-55849-081-7 (cloth : alk. paper). — ISBN 1-55849-082-5 (pbk. : alk. paper)
1. American literature—History and criticism.   2. Temperance in literature.
3. Drinking of alcoholic beverages—United States—History.   4. Didactic
literature, American—History and criticism.   5. Drinking of alcoholic
beverages in literature.   6. Temperance—United States—History.
7. Alcoholism—United States—History.   8. Alcoholism in literature.
I. Reynolds, David S., 1948–   .   II. Rosenthal, Debra J., 1964–   .
PS169.T44S47   1997
810.9'355–dc21   96-53230
CIP

Contents

The Serpent in the Cup

Introduction

▶ Debra J. Rosenthal and David S. Reynolds

EVERY GENERATION ASKS ITSELF THE SAME QUESTIONS ABOUT SUB-
stance abuse: Why do we harm ourselves with addictive substances? When
does use become abuse? Where does the problem of substance abuse come
from? How can we stop it?

Although often taboo and illegal to varying degrees, addictive substances
are nonetheless central to U.S. society and culture. The trade in alcohol and
drugs influences our political structure, social relations, urban geography,
popular culture, and sense of morality. Sharing a drink symbolizes friendship,
seals business transactions, secures political ties, and livens celebratory occasions. Drug and alcohol consumption is an important rite of passage on college campuses; happy hour endures as a popular social mixer on the singles
scene; much of the advertisement industry is supported by brewers, distillers,
and tobacco companies; alcohol-related tragedies inspired such grassroots national movements as MADD (Mothers Against Drunk Drivers); and crimes
linked to substance abuse clog our court system.

While alcohol's widespread influence and historical importance is clear,
national agreement on suitable and unsuitable behavior and the regulation
of alcohol consumption is much more elusive. Religion, ethnicity, class, gender, and race have heavily determined American drinking patterns. Puritans
frowned on drunkenness; immigrants of German and Irish descent in general
drank quite heavily. Expensive liquors and spirits, because of their cost, circulated more widely among those of higher socioeconomic levels, while rotgut
whiskey drowned the sorrows of the destitute. Men drank considerably more
than women; black and white drinking patterns shifted according to historical
changes.[1] Assorted laws, differing from state to state, regulate the legal age of
the drinker and companions, the place where liquor or beer can be sold, the

time and location one can drink, as well as the type and amount of alcohol one can consume. Depending on state laws, a drinker may be able to purchase wine in a grocery store, but not if he or she is under twenty-one, and not on Sunday before noon. Similarly, depending on the jurisdiction, one can drink only at an establishment that serves food, before last call is heralded at 2:00 A.M., and only if the drink remains on the premises.

These countless and varied attempts to limit alcohol consumption signal an American ambiguity with alcohol and its influence on identity, morality, and the reach of the law into everyday lives. Early this century, the desire to restrict drinking culminated in Prohibition; the crusade to curtail imbibing was so strong that the Constitution, which assures rights and freedoms, was altered in 1919 with the Eighteenth Amendment to outlaw the sale of alcohol. This constitutionally mandated morality legislated lifestyle choice and invalidated one's personal decision to drink. Prohibition ultimately proved unsuccessful and was repealed in 1933 with the Twenty-first Amendment.

Since the founding of the thirteen colonies, alcohol and inebriation have been important to American culture and mythology. The role of drink in organizing life in the early republic was so pervasive that to condemn liquor was to denounce the very structure of early society.[2] The tavern and church stood as twin pillars of community life in the eighteenth century, suggesting townfolk's equal devotion to spirits and the Spirit. In the opening decade of the nineteenth century, according to one alarmed observer, the United States was fast becoming "*a nation of drunkards.*"[3] By 1830 the average American consumed the equivalent of over four gallons of absolute alcohol a year—an astonishing amount, especially since many liquors were adulterated by brain-ravaging additives such as lead, logwood, and tartaric acid. Alcoholic beverages were served at virtually all social gatherings. "Everybody was asked to drink," recalled the reformer Thomas Low Nichols of his youth. "There were drunken lawyers, drunken doctors, drunken members of Congress, drunkards of all classes."[4] Walt Whitman, looking back on his childhood from the perspective of old age, ruminated, "It is very hard for the present generation any how to understand the drinkingness of those years—how the 'gentlemen' of the old school used liquor: it is quite incommunicable: but I am familiar with it: saw, understood, it all as a boy."[5] In an era when election days often verged on becoming national drinking sprees and when political leaders from Senator Daniel Webster to President Franklin Pierce waged public battles with the bottle, intemperance was readily identified as a widespread problem.

By the early nineteenth century, public opinion on besottedness began to change as the moral and economic advantages of sobriety became increasingly valued. Leading up to the twentieth-century national ban on the liquor trade was a powerful movement that relied on moral suasion, not governmental intervention, to convert drinkers into abstainers. Temperance reform expanded in early nineteenth-century America as a result of the nation's long history of overindulgence in alcohol. The movement swept through the country, influencing all strata of society and convincing many to put down the bottle. This antiliquor campaign was a major avatar of American ambiguity about drinking and national eagerness to restrict the ravages of intoxication.

Because alcoholism and efforts to combat it were so pervasive in antebellum America, it is not surprising that numerous writers espoused the temperance cause or responded to its images. An immense number of temperance novels and tales were published, many of which sold well, indicating the enormous popularity and cultural significance of reform. Recognizing the capability of temperance fiction to disseminate antialcohol propaganda to large numbers of readers, the American Temperance Union voted in 1836 to endorse the use of such literature to spread its message.[6] By 1865, the National Temperance Society became a publisher of temperance fiction, thus assuring itself a public forum in the fight against intemperance.

America's literary flowering between 1835 and 1860, commonly known as the American Renaissance, produced two temperance best-sellers, George Cheever's *Deacon Giles' Distillery* and Timothy Shay Arthur's *Ten Nights in a Bar-Room*. Hawthorne wrote a popular temperance tale, "A Rill from a Town Pump," Poe chillingly described alcohol's depraved powers in "The Black Cat" and "The Cask of Amontillado," and temperance imagery made its way into various major works of the period, including *Moby-Dick, The Blithedale Romance, Uncle Tom's Cabin*, Emily Dickinson's poems, Frederick Douglass's *Narrative of the Life*, and William Wells Brown's *Clotel*. Scores of lesser-known writers produced temperance novels, stories, poems, plays, and periodicals.

The period of the American Renaissance coincided with dramatic changes in the nation's temperance movement, which originated in the 1820s with the writing of didactic tracts. Although there were many, many stories about the battle with the bottle, they mainly followed formulaic conventions. Each retelling of the same basic story ingrained American literature with temperance imagery. Often didactic, and sometimes insufferably so, temperance literature preached the values of sobriety and castigated the evils of drunkenness. The drinker in the typical story is often either an inexperienced young man who is seduced into the deceptively attractive life of drink, or a miserable father who batters his family physically and economically. In most stories, the first ill-fated taste of liquor leads inexorably to poverty and death. In contrast to the twentieth-century conception of alcoholism as a disease, nineteenth-century temperance stories understood inebriation as a sign of moral weakness and the drinker as the subject of a moral defect. As an antiliquor tract, temperance literature was meant, scripturelike, to show drunkards their sinful ways and to lead them to a life of sobriety which would herald financial and social prosperity. By swearing the temperance pledge, ex-drunkards made an oral testament to their newfound life of sobriety.

Various discourses and strategies were used by American reformers to combat intemperance. The evangelical, Washingtonian, and prohibitionist approaches to the problem used what may be termed, successively, conventional, sensational, and legalistic discourse. Conventional discourse, typified by temperance novels like *Edmund and Margaret* and by the sermons of evangelical preachers like Lyman Beecher, was relatively tame in its imagery, emphasizing the moral and physical rewards of abstinence. Stressing the medical model, Benjamin Franklin and Dr. Benjamin Rush wrote about drink's ill effects on the mind and body.

Sensational discourse was inherited from the eighteenth century and greatly intensified by the Washingtonians, a group of ex-drunkards who regularly held "experience meetings" where they revealed the details of their depraved lives before their conversion to abstinence. Full of graphic descriptions of nightmarish adventures and domestic violence, their titillating confessions drew ever more people to the movement. Washingtonian discourse was often violent and lurid in its renderings of alcohol's ravages, and people were eager to read and hear about the degeneracy and wickedness they supposedly protested. The Washingtonian phase, which started in 1840 and extended in various forms until the early 1850s, had particular relevance to the development of American literature. Few writers escaped the influence of Washingtonian temperance, which was egalitarian in spirit, imaginative in discourse, and riddled with contradictions and ambiguities that made it a fertile source of literary themes and images.

Although sensational discourse persisted into the Civil War period and beyond, it lost dominance in the mid-1850s to the legalistic discourse associated with the prohibitionist movement, which produced a series of state laws banning the sale of alcohol, laws that presaged the advent of national prohibition in 1929.

The prohibitionary rhetoric of temperance literature aligned it with conservative moral reformist efforts, such as the male purity movement, that sought to limit individuals' actions. With its emphasis on constraint and control, the antialcohol crusade's ideals opposed the national mythology of the country: the American Revolution was fought to secure individual liberty and the Declaration of Independence was composed to assure freedom of choice. Thus, the American temperance movement's tenets sometimes conflicted with foundational American identity.[7]

In some senses, this conservative climate of self-moderation through discipline, humility, and self-restraint stood in contrast to the contemporaneous progressive reform movements of suffrage and abolition. In its emphasis on mastery of the self, the temperance movement appeared traditional and conservative when compared to the liberal and society-changing ambitions of the drive to enfranchise women and blacks. Whereas temperance fiction advocated the retraction of rights, the suffrage and abolition efforts championed the expansion of rights.

At the same time, however, temperance rhetoric did not contrast entirely with the rhetoric of women's and blacks' rights. Many prominent members of the Whig Party and its successor, the Republican Party, simultaneously supported antislavery and temperance; Lincoln was the most famous example of this dual allegiance. Within abolitionist and feminist circles there were many who endorsed temperance. For abolitionists, the enslavement of southern blacks was paralleled metaphorically by the drunkard's enslavement to the bottle. For feminists, man's injustice against woman was often figured in the image of the oppressed wife, brutalized by an intemperate husband from whom she could not escape because of the legal difficulty of procuring a divorce.

Whether considered conservative or progressive, the discourses of temperance, suffrage, and abolition advanced individual autonomy and middle-class esteem. As reform movements they all aspired to overhaul society and valued respectability. Temperance and abolition literature not only presented parallel versions of enslavement, but also leaned on sensational discourse to attract attention: just as drink-related stories often reveled in describing brutal fights and violent crimes, some slave narratives stirred interest with their lurid descriptions of naked slaves being cruelly beaten. Alcohol and slavery shared other pernicious ties: in some parts of the slave trade, rum was bartered for human chattel; also, slaves were needed to harvest sugar for distillation.

While the suffrage and abolition campaigns redressed wrongs suffered by women and blacks, alcoholism disabled equally without regard to race or gender. Although the female alcoholic remained largely invisible in temperance literature, alcoholism was very much a woman's concern: beholden to her husband, a woman's security depended on having a sober and responsible spouse. Tavern culture lured intemperate husbands away from domesticity and emptied their pockets of the money their wives needed to run a home. Numerous temperance stories, many written by women, contrast the ruin and loneliness of the drunkard's family with the bliss and strength of the temperate man's family.

The temperance movement galvanized women as a political force. Such suffrage leaders as Susan B. Anthony and Elizabeth Cady Stanton, committed to overhauling women's position and rights in society, were also forceful temperance activists. One of the most powerful groups within the temperance movement was the Women's Christian Temperance Union, founded in 1874. Although not as influential as the WCTU, a woman headed the most colorful antiliquor crusade and became a folk heroine in the process. Angry at alcohol's power to destroy families and lives, Carrie Nation led a turn-of-the-century antisaloon campaign of hatchet-bearing women who chopped and smashed drinking establishments.

Even though alcoholism did not discriminate against African Americans, the temperance movement did. The temperance and abolition movements shared much the same energies, strategies, gatherings, and rhetoric, but antiliquor activists did not permit blacks to join their ranks. Blacks were forced to form their own temperance societies; black women formed an auxiliary to the WCTU. Such writers and orators as Frederick Douglass and Frances Ellen Watkins Harper espoused the importance of temperance to African Americans.

Ultimately, the battle with the bottle was a failed movement. While the suffrage and abolition causes achieved their goals, the temperance movement did not turn America into a dry republic. But the literature inspired by the temperance movement successfully converted many and made an indelible mark upon American literary history. Surprisingly, literary scholars have largely ignored this vast popular movement. The purpose of *The Serpent in the Cup: Temperance in American Literature* is to gather new scholarship by leaders in the field to probe the pervasive influence of antialcohol reform on American literature. The title of the volume alludes to two images in the epigraphs to chapters 16 and 4 of Walt Whitman's 1842 temperance novel, *Franklin Evans: or, the Inebriate*: "a stinging serpent [that] unseen, sleeps" and the warning that "within that cup there lurks a curse." Primarily emphasizing nineteenth-century literature, the volume is bookended by David Shields's essay on alcohol and temperance in the eighteenth century and by Ed O'Reilly's study of contemporary recovery narratives. As a coda, Joan Hedrick addresses pedagogical strategies for teaching about alcohol and drinking culture in a gender studies course.

David S. Shields opens the collection with his essay "The Demonization of the Tavern." Providing a historical survey of alcohol in the eighteenth century, Shields diagnoses the importance of tavern and alehouse culture to early America. As "institutions of disorder," drinking establishments brewed public opinion and action as well as political discourse. Shields also discusses the beverage and its followers that challenged drunken male society: women tea takers who attacked the tavern and its culture.

In "Black Cats and Delirium Tremens: Temperance and the American Renaissance," David S. Reynolds argues that sensational temperance rhetoric was essential to the creative output of both Whitman and Poe, though in very different ways. The temperance movement's vilification of alcohol tempted Whitman to explore grim yet titillating themes that served as rehearsals for his later exuberant poetry. Concerned more with the energetic, brazen spirit of reform than with its moral underpinnings, Whitman valued temperance themes for their creative potential. Poe, too, was influenced by the dark-temperance conventions of the Washingtonians, but he reworked their popular formulas into penetrating psychological studies of the horrors of alcohol.

Another popular narrative formula, a child's love that converts a drunken father, is the focus of Karen Sánchez-Eppler's essay "Temperance in the Bed of a Child: Incest and Social Order in Nineteenth-Century America." Reading the scenes of pedophilia and child abuse in temperance fiction as simultaneously culturally subversive and culturally conservative, Sánchez-Eppler explores the erotics of disciplinary intimacy and suggests that youthful love that redeems an intoxicated father nonetheless exploits the child's defenselessness.

Robert S. Levine discusses the conflation of temperance, slavery, and race in the first novel published by an African American. In " 'Whiskey, Blacking, and All': Temperance and Race in William Wells Brown's *Clotel*," Levine situates *Clotel* in the midst of cultural debates on liberation from bondage both to alcohol and the slavocracy system. Focusing on free blacks' aims to reclaim black bodies from slavery and from enslaving appetites for alcohol, Levine shows how Brown portrays intemperate behavior in whites and blacks, thereby destabilizing facile alignments of temperance and race.

Similarly interested in ideas of alcohol and race, John W. Crowley addresses the ideological congruence of temperance and slave narratives in his essay "Slaves to the Bottle: Gough's *Autobiography* and Douglass's *Narrative.*" Using as examples the best-known temperance tale and the most important slave narrative, which were published in the same year, Crowley suggests the influence of the prohibitionary rhetoric of the antialcohol movement on Frederick Douglass's representation of human bondage.

Although Harriet Beecher Stowe is most famous for her antislavery novel that features an unregenerate drunkard, she also treated images of drink in other works. In "Temperance, Morality, and Medicine in the Fiction of Harriet Beecher Stowe," Nicholas O. Warner argues that Stowe's medical understanding of alcoholism provided a more sympathetic view of the drunkard, thereby challenging the temperance movement's disdain for inebriates. To contextualize Stowe's literary production, Warner outlines the nineteenth-century moral-medical debate over intemperance.

Intemperance was also of great concern to the African American community. In two of her works, Frances E. W. Harper empties her narratives of racial markers, a politically astute move. In her essay "Deracialized Discourse: Temperance and Racial Ambiguity in Harper's 'The Two Offers' and *Sowing and Reaping*," Debra J. Rosenthal investigates this renunciation of racial difference and its implied normalizing of black identity, especially in light of Harper's temperance reform ambitions.

Moving to the twentieth century, John W. Crowley crowns drunkenness the modernist vice. Coming of age during Prohibition, writers of the Lost Generation rebelled against the mandates of their predecessors and drank to signify their independence and solidarity. With nods to works by London and Fitzgerald, Crowley delineates the confluence of modernism and alcoholism and the modernist sensibility that generated the formation of Alcoholics Anonymous.

The genre of A.A. recovery narratives has much in common with nineteenth-century Washingtonian meetings: alcoholics gather together to disclose personal accounts of their battles with the bottle in order to help each other achieve sobriety. The story of Bill W.'s founding of A.A. and the Twelve Step method has secured near-mythic status among followers, and Edmund O'Reilly, in "'Bill's Story': Form and Meaning in A.A. Recovery Narratives," analyzes the role of this story and the "Big Book" in establishing an indigenous American genre.

While all of the essays suggest a link between identity and alcohol consumption, Joan Hedrick makes this connection explicit in an undergraduate course she teaches at Trinity College. In her essay "Drink and Disorder in the Classroom," Hedrick discusses pedagogical strategies for teaching about the culture and institution of drinking, as well as her scheme of using the history of alcoholism and temperance to attract men to a gender studies course.

Temperance has been a leading preoccupation of Americans from colonial times to the present. In its many avatars, it stands as one of the longest-lasting and most broadly influential reform movements of all time. Today, with substance abuse an ever-increasing social concern, it behooves us to reconsider the significant body of literature that such abuse has prompted throughout American history.

Notes

1. More detailed studies of the history of American drinking and temperance include Ruth Bordin, *Woman and Temperance: The Quest for Power and Liberty, 1873–1900* (New Brunswick, NJ: Rutgers UP, 1990); Norman H. Clark, *Deliver Us from Evil: An Interpretation of American Prohibition* (New York: Norton, 1976); Jed Dannenbaum, *Drink and Disorder: Temperance Reform in Cincinnati from the Washingtonian Revival to the WCTU* (Urbana: U of Illinois P, 1984); Barbara Leslie Epstein, *The Politics of Domesticity: Women, Evangelism, and Temperance in Nineteenth-Century America* (Middletown, CT: Wesleyan UP, 1981); Joseph R. Gusfield, *Symbolic Crusade: Status Politics and the American Temperance Movement* (Urbana: U of Illinois P, 1963); Mark Edward Lender and James Kirby Martin, *Drinking in America: A History* (New York: The Free Press, 1982); W. J. Rorabaugh, *The Alcoholic Republic: An American Tradition* (New York: Oxford UP, 1979); Ian R. Tyrell, *Sobering Up: From Temperance to Prohibition in Antebellum America, 1800–1860* (Westport, CT: Greenwood P, 1979). For more information on black drinking and temperance, see Denise Herd, "Ambiguity in Black Drinking Norms: An Ethnohistorical Interpretation," in *The American Experience with Alcohol: Contrasting Cultural Perspectives*, ed. Linda A. Bennett and Genevieve M. Ames (New York: Plenum P, 1985); Jane H. Pease and William H. Pease, *They Who Would Be Free: Blacks' Search for Freedom* (New York: Atheneum, 1974), 124–26; and Donald Yacovone, "The Transformation of the Black Temperance Movement, 1827–1854: An Interpretation," *Journal of the Early Republic* 8 (Fall 1988): 281—97.
2. Tyrell, *Sobering Up*, 16.
3. *A Letter to the Mechanics of Boston, Respecting the Formation of a City Temperance Society* (Boston: Society for the Suggestion of Intemperance), 5.
4. *Forty Years of American Life* (1864; rpt., New York: Negro UP, 1967), I: 87.
5. Horace Traubel, *With Walt Whitman in Camden*, IV (1953; rpt., Carbondale: Southern Illinois UP, 1959), 486.
6. Herbert Ross Brown, *The Sentimental Novel in America, 1789–1860* (Durham, NC: Duke UP, 1940), 201–3.
7. We are indebted to Karen Sánchez-Eppler for this insight.

The Demonization of the Tavern

☙ David S. Shields

At the beginning of the eighteenth century many English-men reckoned the tavern the central institution of their culture. A joke that circulated in the West Indies during the 1710s conveys this estimation: "When first entering upon a colonial design, the first building the Spanish erect is a church; and the first building the Dutch erect is a fort. But the English, when settling anew, the first building that they erect is a tavern" (Thomas Walduck, letter to James Petiver, London, 1710; British Library). By the end of the eighteenth century, the tavern would be the center of the war of beverages and subject to attack in England and America as a site of corruption—a space where libertinism, drunkenness, lewdness, and sharping perverted public morality. This essay is a speculation about the conditions leading to the demonization of the tavern in Anglo-American culture.

First we must consider the alteration in the institution itself. At the beginning of the seventeenth century, the tavern was a gentry institution.[1] It was deemed a necessity everywhere, "for the Entertainment and Refreshment of Strangers and Travellers." While inns served the nobility and coaching trade, and alehouses and dram shops provided drink to the tramping classes and urban commoners, the tavern sated the thirsts and appetites of gentlemen and some women. It was distinctive in that it featured wine as the drink of choice, rather than ale, beer, or strong spirits. That is, the tavern vended a foreign tipple instead of home brew. In London the city's taverns were licensed through the society of vintners, not the local corporation or the state. The alehouse, not the tavern, was trouble to the peace and the object of police scrutiny. This low estimation of the alehouse is reflected in the American colonies; in Michael Wigglesworth's "The Day of Doom," the frequenters of the alehouse, not tavern-goers, were marked as logs for the burning among a lurid crew: "Murd'rers, and Men of blood, / Witches, Inchanters, and Ale-house-haunters, / beyond account there stood."[2]

But this would change by the 1680s in England. The tavern became the scene of riot, the lair of libertinism. It became the space of disruption as the result of a peculiar set of developments. The initiating development was the emergence of the coffeehouse as a rival arena in the developing public sphere. The coffeehouse, because of its liberty of conversation, became the principal political institution to disrupt the project of Restoration.[3] Charles II's attempts in 1675 to quash the political ferment in the public rooms by suppressing the coffeehouses resulted in so sharp an outcry from the citizenry that he was forced to rescind his order in a scant eleven days.[4] When the Whig opposition finally coalesced, it drew its operatives from the coffeehouse politicians. The Tory reaction in urban politics emanated from the taverns, as gangs of Tory gents dispersed from their tavern meeting places to trouble the town. Scowering— the premeditated disturbance of the peace with rakehell incivility for political purposes—broke out in the wake of the Glorious Revolution. Restoration libertinism had been displaced from the court and the theater into the tavern and street, its new political character characterized by Thomas Shadwell in his 1690 hit, *The Scowrers*.[5]

With the Glorious Revolution, the dispossessed Tories, particularly the recent graduates of the universities who saw their chances at preferment blown, gravitated to the metropolis, and there supported themselves by the one bankable skill they possessed: their ability to write. Tom Brown, Richard Ames, and their confrères were the hired penmen for the commercial print culture that flourished in London under the name Grub Street.[6] They resided (indeed some were kept under virtual house arrest by bookseller Charles Gildon) in the taverns, and a tavern-keeper, Ned Ward, was a principal member of the brotherhood.[7] Grub Street's scabrous attack on the Williamite/Whig commercial culture—with its Dutch credit schemes, lotteries, national debt, banks—also extended to its cultural institutions—the spas, the exchange, the coffeehouse.[8] Ward's satire "The Humours of a Coffee-House" is well known to students of the period.[9] Yet the campaign was extraordinarily elaborate. Symbolically it extended to the tipples that identified the institutions themselves. Ned Ward contributed *A dialogue between claret & darby Ale* (1692), Richard Ames combined commercial satire with cultural satire in his *The last search after claret in Southwark, or, A visitation of the vintners in the mind: with the debates of a committee of that profession thither fled to avoid the cruel persecution of their unmerciful creditors* (1691). He later capped Ward's dialogue with his own disingenuous *The bacchanalian sessions, or, The contention of liquors: with a farewell to wine* (1693).

The counterdiscourse to the Grub Street screeds against Whiggery, commercialism, coffeehouses, and darby ale, was a bumptious celebration of native British fare that became part of the creed of the clubs. "The Rare Roast Beef of Britain" became the byword of the Roast Beef Society, the nut-brown ale of Britain became the toast of the "October Club," while wine became a sign of Stuart loyalty and French sympathies, to be denigrated along with ragouts, fricassees, and other innovations of French cookery. William King, the laureate of the Roast Beef Society, became one of the great literary popularizers of the discourse.[10]

The war of English ale against French wine, of alehouse against tavern, would reach its climax in the aftermath of the accession of George I. Then the Whig adherents to the house of Hanover organized their opposition to the Jacobite mob through a series of mug clubs in Long Acre, in Salisbury Court, in Fleet Street, Tower Street, and Whitechapel.[11] In a mug-house like the Roebuck in Whitechapel "nothing [is] drunk but Ale, and every Gentleman hath his separate Mug, which he chalks on the Table where he sits as it is brought in; and every one retires when he pleases, as from a Coffeehouse."[12] The beer mugs were originally fashioned in a grotesque resemblance of Lord Shaftesbury's face—his "ugly mug," as it was called—suggesting the political genealogy of the assemblies. Besides engaging in celebrations of the Hanoverians and lauding King William, the mug clubs provided the muscle in the street wrangles with the Jacobite mob. Throughout 1715 and 1716 riots occurred on November 4 (King William's birthday), November 17 (the accession of Queen Elizabeth), and March 8 (the anniversary of King William's death). This last proved so volatile that street disturbances continued for two days, culminating in the murder of a Jacobite rioter by the proprietor of a mug-house and the burning of the house. Five of the Jacobite rioters were executed at Tyburn for rebellion. Parliament was forced to intervene, repressing the clubs.[13]

Among polite Whigs, among pietists, among peace-loving citizens, a perception grew that somehow alehouse mug clubs and Jacobite tavern cabals did not much differ—both were institutions of incivility.

Peter Clark has noted a gradual coalescence of the alehouse and the tavern during the eighteenth century—a blurring of distinctions in terms of scale of business, clientele, and cultural function.[14] This convergence was marked by their frequent subsumption under the term "public house" in popular and legal parlance. In the metropolis and in the provinces this convergence was a function of government attempts to legislate the low end of the business out of existence. In London, the vintners lost their dominion over licensing.[15] In the colonies no independent company or guild was permitted to have it. Colonial governments oversaw the licensing and regulated the activities of taverns. Proprietors and governors warned of the dangers to the peace posed by public houses, particularly "the growth of vice and looseness."[16] In Pennsylvania, the governor licensed taverns, while the provincial council regulated what could take place on the premises.[17]

The port cities of British America abounded in places that claimed the name "public house." Some were unlicensed dram houses, dispensing hard spirits to a clandestine clientele in someone's dwelling. The low end of the legal business was held by the alehouses, one- or two-room public houses with a keg of porter and sleeping pallets.[18] Philadelphia's first licensed house, the Blue Anchor, was barely the size of a present-day living room, twelve by twenty-five feet.[19] Most of the lower-end establishments tolerated the usual sorts of urban vice—gambling, drunkenness, and prostitution—the sorts of activity that kept a city constabulary in business. A greater threat to the public order was posed by the habitués of the high-end establishments, the inns, taverns, and alcohol-serving coffeehouses. There merchants, ship captains, traders, and traveling officials congregated. These were strangers for the most part to local customs, mores, and laws. Colonial executives looked anxiously toward the cosmopolitan coteries that formed in the taverns, knowing that the economic health of the colony depended upon their aid, yet mindful that their loyalties and interests lay elsewhere. Two fears predominated: that the tavern crowd would organize a black market trade; that in the taverns a political opposition might form. Sometimes these fears were justified. In Pennsylvania, for instance, an anti-Quaker political faction formed among the young gentry who frequented Enoch Story's tavern. Story's, along with the London Coffeehouse and the Pewter Platter Inn, made up the highest rank of Philadelphia's public houses.[20]

Penn had tried to counteract the concentration of the upper classes in certain taverns by legislating uniformity in beverages, prices, and hours in the city. He restricted operating hours in the evenings, mandating an 8:00 P.M. closing time. No local resident could stay at a tavern more than an hour, unless meeting on business.[21] Since 6:00 P.M. marked the beginning of prime time business activity to the transatlantic world, Penn was allowing only two hours for evening enterprise. The laws were overseen by the city corporation and enforced aggressively by a Quaker constabulary.

Merchants boarding at inns could evade the restrictions on evening business. Local residents who frequented the taverns suffered. They organized a resistance to Quaker control of public life in 1703. The date was significant. In 1693 the merchant community in Philadelphia was largely Quaker; a decade later, sizable contingents of Anglicans and Presbyterians had entered its ranks.[22] In the summer of 1703 the youngest of these merchants met with some of the young gentry at Story's and commenced a tavern war against the city corporation.[23]

The flashpoint for the war was probably a repressed play. Colony statutes prohibited "stage-plays, masques, revels, bull-baiting, cockfightings." The itinerant player Tony Aston had arrived in Philadelphia fresh from success in Charleston, South Carolina.[24] He stayed at Story's but did not perform there, as he had at Gignilliat's tavern in Charleston. He was probably prevented from appearing. Shortly after Aston's departure, the young blades at Story's rioted in the streets, attacking the watch, breaking windows, bashing doors, and rolling citizens in hogsheads through Philadelphia's muddy streets. An episode in late August led to several arrests "for raising a great disturbance and riot in the city at dead of night."[25] (Note the time—well after legislated closing hours.) One of the detainees, Henry Brooke, was the colony's foremost wit, custom's collector at the mouth of the Delaware River, an Anglican, and a foe of the Quaker pacifists in the Pennsylvania legislature. He was also friend of Governor John Evans, a young ex-military officer who shared Brooke's contempt for Quaker inaction during the War of Spanish Succession. In September another mass arrest occurred, this time bringing in Billy Penn, the proprietor's son and heir. Two months later, the constabulary invaded Story's, discovering to their dismay Governor Evans who throttled Watchman Solomon Cresson. Word of the melee exploded through town, bringing reinforcements for the constabulary in the persons of the mayor, recorder, and several aldermen. Many, including Evans, were injured.

Governor Evans played upon the heightened tensions in the city in the wake of the tavern war by staging a hoax in collusion with Henry Brooke. Brooke and others sent dispatches from various points along the Delaware River warning that the Spanish had landed and were marching toward the Quaker capital. Evans intended to panic the Assembly into funding an army. The ruse failed, but created such an anxiety about the colony's security that a cosmopolitan opposition came into being that would operate for the duration of the proprietary period.

The Pennsylvania case is interesting because in it both governmental and sectarian objections to the tavern coincide. As print consolidated a sense of the

public distinct from state and church, particularly after the founding of newspapers in the provincial metropolis, the old objectors were supplied a new
mask through which to voice their criticisms: the "sober citizen." The sober
citizen was a figure of sufficient generality to encompass both religious and
state interests. One example of the type speaks in a letter of February 1726 to
the *New England Courant.* "It is a Complaint no less true than Common,
among Sober People *that the abuse of strong Drink is become Epidemical among
us.* And it is very justly Suppos'd by Judicious People, that the Multiplication of
Taverns has Contributed not a littel to this Excess of Riot and Debauchery."[26]
For the sober citizen, the tavern had become the haunt of a growing population of local sots and tipplers whose indulgences offended both godliness and
government. "Certainly the Bacanalian Revels which are too Frequent in our
Publick Houses, are a Reproach to Men, and much more so, to a People
Professing Godliness. So also the Nocturnal Frolicks of Young Men afford us
but a very Indifferent opinion of the Family order and Government of this
great Town, for which it has formerly been deservedly Famous." Thus the
tavern becomes a sign in the rhetoric of cultural jeremiad. The distinction in
terms of age in the sober citizen's critique—Men and Young Men—becomes
transformed into a critique of clubs—that is, tavern companies whose behavior operates as an intentional program. The analysis, however, has become
formulaic. We see the London scowerers of 1690 in Boston 1720s dress: "the
Young Club, or the Club of Rakes . . . spend whole Nights In Drinking and
Gaming, it is to be fear'd at their Fathers and Masters Expence. The quantitys
of Wine and Brandy-Punch drank (or rather destroy'd) by these Clubs, is
incredible. So that their practice is an excess of Riot."

The charges of religious and political subversion first leveled at coffeehouses
and later at the mug clubs were laid against the "Senior Club," composed of
gentlemen among whom "vast affairs of State and Governments are Survey'd
and settled and Honest Schemes of Rulers are arraing'd and traduc'd, and their
Arcana too freely intermeddle with. . . . and Finally, 'tis to be fear'd that too
often the Mysteries of Religion, which are too Sacred and Sublime to be droll'd
on over Muggs and Bowls, make up part of the Conversation." To this was
added a third group, the "Tippling Club" made up of men who drink for
drinking's sake.

These publicly recognized institutions of disorder were supplemented by a
further, even more pernicious, entity, the unlicensed house. In these secret
places the character of vice as rebellion from good order was made apparent in
the design of eluding moral and governmental scrutiny. "Our Young Sparks

Drink and Game, and Revel for whole Nights together, and Perhaps Every Night. And such Vile Houses will be kept, and such Devilish clans Abetted, by evil minded Persons, whose wicked Arts elude the Care and Vigilance of them whose proper Business it is to look after and suppress them."

The enmity of unlicensed houses to the established order was no figment of the sober citizen's imagination. In 1737 Georgia, the paternalistic rule of the Trustees was resisted by the "malcontents," a gentry cabal of Scottish settlers who conducted a publicity campaign against the charter of the colony from one such house. William Stephens, the Trustees' informant in Savannah, provides a glimpse of the place and its company: "In the Evening I understood there was a little Assembly of some of the Malecontents, at the House of one Townshend, where probably (as I conceived) no Good was contriving, especially as Aglionby was one of the Company, who was bred a Smatterer in the Law, lodges at present in that House, and is looked on as one of the greatest Mischief-makers in the whole Town; being consulted with frequently by those of the Faction. It is to be noted, that this House of Townsend's is where they commonly resort; being a publick House, though unlicens'd."[27] When Aglionby died in August 1738, Stephens observed, "he was a great Devotee to Rum . . . using it to Excess brought a Flux upon him, which after all Endeavours to the contrary, at length carried him off; wherein the Colony (I conceive) sustained no Loss." Stephens's association of intemperance with political subversion was a commonplace among sober, God-fearing citizens.

Beginning in the 1710s, a domestic voice was added to the critiques by the sober citizen. This domestic critic was a devotee of a beverage that in the eighteenth century would rival ale and wine—tea. The voice of tea was feminine, Christian, and censorious. In Boston in 1722 one member of the tippling set, who styled himself "Sisyphus," complained of his wife: "Her companions are sure at every visit not to miss of a bellyful of Tea, whereas when I return from taking my glass with my friend, my ears are immediately filled with sot & drunkard, and other such like opprobrious expressions which render my life utterly burdensome."[28]

The campaign of the tea tables was two-pronged. It railed against coffee and the coffeehouses for having taken men and business out of domestic spaces and family interactions into separate commercial spaces that were largely homosocial.[29] It rebuked indulgence in alcohol as intemperate incivility. The consumption of tea was a phenomenon associated with the propertied classes until the mid-eighteenth century. Its ceremonies were superintended by women in domestic spaces. From the 1690s in London and 1710s in Boston and New York City, elite circles of women formed about the tea table.[30] These circles promulgated "polite" manners and enforced their reign over the beau monde by gossip and scandal. Bellona, a female vindicator of Boston tea tables, chastised a male critic of the reign of feminine opinion in the city: "I would have you know, Sir, that some of us can handle our Pens as well as our Tongues, and it will be your wisest way to be quiet, or treat us with better Manners in the future. . . . We can discover, if we will, all the excellent Qualities you are endowed with over a Cup of Drink with your Companions, and let the World see, that your Knowledge is as universal as that of Gossips, only with this Difference, that yours comes and goes with the Liquor, and theirs is always the Same."[31] Here we come to the gist of the war of beverages. Tea enables a durable knowledge and sense. Wine and ale offer only transient illumination.

By the end of the 1720s, the woman tea-drinker, the sober citizen, the minister, and the state in British America stood arrayed in common cause against the tavern and its inhabitants. They were the animators of publicity campaigns ventured during the eighteenth century against rum, public drunkenness, and dram-drinking. The woman tea-drinker militated against intemperance among the elite, the gentleman's indulgence in the "friendly glass." The clergyman spoke to the public at large in tracts such as Cotton Mather's *Sober Considerations, on a Growing Flood of iniquity* (1708), Samuel Danforth's *Woful Effects of Drunkenness* (1710), and Benjamin Wadsworth's *Essay to Do Good: Being a Dissuasive from Tavern Hunting and Excessive Drinking* (1710). The sober citizen addressed the middling and lower classes.

The newspaper and almanac addresses of these civic moralists projected "temperance" into an explicit cultural ideal. Benjamin Franklin was the most famous of these ethical campaigners. His various writings against public intoxication, beginning with Silence Dogwood #12 through his "Drinker's Dictionary" and his *Pennsylvania Gazette* essay "On Drunkenness," suggest why he made temperance the first of his twelve virtues to be cultivated in self-improvement.[32] The burden of Franklin's argument was that intemperance assured one's subjection to poverty and one's fixed station in the lower ranks of society. Franklin's was a consequentialist ethical scheme—temperance was valued not as a virtue in itself, but for its effects on one's worldly condition. An anonymous contemporary of Franklin's composed a poem that might stand as the creed of ethical pragmatism in regard to temperance: "The Credit and Interest of America, Considered: Or, The Way to Live above Want. Wherein

Temperance is commended for her Decency, and being Provident." Intemperance was by synecdoche visualized throughout the poem as swallowing. The rewards of restricting consumption:

> To Save our Money and to Keep our Land;
> And that's the Credit every Man should price,
> The Saving Hard to good Estates doth rise:
> In all Concerns she [temperance] is a certain Guide,
> And from our Presence will at no time slide;
> Whoso is bent her Counsel for to follow,
> Preserves in Store, what others lightly Swallow.[33]

The tavern was a gaping maw that consumed men's savings and gnawed at their credit in the eyes of the public. This idea, and all the kindred images that contributed to the demonization of the tavern, were the rhetorical ammunition employed in an early exercise in molding opinion in several arenas of the nascent public sphere. The publicity campaigns of the tea tables, clergymen, and sober citizens made the haunting of taverns a demerit in polite society, in the kingdom of God, and in the credit market. Their elaboration of a complex of negative associations about taverns, tavern beverages, and tavern-goers would inform much of the subsequent discourse of temperance. The same cast of critics—ministers, tea-totaling women, and sober citizens—would people the later armies marshaled against Demon Rum, Satan's Suds, and France's Wicked Wine.

Notes

1. Peter Clark, *The English Alehouse: A Social History 1200–1830* (London and New York: Longman, 1983), 12–14.
2. Michael Wigglesworth, "The Day of Doom," in *Seventeenth-Century American Poetry*, ed. Harrison Meserole (Garden City, NY: Anchor Doubleday, 1968), 64.
3. Lawrence E. Klein, "Coffee Clashes: The Politics of Discourse in Seventeenth- and Eighteenth-Century England" (paper presented at American Historical Association meeting, Chicago, IL, December 27–30, 1991).
4. "WHEREAS it is most apparent that the multitude of coffee houses of late years set up and kept within this kingdom, the dominion of Wales, and town of Berwick-upon-Tweed, and the great resort of idel and disaffected persons to them, have produced very evil and dangerous effects; as well for that many tradesmen and other, do herein mispend much of their time, which and probably would be employed in and about their Lawful Calling and Affairs; but also, for that in such

houses . . . divers false, malitious and scandalous reports are devised and spread abroad to the Defamation of his Majesty's Government, and to the Disturb and of the Peace and Quiet of the Realm; his Majesty hath thought fit and necessary, that he the said coffee Houses be (for the future) Put down, and suppressed." "A Proclamation for the Suppression of Coffee Houses" [Dec. 23, 1675]. Quoted in William H. Ukers, *All About Tea*, 2 vols. (New York: The Tea and Coffee Trade Journal Co., 1935), 1:45.

5. Thomas Shadwell, *The Scowrers. A Comedy, Acted by Their Majesties Servants* (London: Knapton, 1691). The play was produced in December 1690. It is noteworthy that it was revived in 1717 in the wake of the mug club clashes.

6. For a prosopography of Grub Street, see Robert Pinkus, *Grub St. Stripped Bare* (Hamden, CT: Archon, 1968); also Benjamin Boyce, *Tom Brown of Facetious Memory: Grub Street in the Age of Dryden* (Cambridge, MA: Harvard UP, 1939).

7. For Ward's politics and career, see Howard William Troyer, *Ned Ward of Grubstreet: A Study of Sub-Literary London in the Eighteenth Century* (Cambridge, MA: Harvard UP, 1946).

8. David S. Shields, "The Rise of Grubstreet and the Williamite Imperium Pelagi" (paper presented at American Historical Association meeting, Washington, DC, Dec. 26–29, 1992).

9. Edward "Ned" Ward, *The Humours of a Coffee-House: A Comedy as it is Daily Acted* (London: for the benefit of Bohee, the Coffee-Man, 1707). This work was a revision of *The Weekly Comedy, As it is Dayly Acted at most Coffee-Houses in London* (London: J. How, weekly installments May 10–July 12, 1699).

10. William King, *The Art of Cookery: in Imitation of Horace's Art of Poetry* (London, 1708).

11. Sir H. M., *Down with the Mug; or Reasons for suppressing the Mug-houses* (London, 1717).

12. *A Journey Through England* (London, 1722).

13. John Timbs, *Clubs and Club Life in London* (Detroit: Gale, rpt. of 1872 ed.), 43–47.

14. Clark, "The Alehouse Improved," in *The English Alehouse*, 195–221.

15. Ibid., 190–95.

16. William Penn, *The Papers of William Penn*, ed. Mary Maples Dunn, 5 vols. (Philadelphia: U of Pennsylvania P, 1981–86), 2:45.

17. Peter J. Thompson, "A Social History of Philadelphia's Taverns, 1683–1800 (Ph.D. diss., University of Pennsylvania, 1989), 128–49. This study provides the best description and analysis of the business and social function of the taverns in any colonial metropolis.

18. Ibid.

19. Harold D. Eberlein, *Portrait of a Colonial City: Philadelphia 1680–1839* (Philadelphia: Lippincott, 1939). 10.

20. The antiquarians Benjamin and Mary Boggs in 1914 identified the following public houses as operating in Philadelphia during the first decade of the eighteenth

century: The Blue Anchor, The Broadaxe, Carpenter's Coffeehouse, The Crooked Billet, Enoch Story's, The George, The Globe, The Pewter Platter, The Scales, Thomas Hooten's, The Three Tuns, The Tun, William Frampton's, and Whitpain's. "Inns and Taverns of Old Philadelphia," ms., Boggs Collection, Historical Society of Pennsylvania.

21. William Penn, "Tavern Regulations," in *William Penn and the Founding of Pennsylvania, 1680–1684: A Documentary History*, ed. Jean R. Soderlund (Philadelphia: U of Pennsylvania P, 1983), 205–18.

22. Gary Nash, "The Early Merchants of Philadelphia: The Formation and Disintegration of a Founding Elite," in *The World of William Penn*, ed. Richard S. Dunn and Mary Maples Dunn (Philadelphia: U of Pennsylvania P, 1986), 337–62.

23. Enoch Story's Tavern was located on the corner of Market and Front streets, contiguous to the Pewter Platter Inn. Its proprietor, Enoch Story, was the son of New York merchant Robert Story, who died in 1683. His widowed mother Patience married Thomas Lloyd of Philadelphia, a member of the governing council of Pennsylvania.

24. "The Life of Tony Aston," in *Church Music and Musical Life in Pennsylvania in the Eighteenth Century*, 3 vols. (Philadelphia: Publications of the Pennsylvania Society of the Colonial Dames of America IV, 1938), 3:134. The memoir makes no mention of a performance in Philadelphia, whereas accounts of other towns visited note the nature and success of Aston's theatrical offerings. The editor's speculation (3:92–96) about what Aston performed at Story's is entirely fanciful. In the wake of the 1701 prosecution of a costumed Boxing Day revel at John Simes's tavern, it is highly unlikely that Aston would have risked arrest. The editor's dating of Aston's appearance in November is also incorrect; he probably appeared in Philadelphia in early summer.

25. John F. Watson, *Annals of Philadelphia, and of Pennsylvania in Olden Times*, ed. Willis P. Hazard, 3 vols. (Philadelphia: J. M. Stoddart, 1881), 1:327.

26. "To the venerable Father Janus," *New England Courant*, Feb. 26, 1726. All subsequent quotations of this writer will refer to this text.

27. William Stephens, *A Journal of the Proceedings in Georgia*, vol. 1 (London: Meadows, 1742), 77.

28. Sisyphus, [Letter complaining of Wife & Tea Companions], *New England Courant* 35 (April 2, 1722).

29. Beth Kowalski-Wallace, "Tea, Gender, and Domesticity in Eighteenth-Century England," in *Studies in Eighteenth-Century Culture*, vol. 23 (Colleague's Press, 1994).

30. Rodris Roth, "Tea Drinking in 18th-Century America: Its Etiquette and Equipage," *United States National Museum Bulletin 225, Contributions from the Museum of History and Technology* (Washington, DC: Smithsonian Institution, 1961), 84.

31. Bellona, [A Reply to Z.Y.'s Remarks upon Gossip], *New England Courant* 112 (Sept. 23, 1723).

32. Robert Arner, "Politics and Temperance in Boston and Philadelphia: Benjamin Franklin's Journalistic Writings on Drinking and Drunkenness," in *Reappraising Ben Franklin, A Bicentennial Perspective*, ed. J. A. Leo Lemay (Newark: U of Delaware P, 1993), 52–77.

33. "The Credit and Interest of America," *American Weekly Mercury* 735 (Jan. 29, 1733/34).

Black Cats and Delirium Tremens

Temperance and the American Renaissance

✒ *David S. Reynolds*

America's literary flowering between 1835 and 1860, commonly known as the American Renaissance, owed much to the temperance movement that burgeoned in several forms during these years. No other single reform had so widespread an impact upon American literature as temperance, largely because of its extraordinary cultural prominence. In particular, the Washingtonian movement, which during the 1840s infiltrated nearly every area of working-class life, made temperance an inescapable phenomenon. As one popular writer noted in 1846, the typical American town had not only frequent temperance lectures but also "temperance negro operas; temperance theaters; temperance eating houses, and temperance every thing, and our whole population, in places, is soused head-over-heels in temperance."[1] Although the campaign against drink did affect alcohol consumption, which dropped from the equivalent of around ten gallons of absolute alcohol per American yearly in 1830 to just over one gallon by 1855, the temperance movement became riddled with contradictions and ambiguities that made it a fertile source of literary themes and images. Temperance produced two best-selling novels, George B. Cheever's *Deacon Giles' Distillery* and Timothy Shay Arthur's *Ten Nights in a Bar-room*, and provided a rich fund of images and character types that were adopted by all of the major authors.

Four main types of temperance-related discourse developed during this period: what may be called conventional, dark temperance, ironic, and transcendental.

Conventional temperance literature featured straightforward, didactic expositions or exempla against drinking, with emphasis on the benign rewards of virtue rather than the brutal results of vice. Rooted in the relatively restrained evangelical tracts, novels, and newspapers of the 1820s, the conventional mode, which determinedly avoided excessive sensationalism, waned during the 1830s and especially after 1840, the year that witnessed the arrival of Washingtonianism. Initiated by a group of reformed drunkards from Baltimore whose repentance led to nationwide appeals for total abstinence, the Washingtonian movement spread with incredible rapidity, largely because its antialcohol message was typically delivered in diverting, often highly sensational stories about the horrors of drink, stories that had high entertainment value for an American working-class that feasted on crime-filled penny papers and P. T. Barnum's gallery of freaks. Canny publishers, grasping the opportunity to peddle blood and violence under the guise of morality, issued a series of temperance novels and story collections in which didacticism was muted and sensationalism was exaggerated. This dark-temperance mode placed new emphasis on the pathological behavior and diseased psychology associated with alcoholism. It is against this ambiguous background of dark temperance that several works by major authors—Whitman's *Franklin Evans*, Poe's "The Black Cat" and "The Cask of Amontillado," and some of Hawthorne's and Melville's fiction—can be profitably viewed.

A corollary of dark temperance was the ironic mode, which refers to the widely noted irony of supposedly virtuous temperance reformers who were involved in dissipation or debauchery on the sly. The intemperate temperance reformer became a common character type in popular fiction and contributed to the paradoxes of familiar works by Hawthorne and Melville.

The indulgent sensationalism of dark temperance and crippling paradoxes of the ironic mode contributed, on the popular level, to the replacement of moral suasion by legalistic temperance reform and, in the major literature, to transcendentalist reconstructions of temperance by Thoreau, Whitman, and Dickinson. The transcendentalist response consisted of affirmative, individualistic versions of alcohol-related images by those who perceived the flaws or ironies of temperance reform and who wished to redirect temperance, usually by associating it with such positive things as deliberate living and reveling in nature's beauty.

The Popular Scene

Early in this period, popular temperance reformers made a deliberate effort to communicate their animus against spirits without overstepping the bounds of what they perceived as propriety. The language and style of what I call conventional temperance is epitomized by the influential New York newspaper *Genius of Temperance*. Founded in Boston in 1826 as the *National Philanthropist*, this evangelical organ moved to Providence in 1829 and the next year to Manhattan, where it ran until 1833. Establishing the conventional approach to temperance, it repeatedly warned against tippling but avoided graphic descriptions of drunkenness and inveighed against novels and the sensational press. Alarmed by the rising popularity of the latter, the editors asked in exasperation, "Is it because men are so superficial, volatile, and vicious, that they can neither understand nor relish a sober solid essay on morals?"[2] In opposition to what they termed "licentious literature," they filled their paper with "sober solid essays" denouncing drinking, gambling, and other social vices. In the many issues of the newspaper I surveyed, I found only one piece of fiction, a short story entitled "Henry Wallace; or, The Victim of Lottery Gambling." This deemphasis of fiction was reflected in several articles attacking novels and the reportage of crimes in the popular press. Lamenting that crimes formed "the great burden of the 'Domestic News' of almost every journal," the editors believed that vivid depictions of evil, even if motivated by reform, tended to make evil attractive.[3] "In an age when vice is popular," they argued, "and men hasten to sin as with a cart-rope—drinking in iniquity like water—there is sometimes a danger of making bad men and bad measures and systems *popular*, by merely demonstrating their iniquity."

Such cautious avoidance of descriptions of vice was shared by temperance novelists of the 1820s. *Edmund and Margaret; or Sobriety and Faithfulness Rewarded* (1822) established a basic situation often used in later temperance fiction—a marriage threatened by the husband's drinking habit—and handled the theme with explicit didacticism reinforced by many quotations from the Bible. The novel ends with a moralistic affirmation of social reintegration, as the married pair, having learned to eschew alcohol, "become useful members of society, and, by honesty and sobriety in their callings, and a desire to do the will of their Maker, . . . deservedly have the respect of the wise and good, and may look forward with cheering hope in the mercy of God, unto everlasting life, by his beloved son, Jesus Christ."[4]

The preachy, nonsensational tone of conventional temperance was equally visible in another novel of 1822, *The Lottery Ticket: An American Tale*. Again we witness the decline and fall of a good family man, and again we follow his carefully described religious recovery and reintegration into his family and society. In the novel, a New Hampshire farmer, Meriam, falls into "every species of dissipation and licentiousness" as a result of gambling and drinking.⁵ Forced to sell his farm and sent to jail, Meriam is nurtured back to moral health by his long-suffering but sturdy wife, whose Bible-reading brings about his renunciation of vice and his embrace of Christianity. While Meriam's temporary fall from virtue is described only cursorily, much space is devoted to his reentry into the peaceful family circle and his recovery of spirituality and social respectability.

The continuance of conventional temperance into the 1830s was marked by two works of 1836, *Tales of Intemperance* and William Dunlap's *Memoirs of a Water Drinker*. The former, a story collection issued by the Massachusetts Sabbath School Society, featured six tales of people who fell into excessive drinking but then were successfully recalled to sobriety and religion after pledging abstinence at temperance meetings. Dunlap's long, two-volume *Memoirs of a Water Drinker* was likewise notable for its restraint in describing aberrant behavior caused by drink. In the middle of the novel there appears an interpolated essay on alcohol-related evils such as wife-beating, suicide, and murder, but these are disposed of in a vague paragraph and, as Dunlap stresses, are "softened in feature and coloring, rather than exaggerated, or even exhibited in a strong light."⁶

Although the conventional approach would never totally disappear from American temperance writing, it began to be challenged in the 1830s by more sensational modes. This was the decade that saw the rise of the penny papers as well as a notorious case of what I call "immoral reform," involving a New York antiprostitution reformer, Rev. John McDowall, who described illicit sex so vividly that he was brought to trial as a pornographer and later defrocked. Temperance writers saw the need to compete against the penny press and perfervid reformers like McDowall. As the *Genius of Temperance* noted: "That which was once too shocking for recital, now forms a part of the intellectual regalia which the public appetite demands with a gusto that will scarcely brook a disappointment, should the mails provokingly bring fewer murders than temperance meetings!"⁷

This movement toward the sensational was reflected in temperance novels with a significantly dark coloration. *Intemperance Illustrated* and *The Catastrophe*, two novels that appeared in 1833 (the year of America's first penny newspaper), heightened horror and deemphasized regeneration. *Intemperance Illustrated* traced a drunkard's progression from sipping medicine as a baby through abandoning his family on drunken sprees, brutalizing his wife and children, and ending up a murderer on the gallows. Similarly dark is *The Catastrophe*, which followed the life of Edward L——, initially the model citizen of a dry community who turns into a wife-murderer because of alcohol. Anticipatory of Poe's "The Black Cat," the tale reaches a gory climax when L——, driven to a frenzy by drink, brains his wife with an axe: "There she lay in her blood! The axe by her side with which the murderous deed had been accomplished, and Edward L—— was the murderer!"[8]

Several other works of the 1830s sped the shift toward dark temperance. Anna Fox's *The Ruined Deacon* (1834) pictured the steady descent of a Connecticut deacon after he begins drinking; his wife becomes a gloomy skeptic and finally a raving maniac as a result of her husband's habit. Fox's next novel, *George Allen, The Only Son* (1835), ends in Hawthornesque gloom, as a man whose son had become a drunken criminal and whose wife died of grief survives as a melancholy doubter. Similarly bleak is *Deacon Giles' Distillery* (1835), by Hawthorne's friend George B. Cheever, which stirred up an immense controversy because of its graphic portrait of devils gathering nightly in a distillery to produce barrels of alcohol labeled "death," "madness," "murder," and so on. McDonald Clarke, a Manhattan poet Whitman greatly admired, used horrific images in temperance verse, as when in "The Rum Hole" he called a grog-shop "The horrible Light-House of Hell / . . . built on a ledge of human bones, / Whose cement is of human blood."[9]

The stage was set, then, for the intensified sensationalism that accompanied the Washingtonian movement, which began in April 1840 when six men drinking in a Baltimore bar sent some of their number to a temperance lecture that led to their repentance. These men became the core of a movement of reformed drunkards that gained one hundred thousand members by 1841 and half a million two years later. Working-class in origin, the Washingtonians appealed to the masses by acting out the miseries of drunkenness. Their tawdry scare-tactics shortly came under fire. A New England journalist generalized: "Very many of the temperance stories that are narrated by teetotal lecturers are mere fables, and told merely for the effect they are expected to produce."[10] Another commentator sarcastically described the Washingtonians as "itinerants, who wander about in very eccentric orbits, and narrate their *rum* days at so much *per diem*."[11] Theodore Parker called the Washingtonians "violent, ill-bred, theatrical," noting the irony that there had been "more preaching against the temperance movement than in its favor."[12] Another observer lamented "the narration of horrible 'experiences'" by "the scurrilous army of ditch-delivered reformed drunkards (whose glory was in their shame)."[13] Washingtonianism was also criticized because of highly publicized instances of backsliding among both the leaders and the general members of the movement. According to an estimate made in 1848, 80 percent of those who had taken the temperance pledge in 1840 had resumed drinking.

Many of the inconsistencies of Washingtonianism were embodied in its leader, John Bartholomew Gough. One of the most popular orators in American history, this ex-actor and reformed drunkard put his histrionic talents to use on the lecture platform, terrifying his hearers with spine-tingling accounts of alcohol-induced crimes and horrid visions spawned by delirium tremens. His lectures were typically strings of short stories—some based on fact, others fictional—filled with grotesque humor, vernacular language, and horror. Known as "the poet of the d.t.s," he was expert at enacting "the trembling madness," picturing hairy spiders crawling over a crazed drunkard's body, or hundred-bladed knives that tore into the flesh. In a typical lecture he asked, "Did you ever see a man in *delirium tremens*, biting his tongue until his mouth was filled with blood, the foam on his lips, the big drops on his brow? Did you ever hear him burst out in blasphemy which curdled your blood, and see him beat his face in wild fury?"[14]

Such theatrics, predictably, lay Gough open to the charge of crass sensation-mongering. Gough conceded in his autobiography, "I have been called a 'humbug,' a 'theatrical performer,' a "mountebank, a 'clown,' a 'buffoon,' . . . my lectures have been called 'idiotic ravings."[15] In addition to bringing a new sensationalism to the temperance movement, he became the era's most notorious example of backsliding when in 1845 he disappeared for a week and was found in a Manhattan whorehouse in a stupor that he attributed to drugged cherry soda but which almost certainly resulted from an alcoholic binge.

With the rise of Washingtonians, popular temperance novelists became unabashed in their sensationalism, often using temperance as a mere pretext for concocting diverting tales. The author of the Washingtonian novel *Letters from the Alms-House, on the Subject of Temperance* (1841) proclaims he has known intemperance "in its darkest and most hideous shades, and I shall paint it all, let who will be offended."[16] In a section on families ruined by alcohol, the author writes: "There was a man drawing his wife by the hair. There was another with a club, driving a woman and children out of doors. There was a man and woman fighting with shovel and tongs. There was a man with an axe running after a woman, and cutting his wife's throat with a carving knife." Another Washingtonian novel, *John Elliot, the Reformed. An Old Sailor's Legacy* (1841) switches between moralizing and sheer escapist adventure, repeatedly interrupting the main narrative of a tippling tar's doom with unrelated episodes about pirate battles, shipwrecks, and so on. *The Drunkard's Orphan Son*

(1842) leaves temperance altogether behind, tracing a drunkard's abandoned son who becomes a sea captain, is shipwrecked in the South Seas, and, anticipatory of Tommo in Melville's *Typee*, lives among the cannibals and falls for a native woman. *The Confessions of a Rum-seller* (1845) depicts a bibulous liquor merchant who murders his father-in-law for money, driving his mother-in-law insane; he then sells rum to his brother-in-law, whose turn to alcoholism results in these horrid events described by the narrator: "My sister's husband,—the man I had ruined,—murdered his own daughter, a beautiful child of eight years old, because she wept when he struck her mother. He was hanged, and Mary became a maniac. She soon died."[17] In Maria Lamas's *The Glass; or, The Trials of Helen More. A Thrilling Temperance Tale* (1849), dark-temperance sensationalism reached what may have been its nadir. At the climax of the novel, a drunken mother locks her child in a clothes room, leaves for several days of drinking, and returns home only to find that the boy, in an effort to keep from starving, has eaten the flesh off his own arm and has died in the process. The mother reports:

> I unlocked the clothes room door, and there—oh! there bathed in his blood, lay the mangled corpse of my child—murdered by his mother. There he lay, poor slaughtered innocent! starved! starved! starved! His left arm gnawed to the bone—gnawed till the artery had been severed, and he had bled to death.[18]

Delirium tremens, that staple of Washingtonian lectures, became an almost obligatory feature of dark-temperance novels. The inebriated protagonist of *Letters from an Alms-house* believes he is being chased by dogs, cats, rats, and devils. The 1844 novel *Confessions of a Reformed Inebriate* pictures one drunkard assaulted by imaginary "slimy reptiles and creeping vermin" and another haunted by "the specters of departed friends, in all the hideous and disgusting aspects of death and the grave."[19] The lead character of *Autobiography of a Reformed Drunkard* (1845) is tortured by "all sorts of visions, the most ludicrous, and the most painful," including dancing cats, fiddling monkeys, and a devil covered with skulls.[20] In Lamas's *The Glass*, a dying drunkard screams, "See! look! the lizards—green, slimy lizards are crawling all over me! Take them away! Will nobody kill the reptiles?"[21]

While some popular writers were exploiting Washingtonian temperance for its sensationalism, others went beyond exploitation to outright satire, aimed mainly at the backsliding of temperance reformers. What I call the ironic mode was popularized by those who perceived a wide gap between the professions and practice of many who preached temperance. In *Beneath the American Renaissance* I show that subversive popular fiction generated oxymoronic character types—including the Christian slaveholder, the fighting Quaker, the churchgoing capitalist, and the pious Indian-hater—that undermined clear moral signifiers and contributed to the paradoxes of the major literature.[22] One such oxymoronic type was the intemperate temperance advocate.

We are all familiar with Mark Twain's Dauphin, the bald-pated con artist who, upon meeting Huck Finn, boasts that he has "ben a-runnin' a little temperance revival" in order to raise funds to buy whiskey.[23] The Dauphin had many predecessors in American fiction and humor of the antebellum period, when hypocritical temperance advocates were a favorite butt of ridicule. George Lippard in *The Quaker City* sneered at "intemperate Temperance lecturers," caricaturing them in his portrait of the Rev. F. A. T. Pyne, who preaches against drinking while secretly enjoying brandy, opium, and illicit sex.[24] In his "study" in Monk Hall, Parson Pyne gleefully opens packets of opium and snickers, "We temperance folks must have some little excitement after we have forsworn intemperance. When we leave off alcohol, we indulge our systems with a little Opium. That's what I call a capital compromise." Although most of Pyne's lecture audiences believe in his probity, one man, an old Revolutionary War veteran, sees through him and openly confronts him, decrying "that foul-mouthed temperance in public—wine-drinking in private" which Pyne embodies.

Other popular writers followed Lippard in developing the ironic mode. The city-mysteries novelist George Thompson returned insistently to the figure of the intemperate temperance advocate. In *New-York Life* he portrayed a reformer, Bob Towline, who starts a paper devoted to stamping out intemperance, gambling, and whoredom—vices that are his favorite pastimes. Bob "made love to prostitutes" and "got intoxicated on champagne," Thompson writes, "but his mission was to reform the age, and he did not stand above a little inconsistency."[25] He regularly drank too heavily, "but then Bob was a model reformer of whom these little slips are expected." In another novel, *City Crimes*, Thompson featured a hypocrite who first becomes a doctor who fornicates with his female patients, then a preacher, and finally, in his words, "growing tired of piety, I kicked it to the devil to join the ranks of temperance. For over a year I lectured in public, and got drunk in private—glorious times! But at last people began to suspect that I was inspired by the spirit of alcohol instead of the spirit of reform."[26] One of the real-life hypocrites Thompson had in mind was John B. Gough, who appears in this novel as Samuel Cough and who explains a recent "scrape" as follows: "I got infernally drunk, and slept in a brothel, which was all very well, you know, and nothing unusual— but people *found it out*! Well, I got up a cock-and-bull story about drinking drugged soda," so that "Now when I get *corned*, I keep out of sight.—Ah, temperance spouting is a great business." Thompson's *Adventures of a Pickpocket* depicted a man who preaches temperance even as he begs for liquor, saying, "A drop more, if you—hic—please, Mr. Whanger. The sin of intemperance brings many—many souls within the clutches—hic—of Satan."[27]

It is understandable, in light of the unrelenting assaults on Washingtonianism, that by 1845 it had already fallen into disrepute, and soon thereafter it lost dominance to the Sons of Temperance, which demanded respectable dress, language, and comportment. The inconsistencies and paradoxes of Washingtonianism brought into question the entire idea of the use of persuasion (then called "moral suasion"), as opposed to law, for social reform. Just as the ironic mode undercut the authority of temperance orators, so the dark-temperance mode brought attention to the grim fatalism surrounding alcohol, which was increasingly described in metaphors that emphasized its overpowering force. The fact that most who took the temperance pledge soon violated it underscored what seemed to be the almost uncontrollable nature of alcohol obsession. The behavior of Mark Twain's Pap, who takes the temperance pledge but then immediately trades his new coat for a jug of whiskey and gets "drunk as a fiddler," was a comic version of a painfully real phenomenon.[28] In the late 1840s, due to the lapses and failures of Washingtonianism, alcohol came to be widely viewed as a virtually irresistible power: as *Alcohol the Great*, in the title of one temperance tract, or *Prince Alcohol*, in that of another.[29] In the deterministic metaphor of Lamas's *The Glass*, drinkers were "one by one caught in the whirl of that great Maelstrom, more fatal than its Norwegian prototype, and lost forever to society, to themselves and the heaven."[30] Similarly, in John K. Cornyn's *Dick Wilson, The Rumseller's Victim* (1853), alcohol is called "the tide that has swept on, gathering in depth and power, until the debris of human ruin has been left on every shore where human foot has trodden. . . . In the hamlet, the city, the country, or wilderness, the influence has been the same. Nations have been drunken to madness."[31]

Because of the apparent failures of moral suasion, intemperance was increasingly combatted on legal grounds. If alcohol was an irresistible ocean, the argument went, the best way to combat it was to cut it off at its source: in the places where it was produced and sold. The prohibitionist movement of the fifties grew on the ashes of failed Washingtonianism. Thirteen of the thirty-one states adopted so-called Maine laws between 1851 and 1855, with 1855 the peak year in the number of prohibition laws passed.

Signaling, and perhaps accelerating, the prohibitionist movement was the most popular temperance novel ever published in America, Timothy Shay Arthur's *Ten Nights in a Bar-room* (1854). Arthur had formerly been a booster of Washingtonianism, as evidenced by his 1842 novel, *Six Nights with the Washingtonians: A Series of Original Temperance Tales*, but by the fifties he had completely lost faith in suasion as the proper method of reform. *Ten Nights in a Bar-room*, which sold at least four hundred thousand copies, captured the growing interest in prohibition while retaining enough sensationalism to have mass appeal for novel-readers. Suggesting that widespread alcoholism was inevitable as long as spirits were sold, *Ten Nights* called for laws against the sale and distribution of alcohol. Arthur utilized all the gimmicks of dark temperance to make his point: the novel contains three murders, an episode of delirium tremens, an eye-gouging, and a case of a wife's insanity—all resulting from alcohol consumption. He also leaves open the possibility of personal reformation through the urging of family members, as in the plot about a helpless drunkard who embraces sobriety when he promises his dying daughter never to drink again. But the novel's main emphasis is the need for immediate legal suppression of the sale of alcohol. As long as liquor is sold, Arthur indicates, temptation and destruction loom before the unwary at every step. Expressing the deterministic view of the prohibitionists, he writes of the liquor traffic: "The young, the weak, and the innocent can no more resist its assaults, than the lamb can resist the wolf. They are helpless if you abandon them to the powers of evil."[32]

Prohibition, embraced by many states and culminating eventually in the national liquor ban of 1922 to 1933, was immediately attacked by defenders of moderate drinking who labeled the prohibitionists grim naysayers with no faith in human control. "Is this pretended reform movement," asked one critic of prohibition, "to be conducted on the principle that a man is a *nothing*, capable of *no* self-control, and with *no* character, *no* manhood, when temptation is by?"[33] For the moderate-drinking defenders, humans were innately possessed of self-government; to say otherwise was to destroy their will and place them in the grips of an outside power.

With the antiprohibitionists, temperance had come full circle, retrieving the belief in human self-improvement that had once been the province of conventional temperance and that had been undermined by Washingtonianism.

Literary Uses of Temperance and Alcohol

All of the major American Renaissance authors were influenced by the temperance movement. Poe, who had close friends in the movement and actually joined it before he died, used the devices of dark temperance in his tales as a means of probing criminal psychology. For Melville, the dark and ironic modes were useful cultural paradigms that assisted in his delving into human duplicity and philosophical ambiguity. Hawthorne wrote a popular temperance story and explored the paradoxes within dark temperance and the ironic mode in some of his major fiction. Emerson, Thoreau, and Whitman moved beyond what they saw as the narrowness, hypocrisy, and taintedness of temperance reformers to transcendentalist redefinitions of temperance, introducing a process of literary transformation that Emily Dickinson also used.

Poe, in his life and in his fiction, embodied many of the paradoxes of antebellum temperance. An alcoholic whose drinking sprees were interrupted by periods of repentant sobriety, he was ambiguously attracted to the temperance movement. Even as he struggled with his habit, he befriended temperance reformers like John Lofland and Timothy Shay Arthur. In 1843, after a long bout with the bottle, Poe promised a friend he would join the Washingtonians. Whether or not he did so, toward the end of his life he joined the Sons of Temperance. On August 27, 1849, he took the temperance pledge before the group's Richmond branch. Four days later, the *Banner of Temperance* announced his initiation into the order and publicly invited Poe to use his pen on its behalf. But Poe proved to be another intemperate temperance man, for within five weeks after taking the pledge he drank himself to death in Baltimore.

To some of his contemporaries, Poe's tragic end was thoroughly predictable. Despite his sporadic promises to reform his ways, Poe was widely regarded as a backslider doomed by alcohol. Chained to his habit, he was an ideal subject for a dark-temperance novel. One of those who perceived this was a literary enemy, Thomas Dunn English. In English's 1843 temperance novel *The Doom of the Drunkard*, which was serialized in the *Cold Water Magazine* and the *Saturday Museum* before being published as a separate volume, Poe appeared as a bibulous fop who went on public binges. English's next novel, *1844* (later reissued as *Walter Woolfe: or, The Doom of the Drinker*), portrayed Poe as a drunken writer, Marmaduke Hammerhead, who collapsed into insanity and delirium tremens.

Poe, who battled English in the newspapers and eventually filed a successful libel suit against him, retaliated against him by penning a variation on the dark-temperance tale, "The Cask of Amontillado." It has long been surmised that "The Cask" was a vindictive document in the so-called "war of the literati," with the tale's narrator (Poe) getting back at his enemy (English) for a recent insult, using their mutual friend Luchesi (Hiram Fuller, the editor of the *New-York Mirror*).[34] Poe's retaliation was even more subtle than has been guessed, for he skillfully used English's chosen vehicle, dark temperance, to achieve an imaginary victory over him.

In "The Cask of Amontillado" Poe fused a sensational adventure plot with psychologically suggestive dark-temperance images to produce a classic of terror. The tale centers on the diseased psychology associated with drinking. Everything in the main narrative pertains to the ill results of alcohol. The object of the descent into the vault is a bottle of wine. Both of the main characters are wine connoisseurs, as is their mentioned friend Luchesi. Although the narrator's motive for revenge is unclear, a nineteenth-century reader accustomed to reading about alcohol-related criminality would find in Montresor a familiar kind of vindictive psychopath when he boasts: "I was skilful in the Italian vintages myself, and bought largely whenever I could."[35] As for Fortunato, the victim of the revenge plot, the double pun on his name ("lucky" and "fated") had meaning in the dark-temperance sense: from his own viewpoint, Fortunato feels "lucky" to have a friend with a valued bottle of wine; from the reader's viewpoint, he is "fated" (in the deterministic symbology of dark temperance) to be sucked to his doom by his affection for liquor. Like many victims of alcohol obsession in popular temperance stories, Fortunato journeys to his demise with full inevitability. He falls easy prey to Montresor because he maniacally loves wine and takes fierce competitive pride in his connoisseurship. Fortunato is indeed fated by his fascination with the Amontillado. Moreover, he is inebriated at the start and becomes progressively more so as the tale progresses; the more wine he drinks, the more his interest in the Amontillado intensifies. Given the dark-temperance fatalism that governs the story, the narrator, Montresor, is just as degraded as Fortunato. There occurs a kind of evil communion between dissolutes when Montresor breaks open a bottle of Medoc and offers it to Fortunato, who "raised it to his lips with a leer." Poe's contemporary readers would have felt at home with the symbolic interweaving of alcohol and death images, as when Poe described "long walls of piled bones, with casks and puncheons intermingling." They would have appreciated the coupling of drinking and clownlike stupidity in the portrayal of Fortunato (his eyes sparkling with wine as his cap bells jingle), and they would see the appropriateness of the terse tautological exchange that takes place as soon as Fortunato is chained to the wall:

> "The Amontillado!" ejaculated my friend, not yet recovered from his astonishment.
> "True," I replied; "the Amontillado."

The dreary circularity of this conversation, with the repetition of the wine's name, reminds us that all aspects of this crime—the motive, the criminal and his victim, the foil, the instigation—have been closely tied to alcohol obsession and alcohol expertise. The horrid shrieks of both the victim and the murderer as the deadly masonwork is completed suggest the hellish end to which this misled expertise has led. We are left with a tale so morally complex that a modern Poe expert like Thomas Olive Mabbott can write equivocally: " 'The Cask,' on its surface completely amoral, is perhaps the most moral of his Tales."[36] Actually, when viewed in terms of its contemporary popular culture, the tale is a memorable portrait of amorality precisely because it takes to an innovative extreme the twisted dark-temperance morality of the day. The intensification of dark-temperance themes and images, released by Poe from the vestiges of overt moralization, gives rise to an enduring portrait of psychopathic criminality and self-dooming obsession.

Another of Poe's inventive reworkings of dark temperance themes was "The Black Cat," published in 1843, just when Washingtonian temperance was cresting in popularity and was notably darkening popular reform rhetoric. "The Black Cat" is a tale fully in the dark-temperance tradition, with reform images retained but an explicit moral message eclipsed. Many dark-temperance tales of the day dramatized the shattering of a happy family after the husband takes up the bottle. By exaggerating both the happy prologue and the horrific aftermath of the husband's tippling, Poe converts a popular reform formula into an intriguing study of the subversive forces unleashed by alcohol. The tale's narrator has long been known for his gentleness and humaneness, especially displayed in his affection for his pet cat. But, as he explains, alcohol changes his character inalterably. He declares that his temperament—"through the instrumentality of the Fiend Intemperance—had (I blush to confess it) experienced a radical alteration for the worse. I grew, day by day, more moody, more irritable, more regardless of the feelings of others."[37] To describe this mental change, Poe uses popular dark-temperance metaphors: the narrator says that "my disease grew upon me—for what disease is like Alcohol!" One night, when "a more than fiendish malevolence, gin-nurtured, thrilled every fibre of my being," the narrator cuts out his cat's eye with a penknife. To forget his action, "I again plunged into excess, and soon drowned in wine all memory of the deed." In the crescendoing perversity that leads to the murder of his cat and finally his wife, the narrator is driven by alcohol to the depths of paranoia, misanthropy, and criminality. The climax of the story, in which the narrator's grisly murder of his wife is revealed to the police by his own perverse game-playing and cockiness, has a somewhat moralistic overtone recalling the con-clusion of many dark-temperance tales—the drunkard, after all, will get his due and is already crying out in fear of "the fangs of the Arch Fiend!" But Poe, who in many tales exploited different popular genres purely for the *effect* they could produce, is here avoiding didactic statement and exploring the shattered homes and self-lacerating demonism made available by the dark-temperance mode.

Like Poe, Melville in his fiction exploited the paradoxes surrounding tem-perance reform as a means of escaping narrow didacticism and probing dark psychology. Melville's main concern, however, was not with psychopaths but with ordinary human beings whose backsliding or habitual intemperance represented the potential failings of all humankind.

Melville's first novels, published in the mid-1840s, coincided with the widely publicized problems within the ranks of the Washingtonians, particularly the Gough scandal. Quick to make literary capital out of ironies he saw in his contemporary popular culture, Melville found some of his richest ones within the temperance cause. In his first three novels he explored the popular paradox of the intemperate temperance reformer. In *Typee* (1846) he drew an ironic portrait of the pagan King Mehevi, who, "although a member of the Hawaiian Temperance society, is a most inveterate dram drinker."[38] In *Omoo* (1847) Melville himself played the paradoxical temperance reformer, since the novel protests frequently against intemperance and yet contains many playfully de-scribed scenes of excessive drinking.

Melville's next novel, *Mardi* (1849), similarly probed the ironic mode and also made use of the kind of oceanic imagery that in the late forties was increasingly associated with alcohol. The intemperate temperance reformer reappears here as Donjalolo, the Prince Juam, who is one of the first figures the protagonists meet on their island travels. Like John Gough and other backsliding temperance reformers of the decade, Donjalolo vacillates between extreme professions of temperance and private bouts with the bottle. In Chapter 84 we see Donjalolo getting totally drunk, but in the next we hear him cursing alcohol as a "treacherous, treacherous fiend! full of smiles and daggers."[39] Melville makes a point of saying that Donjalolo was "famed for his temperance and discretion" but periodically "burst into excesses, a hundred fold more insane than ever. Thus vacillating between virtue and vice; to neither constant, and upbraided by both; his mind, like his person in the glen, was continually passing and repassing between opposite extremes." This fascination with the ambiguities of the intemperate temperance character is linked in *Mardi* with Melville's growing interest in the mythic, larger-than-life images associated with revelry scenes. Note the energetic images (some of them giving a foretaste of *Moby-Dick*) in this account of Donjalolo's drunken feast: "The mirth now blew into a gale; like a ship's shrouds in a Typhoon, every tendon vibrated; the breezes of Omi came forth with a rush; the hangings shook; the goblets danced fandangos; and Donjalolo, clapping his hands, called before him his dancing women." Here and in several other drinking scenes in the novel Melville becomes swept up in the metaphorical excitement of the moment, allowing his imagination to revel in the kind of oceanic images that the temperance reformers were using. In this context, it is significant that his philosophical mouthpiece, Babbalanja, toward the end of the novel praises wine, which he says opens the heart, brings "glorious visions" to his mind, and stimulates his poetic imagination. It would seem that Melville in *Mardi* is stepping beyond the ironic mode toward a poeticizing of the creative powers this mode releases.

Melville continued to dramatize the ironies surrounding temperance reform in *Redburn* (1849) and *White-Jacket* (1850). In the former novel, breaking the temperance pledge is a key symbolic element in the protagonist's initiation into evil. Redburn explains his "scruples about drinking spirits" by reporting that as a youth he had been a member of the Juvenile Total Abstinence Association and had taken the temperance pledge.[40] Most of Melville's contemporary readers would have been fully aware that such simple devotion to total abstinence was almost surely doomed to failure, since by the late forties pledge-signing was widely in disrepute and alcohol was increasingly viewed as an overwhelming force, a kind of updated version of the Calvinist God, driving humanity inexorably to earthly hells. Ominously, when Redburn boards the Liverpool-bound merchant ship, he sees two drunken sailors, another one who has passed out, and two more who have gone below to sleep off their inebriation. The first token of Redburn's descent into evil is his breaking of the temperance pledge. When he accepts grog to relieve seasickness, he wishes guiltily "that when I signed the pledge of abstinence, I had not taken care to insert a little clause, allowing me to drink spirits on the case of sea-sickness." But break the pledge he does, and, as he puts it, violating the pledge "insidiously opened the way to subsequent breaches of it, which . . . carried no apology with them." He has a similar experience with smoking, at first refusing a cigar because he was a member of an antismoking society but then joining the rollicking sailors in their cigar puffing.

After his first sip of alcohol, Redburn is prepared to associate with drunken sailors, to explore the London slums, and to accompany his friend Harry Bolton into a lavish den of vice. That Melville seemingly shares his contemporaries' deterministic vision of alcohol is made clear in a passage in which he emphasizes that all efforts by temperance societies or tract writers to reform alcoholic sailors are vain, since the sailors are virtually predestined to remain addicted to their vice. But Redburn never gives himself up to bestiality or perversity, as do the typical protagonists of dark-temperance works. Instead, he remains a sometimes bewildered but usually sensitive and sympathetic recorder of dark-reform horrors. Accordingly, Melville is able to treat these horrors with greater detachment, with more attention to symbolic and psychological implications, than had most popular writers. To be sure, the novel contains sheer sensationalism that resembles dark-temperance writing of the crassest variety, such as the account of the sailor who leaps overboard while suffering from delirium tremens or the improbable description of another sailor who is burned alive in flames produced by the internal spontaneous combustion of cheap liquor he has drunk. But even such meretricious moments are significant, for Melville exploits them as convenient exercises in post-Calvinist image-making. Of the spontaneous combustion scene, Redburn declares: "I had almost thought that the burning body was a premonition of the hell of the Calvinists, and that [the burned sailor's] earthly end was a foretaste of his eternal condemnation."

In *White-Jacket*, alcohol is again described in vivid post-Calvinist imagery, as Melville insists that the sailor who leaves the navy is predestined to return, "driven back to the spirit-tub and gun-deck by his old hereditary foe, the ever-devilish god of grog."[41] Although such typical dark-temperance moments may explain why *White-Jacket* was favorably reviewed by a temperance journal, the Honolulu *Friend*, Melville is moving in this novel toward a freer treatment of alcohol and its devotees. He paints notably sympathetic portraits of two heavy drinkers, the gruff, likable Mad Jack and a "wry old toper of a top-man" who, in answer to White-Jacket's appeal that he give up the bottle, replies that he is too much "a good Christian" to give up drinking, because he loves his "enemy too much to drop his acquaintance." Melville is turning evangelical temperance against itself, as he does differently in *Moby-Dick* when he has Ishmael hop into bed with Queequeg with the pious rationalization: "Better sleep with a sober cannibal than a drunken Christian."[42] In short, Melville is now beginning to toy objectively with protemperance and antitemperance to reach new levels of literary irony.

By the time Melville wrote *Moby-Dick* (1851), the imagery of temperance reform had become for him a colorful shell, largely devoid of didactic content, that could be arranged at will in the overall mosaic of a subversive novel. He repeats the oxymoronic character of the intemperate temperance advocate in his sketch of Jack Bunger, the captain of the *Samuel Enderby*, who boasts that he is "a strict total abstinence man" even though he gets drunk on the sly.[43] But, perhaps because this character was becoming a bit hackneyed, Melville gave some new twists to it, as in his updated version of the biblical rich man Dives, who, "a president of a temperance society, . . . only drinks the tepid tears of orphans" (19). He developed other oxymoronic characters as well, such as the Quaker captain Bildad (the penny-pinching philanthropist and squabbling peace advocate) and Ahab, described as an "ungodly, god-like man" and a "swearing good man."

Melville was now so sensitively attuned to all possible permutations of the dark-temperance mode that he could shift with ease between protemperance and antitemperance stances, giving full moral credence to no single viewpoint and always seeking the stylistic potentialities of whatever stance he assumed. In his portrait of the blacksmith Perth he sounds like the typical dark-temperance writer showing how alcohol can destroy a family and lead to suicide. Melville tells how Perth had been a churchgoing family man until "a desperate burglar slid into his happy home, and robbed them all of everything. And darker yet to tell," Melville cautions, "the blacksmith himself did ignorantly conduct this burglar into his family's heart. It was the Bottle Conjurer! Upon the opening of that fatal cork, forth flew the fiend, and shrivelled up his home" (401–2). "Oh, woe on woe!" Melville laments as he describes the steady demise of the whole family as a result of Perth's drinking. Perth is left a stolid relic, a man "past scorching" who is well fitted to forge the harpoon that Ahab will baptize in the devil's name and hurl at the white whale.

If the Perth episode shows that the dark-temperance mode could be used as an appropriate entrance to gloomy message and mythic imagery, so an incident involving the harpooner Queequeg and the mate Stubb shows that the flexible Melville could readily use antitemperance images for humorous purposes. Just after he has emerged from his perilous descent into the whale in Chapter 72 ("The Monkey-Rope"), the exhausted Queequeg is handed a drink of ginger and water by Dough-Boy, the steward. The onlooking Stubb, a boisterous advocate of grog, furiously declares, "There is some sneaking Temperance Society movement about this business" (272). When Dough-Boy tells him that the social worker Aunt Charity has sent aboard ginger to enforce temperance among the harpooners, Stubb throws the ginger to the waves and ensures that Queequeg benefits from the captain's command: "grog for the harpooner on a whale" (273).

The fact is that Melville is now interested in temperance reform chiefly as it can provide ironic or dark images for subversive fiction. In the course of the novel the temperate characters (Bulkington, Aunt Charity, Starbuck, Dough-Boy) prove powerless before the wickedly uproarious, spirit-quaffing ones (the *Grampus* crew, Ahab, most of the *Pequod* crew). Melville neatly dramatizes this conflict and its outcome early in the novel, when Ishmael witnesses the *Grampus* crew, just home from a three years' voyage, rushing straight into the Spouter-Inn bar (the entrance to which is a huge whale's jaw) and getting drunk on drinks poured by the bartender Jonah, while the temperate Bulkington watches aloof and then disappears. Just as the popular reformers described alcohol as a ferocious, hope-destroying "Giant" or an all-consuming "destiny," so Melville described the *Grampus* crew entering through "jaws of swift destruction" to be served "deliriums and death" by a prophetically named bartender (21). Just as the reformers had emphasized the illusoriness of alcohol's pleasures, so Melville writes: "Abominable are the tumblers into which he pours his poison. Though true cylinders without—within, the villainous green goggling glasses deceitfully tapered downward to a cheating bottom" (23). Just as dark-temperance literature had stressed the orgiastic extremes of inebriation rather than remedies for it, so Melville suggests the relative impotence of Bulkington in the face of his shipmates' obstreperous carousing, which Bulkington watches with a "sober face" before he slips away unnoticed.

The disappearance of Bulkington here, presaging his later disappearance from the novel, epitomizes the victory of dark temperance, with its boisterous irrationalism and its mythic imagery, over the forces for conventionality. This imagistic victory is repeated throughout the novel, as when Ahab toasts his demonic crew and mates on the quarterdeck (Chapter 36) or when the sailors hold a midnight orgy in the forecastle (Chapter 40). Indeed, Ishmael experiences a kind of conversion to the subversive during the drunken orgy scene, as the formerly blithe narrator begins Chapter 41 by declaring that "my shouts had gone up with the rest; my oath had been welded with theirs. . . . Ahab's quenchless feud seemed mine" (155). Given the number of dark-temperance images in the novel, it is possible to read the Spouter-Inn barroom scene as a preparatory literary exercise: just as the bartender pours poisonous drinks to rambunctious sailors who are inside symbolic whale's jaws, so in a sense dark temperance "pours" many of the subversive images in *Moby-Dick*.

For Melville's friend Hawthorne, temperance reform similarly provided a number of themes and images that he used in his fiction. Many of these images were visible in his temperance tale, "A Rill from the Town Pump," published in the *New England Magazine* in May 1835. The tale merits more attention than it has received, because it is a kind of ur-source for some of the main concerns of Hawthorne's later fiction. The tale is an imaginary monologue by a town water pump, who boasts that the water it yields can cure many of the ills that beset humanity. The pump says that, along with the cow, it is "the grand reformer of the age," since water and milk form "that glorious copartnership, that shall tear down the distilleries and brew-houses, uproot the vineyards, shatter the cider-presses, ruin the tea and coffee trade, and, finally, monopolize the whole business of quenching thirst."[44] The pump predicts that when water gains supremacy over alcohol, poverty, disease, and sin will diminish, and temperance will heal both public and private ills:

> Until now, the phrensy of hereditary fever has raged in the human blood, transmitted from sire to son, and re-kindled, in every generation by fresh draughts of liquid flame. When that inward fire shall be extinguished, the heat of passion cannot but grow cool, and war—the drunkenness of nations—perhaps will cease. At least, there will be no war of households. The husband and wife, drinking deep of peaceful joy—a calm bliss of temperate affections—shall pass hand in hand through life, and lie down, not reluctantly, at its protracted close. To them, the past will be no turmoil of made dreams, nor the future an eternity of such moments as follow the delirium of the drunkard.

When the world is regenerated by its work, the pump announces, "you will collect your useless vats and liquor-casks into one great pile, and make a bonfire, in honor of the Town-Pump." The pump insists that it is the most effective temperance advocate, since most temperance reformers are bizarre hypocrites. The pump asks the reader whether it is decent, "think you, to get tipsy with zeal for temperance, and take up the honorable cause of the Town-Pump, in the style of a toper fighting for his brandy-bottle? Or, can the excellent qualities of cold water be no otherwise exemplified, than by plunging, slap-dash, into hot-water, and woefully scalding yourselves and other people?" Pointing to itself as the example of cool detachment needed for temperance reform, the pump insists, "In the moral warfare which you are to wage—and indeed, in the whole conduct of your lives—you cannot choose a better example than myself, who have never permitted the duct, and sultry atmosphere, the turbulence and manifold disquietudes of the world around me to reach that deep, calm, well of purity, which may be called my soul. And whenever I pour out my soul, it is to cool the earth's fever, or cleanse its stains."

In this tale lie the seeds of many of Hawthorne's later themes. The image of alcohol vats being cast into a huge bonfire would be repeated and amplified in his tale "Earth's Holocaust." The idea of sin being transmitted through generations as a "hereditary fever" that has "raged in the human blood" presages the long-standing sins of the Pyncheon family, who in *House of the Seven Gables* live under Matthew Maule's dark prophecy that the family would have blood to drink. The Maule-Pyncheon warfare is anticipated in the reference to a "war of households." The image of the past as a "turmoil of mad dreams" and the future as "delirium" participates in the nightmarish atmosphere of many Hawthorne works, from "Young Goodman Brown" through *The Scarlet Letter* to *The Marble Faun.* The pump's championing of the "deep, calm well of purity" of its soul, in contrast to the "plunging, slap dash" people around him, parallels Hawthorne's own cool, somewhat distanced position with regard to the gallery of hypocrites, fanatics, and criminals that figure so largely in his fiction.

The latter point needs developing, since the quietness and repose that Henry James and others have valued in Hawthorne seem to have derived in large part from the latter's success in forging an equanimity in response to the turbulent reform culture around him. The town pump's pointed complaint about those who "get tipsy with temperance . . . in the style of a toper fighting for his brandy bottle" is one that Hawthorne often made. In an 1835 notebook entry, he wrote: "A sketch to be made of a modern reformer,—a type of the extreme doctrines on the subject of slaves, cold water, and other such topics." Hawthorne imagines this temperance/abolitionist orator haranguing on the streets "when his labors are suddenly interrupted by the keeper of a mad-house, whence he has escaped. Much may be made of this idea."[45] The stereotype of the intemperate temperance advocate, and the larger one of the mad reformer, would reappear throughout his writings: in Judge Jaffrey Pyncheon, the seemingly model citizen who gives money to the temperance cause but is secretly corrupt; in Holgrave, who initially appears amidst "reformers, temperance-lecturers, and all manner of cross-looking philanthropists"; in the drunken preacher of the *Septimus Norton* manuscripts, whose preaching was "only a diabolical covering" for many sins, as he had a "propensity for strong drink" and "composed his most powerful sermons under its influence, and always indulged himself after preaching them"; in the American preacher of *Our Old Home* who appears respectably sober at the Liverpool consulate but disappears for a week-long binge, leading Hawthorne to write that "the Arch Enemy" (alcohol) had transformed him "from the most decorous of metropolitan clergymen into the rowdiest and dirtiest of disbanded officers."[46] The latter example of backsliding makes Hawthorne reflect, "The temperance-reformers unquestionably derive their commission from the divine Benevolence, but have never been taken fully into its counsels. All may not be lost, though those good men fail."

Hawthorne was, on some level, attracted to temperance but thought that many of its popular advocates were hypocritical and extreme in their views. In his 1844 tale "Earth's Holocaust," among the things thrown into a huge bonfire are barrels of alcohol. The tale describes "the arrival of a vast procession of Washingtonians—as the votaries of temperance call themselves now-a-days," who, along with other temperance reformers, throw all the world's alcohol into the fire. Sounding a protemperance note, Hawthorne writes: "It was the aggregate of that fierce fire, which would otherwise have scorched the hearts of millions," and the multitude around the fire shout triumphantly as if released from "the curse of the ages." But some did not rejoice, including the Last Toper, who insists that the world would be gloomier than ever without the good fellowship nurtured by convivial drinking. Toward the end of the tale, Hawthorne indicates that in his parable about temperance and other modern reforms he has been describing "the titan of innovation—angel or fiend, double in his nature, and capable of deeds befitting both characters."[47]

This last statement suggests that temperance and other reform movements contributed greatly to the thematic ambiguity and indeterminacy that is so important a feature of Hawthorne's fiction. We think of Hawthorne's many mixed characters: Beatrice Rappaccini, who seems at once an angel and a devil; Pearl, at once lawless and an agent of retribution; Chillingworth, demonic yet curative in that he keeps alive Dimmesdale's sense of sin; Hollingsworth, the beneficent yet cold prison reformer. These and other characters are simultaneously "moral" and "immoral," and thus are allied in spirit to the paradoxical reform movements whose doubleness Hawthorne perceived acutely.

Hawthorne directly took advantage of the doubleness of the temperance cause. On the one hand, he was not above using dark temperance in a manner reminiscent of the popular reformers. "Ethan Brand" (1850) includes a portrait of a village doctor whom brandy "possessed . . . like an evil spirit," making him "surly and savage as a wild beast, and as miserable as a lost soul."[48] In the barroom scene in *The Blithedale Romance* there is a painting of "a ragged, bloated, New England toper, stretched out on a bench"; the only good thing about the drunkard in the painting, Hawthorne tells us, is that he cannot suffer from real headaches or delirium tremens.[49] In these and other instances, Hawthorne borrows from the popular temperance mode in order to reinforce the gloomy themes of his fiction.

On the other hand, Hawthorne knew the excesses of the popular reformers and derided them in his fiction. In his tale "David Hall, A Fantasy" he wryly parodied temperance advocates who were quick to exploit almost any odd human situation, no matter how innocent. When David Hall, a respectable New Hampshire youth, falls asleep by the roadside, he becomes the subject of commentary by several passersby, including the following: "A temperance lecturer saw him, and wrought poor David into the texture of his evening's discourse, as an awful instance of dead drunkenness by the road-side."[50] If Hawthorne's target here is temperance reformers' eagerness to sensationalize commonplace events, in *The Blithedale Romance* it is their lack of human sympathy. One of the main points of this novel is what Hawthorne sees as the appalling gap between various reform programs—including utopian socialism, prison reform, and women's rights—and actual human experience. Temperance reform falls under the general indictment. Miles Coverdale, while waiting for Moodie in the saloon, takes "a boozy kind of pleasure" in seeing people enjoying their drinks. He reflects: "The temperance-men may preach till doom's day; and still this cold and barren world will look warmer, kindlier, mellower, through the medium of the toper's glass. . . . The reformers should make their efforts positive, instead of negative; they must do away with evil by substituting good."[51]

The reconstruction of temperance reform Hawthorne called for—in his words, making it "positive" instead of "negative"—is precisely what Emerson, Thoreau, Whitman, and Dickinson strove to accomplish. What I am calling the transcendental approach was taken by those who knew full well the shortcomings of the popular reformers and who tried mightily to overcome them in their own writings.

In his 1841 lecture "Man the Reformer" Emerson paid homage to the reform movements of the day. "In the history of the world," he generalized, "the doctrine of Reform had never such scope as at the present hour."[52] "These movements are on all accounts important," he declared. Among the specific reforms he mentioned were antislavery, utopian socialism, and temperance. The latter struck him as especially important because of the universal interest taken in it. "The Temperance-question, which rides the conversation of ten thousand circles, is tacitly recalled at every public and private table, drawing with it all the curious ethics of the pledge, of the Wine-question, of the equity of the manufacture and the trade, is a gymnastic training to the casuistry and conscience of the time."

Besides providing mental gymnastics with its moral and legal issues, the temperance movement, in Emerson's view, provided an example of active self-improvement. Emerson confessed in his journal that he felt shamefully in-active when he was approached by an advocate of "Universal Temperance": "I have no excuse—I honor him with shame at my own inaction."[53] Long before he wrote "Self-Reliance," he meditated about the self-mastery attempted by the popular reformers. "Since to govern my passions with absolute sway is the work I have to do," he wrote in his journal in 1831, "I cannot but think that the sect for the suppression of Intemperance or a sect for the suppression of loose behavior in women would be a more reasonable & useful society than the orthodox sect . . . for the suppression of Unitarianism."

Although temperance reform provided impetus for Emerson's notion of self-reliance, it also contained features that he found distinctly disagreeable and that drove him to fashion a highly individualistic version of the reform. His famed hostility toward consistency stemmed directly from what he consid-ered the narrow, programmatic nature of the temperance movement. In an 1839 journal entry that anticipated his indictment of "a foolish consistency" in "Self-Reliance," he wrote: "I wish to say what I think & feel today with the provision that tomorrow I shall contradict it all. Freedom boundless I wish. I will not pledge myself not to drink wine, not to drink ink, not to lie, & not to commit adultery lest I hanker tomorrow to do these very things by reason of having tied my hands." Temperance, although admirable theoretically, seemed to him confining and repressive when pursued as an end in itself. "The reforms whose fame now fills the land with Temperance, Anti-slavery, . . . fair and generous as each appears, are poor bitter things when prosecuted for themselves as an end," he said in an 1841 speech. "To every reform, in proportion to its energy, early disgusts are incident, so that the disciple is surprised at the very hour of his first triumphs, with chagrins, and sickness, and a general distrust."[54]

The "chagrins" and "sickness" of the popular reformers were all too apparent to him. Dark temperance and the ironic mode, which had been a source of literary ambiguity for Hawthorne and Melville, were examples to be avoided for Emerson. He was appalled, not stimulated, by the irony that many temperance reformers peddled sensationalism under the name of morality. "Temperance that knows itself is not temperance," he wrote, "when it peeks and pines, and knows all it renounces."[55] Elsewhere he commented, "The Reformers affirm the inward life . . . but use outward and vulgar means. They are quickly organized in some low, inadequate form, and present no more poetic image to the mind, than the evil tradition which they reprobated."[56] Aware of the liabilities of both moral suasion, epitomized by the Washingtonians, and legal reform, urged by the prohibitionists, he wrote in 1847 that although the importance of temperance "cannot be denied and hardly exaggerated," it "is usually taught on a low platform . . . [I]t is a long way from the Maine law to the heights of absolute self-command which respect the conservatism of the entire energies of the body, the mind, and the soul. I wish to point out some of its higher functions as it enters into mind and character."[57]

Surveying these comments by Emerson on the temperance movement, we see all kinds of negative associations—"sickness," "outward and vulgar," "low, inadequate," "evil tradition"—countered directly by the inwardness, spirituality, and true self-reliance that constituted those "higher functions" he elucidated in his own writings. It is no accident that his major essays appeared in the two volumes of 1841 and 1844, published during the first flush of Washingtonian enthusiasm, just when the potentialities and the problems of this popular reform were becoming readily visible. Vigorously rejecting what he regarded as the impurities of the popular reformers, Emerson forged a fresh brand of reform allied with the spirit and creative individualism.

Emerson's friend and follower Thoreau has gone down to posterity as the era's most powerful reform voice precisely because he too saw both the promise and the perils of his contemporary reform movements. To some degree, Thoreau was a kind of temperance advocate. As Emerson noted in his eulogy of Thoreau, "few lives contain so many renunciations. . . . He ate no flesh, he drank no wine, he never knew the use of tobacco."[58] Sounding like a devoted temperance reformer demonizing alcohol, Thoreau once described "a demon . . . who has acted a prominent and astounding part in our New England life, and deserves, as much as any mythological character, to have his biography written one day; who first comes in the guise of a friendly or hired man, and then robs and murders the whole family,—New England Rum."[59] He combined a distaste for the "demon" rum with a lifelong dedication to water-drinking.

However, Thoreau developed an even stronger horror of reform movements than did Emerson. Indeed, his most striking contribution to reform—the extreme individualism symbolized by his practice of civil disobedience and by his years of contemplative isolation by Walden Pond—resulted largely from what he regarded as the impurity and corruption of reform movements. Thoreau admired certain reformers (particularly Wendell Phillips, Nathaniel P. Rogers, and John Brown, all promoters of both temperance and antislavery) but hated reform societies, which he believed were tainted and low. Throughout his writings runs a keen awareness that reform becomes poisonous and devilish unless enforced by individuals of the most rigorous morality and integrity. American culture taught him an unequivocal lesson: when people grouped together in reform societies, inevitably the reform became diseased or unclean. Having learned this lesson early on, Thoreau committed much of his career to creating a new kind of reform, one which at all costs avoided the "joiner" mentality of reform groups and asserted the power of individual reform.

As early as the mid-1840s, Thoreau expressed disapproval of organized reform movements, largely in reaction to groups like the Washingtonians who were using questionable tactics to advance their views. In an 1845 manuscript he branded "the Reformer" as "the impersonation of disorder and imperfection."[60] He continued: "I ask of all Reformers, of all who are recommending Temperance—Justice—Charity—Peace—the Family, Community or Associative life, not to give us their theory and wisdom only, for these are no proof, but to carry around with them a small specimen of his own manufactures, and to despair of ever recommending anything of which a small sample at least cannot be exhibited:—that the Temperance man let me know the savor of his Temperance, if it be good," and so forth.[61] The reformer, he warned, "should impart his courage and not his despair; his health and ease, not his disease, and take care that this does not spread by contagion." He warned the reformer class: "Be green and flourishing plants in God's nursery, and not such complaining bleeding trees as Dante saw in the Infernal regions." Asking reformers to "deepen their speech, and give it fresh sincerity and significance," he complained that most of them seemed "outward bound, they live out and out," whereas "I would fain to see them inward bound, retiring in and in farther and farther every day." The reformer, he insisted, "must not lecture on Missions & the Temperance" but rather should "read me a more or less simple & sincere account of his life—of what he had done & thought."

Thoreau's point was that temperance agitators, among other reformers, were wallowing in negative images instead of fashioning positive, life-affirming ones. In *Walden* he offered a reform of the spirit and body that was purposefully removed from the popular reformers he regarded as misled. Believing that they expressed despair, he offered the hope of a healthy spirit. Thinking they were spreading contagion, he offered healing. Lamenting the shallowness and directionlessness of their harangues, he wished to supply reform discourse with significance and resonance. Seeing them always plunging "outward" into causes and movements, he wished to retire into the inward depths of his soul, aiming to set a positive example for all. If they harped on the evils of alcohol, he rhapsodized on the pure Walden water. The temperance reformers' insistence on drinking only water took on new meaning when he wrote: "I am glad to have drunk water for so long, for the same reason that I prefer the natural sky to the opium eater's heaven. . . . Of all ebrosity, who does not prefer to be intoxicated by the air he breathes?"[62] Here and elsewhere in *Walden* he suggested his idea of true reform by adopting popular reform images and pointing them toward affirmations of symbolic perception and deliberate living.

Walt Whitman developed attitudes to the temperance movement that were similar to Thoreau's, although he gained these attitudes through the kind of direct participation in popular temperance reform that the more detached Thoreau never had. Whitman became involved in the movement early in his career and kept up an interest in it to the end of his life. Among his earliest periodical contributions were didactic reform works whose tameness reflected the conventional discourse of evangelical temperance. In the fifth essay for his newpaper series "The Sun-Down Papers" he struck the popular reform note in the most straightfoward way, arguing against the use of spirits, tobacco, coffee, and tea. This conventional approach also characterized another Whitman work of 1840, the poem "Young Grimes," a simple portrait of abstinence leading to a happy family life.

Although Whitman always retained a certain allegiance to this simple, conventional kind of temperance, after 1840 the Washingtonians' intensified demonization of alcohol opened the door to his use of more varied types of temperance rhetoric. The populist Whitman was more strongly attracted to the Washingtonians than to other types of temperance reform. He loved the

colorful festivals the Washingtonians put on. "Yesterday was a great time with
the New York temperance societies," he wrote in the March 30, 1842 issue of the
New York *Aurora*. "They had processions, and meetings, and orations, and
festivals, and banners displayed, and a grand blow out at night to cap the
whole."[63] He approvingly noted "the immense number of citizens, formerly
intemperate men, but now worthy members of society." He hated the prohibition movement, believing that reform could be best achieved through persuasion, not legislation. He clung to this belief even in the 1850s, when prohibition
became popular.

The period from 1840 to 1845, when Whitman wrote his main temperance
fiction and poetry, coincided with the Washingtonian craze and the ascen-
dancy of John B. Gough, one of Whitman's all-time favorite speakers. Using
the moral cover of temperance, Whitman in his Washingtonian phase explored an array of dark and erotic themes in his early fiction, preparing the
way for the adventurousness of his mature poetry.

It is not surprising that Whitman's contributions to Washingtonian literature were long on sensation and short on moralizing. His story "Reuben's
Farewell," published in the New York *Washingtonian* in May 1842, was a grim
portrait of a once-happy farmer driven by alcohol to brutalize his wife and
children. "The Child's Champion," a sensational story retooled, with only
slight changes, as the temperance tale "The Child and the Profligate," featured
a barroom scene in which the virtuous hero was pummeled by a rough sailor
who ignored the boy's pleas for sobriety. There were temperance overtones to
another Whitman tale of the period, "Wild Frank's Return," in which a returning prodigal son, falling asleep while tethered to his horse after spending time
in a bar, was dragged to a bloody death when the horse became startled by
thunder.

This kind of moralistic sensationalism, typical of the Washingtonians, was
multiplied exponentially in *Franklin Evans*, the novel Whitman wrote for the
movement in the fall of 1842. Written at the peak of the Washingtonian frenzy,
Franklin Evans embodied all the contradictions of the Washingtonians.

On one level, the temperance message of *Franklin Evans* is sincere. The novel
gives many examples of the dire results of drinking. The young orphan Franklin Evans bears witness to the ravages of alcohol. On the stage from eastern
Long Island to Manhattan he meets a once-happy man who has lost his farm
and his family due to his own drinking. When Evans reaches New York, he is
taken to a bar and has his first drink. A string of tragic events follows. He is
married to a wonderful woman who soon dies from maltreatment and neglect.

He falls in with criminals and is arrested for robbery. The man who procures his freedom persuades him to sign the "old" temperance pledge, forbidding hard liquor but permitting beer and wine. This partial pledge does not prevent him from resuming drinking and falling into deeper troubles. He goes South, where after a drunken revel he marries a mulatto woman, Margaret, whom he soon comes to detest. Margaret eventually murders a rival and then kills herself in prison. These terrible events give Evans an impetus for reform that is strengthened when he hears the sad story of a dying man, Stephen Lee, whose two children died as a result of his wife's drunkenness. Lee convinces Evans to sign the new total abstinence pledge and rewards him by leaving him money. The novel ends with a long paean to the Washingtonians, who are said to be rallying the whole country in their calls for reform. In a guarded reference to the histrionic sensationalism of Washingtonian orators, Whitman writes, "It is true, that the dictates of a classic and most refined taste, are not always observed by these people."[64] Their "want of polish, or grace," he argues, is made up for by their forcefulness and democratic emphasis.

But as was so often the case in Washingtonian writing, there was a good amount of dark theater involved in Whitman's delivery of the temperance message in *Franklin Evans*. The novel was, in his italicized words, "written *for the mass*" (*WEP*, 127), and, like other reformers of the day, he knew that the mass liked violence and sex mixed with their morality. Much of *Franklin Evans* has little to do with temperance. Whitman's publisher promoted the novel by saying it would "create a sensation, both for the ability with which it is written, as well as the interest of the subject" (*WEP*, 124). Most who bought the twelve-and-a-half-cent pamphlet were doubtless looking for one more sensation to go along with their morning *Herald* and their latest visit to Barnum's museum. The novel is filled with scenes that offered diversion to the public and, it would seem, sublimation for Whitman. Homoerotic fantasy seems to enter into the description of the bar Evans is taken to: "It was indeed a seductive scene. Most of the inmates were young; and I noticed no small number quite on the verge of boyhood" (*WEP*, 156). The standard Washingtonian theme that homes can be shattered by alcohol is dramatized no less than four times by Whitman, whose harping on the theme of ruined marriages may reflect his own ambivalence about heterosexual relationships.

Whatever the biographical meanings of the narrative, gratuitous violence and taboo behavior abound. Significantly, the novel was later reprinted in the *Brooklyn Daily Eagle* under the nontemperance title *Fortunes of a Country-Boy; Incidents in Town—and His Adventures at the South*. The boundary between

Washingtonian reform and mere sensationalism was thin indeed. This becomes glaringly evident in the interpolated tale in *Franklin Evans* about two members of rival Indian tribes who kill each other in a bloody fight. This story has nothing to do with temperance reform. Nor do most of the incidents surrounding Evans's marriage to the slave Margaret. Not only does Whitman deal with the risqué topic of miscegenation, but he revels in the perverse results of the flawed marriage, including murder and suicide. Toward the end of the novel Evans admits he had enjoyed reflecting upon even "the very dreariest and most degraded incidents which I have related in the preceding pages" (*WEP*, 219). He adds that the narration has been "far from agreeable to me— but in my own self-communion upon the subject, I find a species of entertainment" (*WEP*, 219).

A species of entertainment. This, ultimately, is what Washingtonian reform was for Whitman. He would later joke that he wrote *Franklin Evans* in three days for money under the influence of alcohol; the type of alcohol was variously reported as port, gin, or whiskey. Given the contradictions surrounding the Washingtonians, it is not surprising that Whitman wrote the novel while under the influence. Nor is it odd that he went on to begin another dark-temperance piece, "The Madman," the opening section of which appeared on January 23, 1842, in the New York *Washingtonian and Organ*. His main goal in all his temperance writings, besides airing private aggressions and fantasies, was to make a connection with the American masses. Peddled as the work of "a Popular American Author," *Franklin Evans* was, in Whitman's words, "not written for the critics, but for THE PEOPLE" (*WEP*, 127). He hoped the story might do some good, issued "in the cheap and popular form you see, and wafted by every mail to all parts of this vast republic" (*WEP*, 127).

This was, Whitman realized, a tawdry way of reaching the masses. His later verdict on the novel would be unequivocal: "It was damned rot—rot of the worst sort—not insincere perhaps, but rot, nevertheless: it was not the business for me to be up to."[65] Significantly, though, Whitman stuck to the business. Throughout the 1840s and 1850s he continued to promote temperance and nearly every other popular reform: antiprostitution, anti–capital punishment, agrarianism, labor reform, and antislavery. Although his sympathies generally stood with the radical side on such issues, he continued to emphasize the imaginative rather than the political possibilities of reform rhetoric, so that popular reform was chiefly important as a training ground in zestful, defiant writing. It was not so much the moral content as the brash spirit of reform that intrigued him. As he wrote in the *Eagle*, "the duty of the promulger of all moral reforms" is "to advocate and illustrate, the more enthusiastically the better, his doctrine."[66] As his newspaper writings show, it was the enthusiasm, rather than the doctrine, that counted most. In the paper Whitman printed many dark-temperance tales with lively titles like "Intemperance and Parricide" or "How Rum Can Change a Young Man into a Brutal Scoundrel," horrid stories about drunken sons killing their fathers with crowbars or besotted brutes knocking down little boys for the sheer sadistic sport of it. This exploitative sensationalism might seem to compromise reformist seriousness, but here again Whitman was moving beyond reform into a neutral ground in which he could playfully juggle moral standards.

Dark-reform rhetoric remained a piquant presence in many of Whitman's later writings, including the poem "Resurgemus" (in which the "bloody corpses" of the poor rise up against wealthy "locusts" [*WEP*, 39–40]), the prose tract "The Eighteenth Presidency!" (filled with images of blood, coffins, excrement, and so on), and the political essay "Democratic Vistas" (in which America is said to be "crowded with petty grotesques, malformations, phantasms, playing meaningless antics").[67] All such Gothicized images tap into the kind of vibrant, sensational discourse Whitman had first used in his writings for the Washingtonians.

If Washingtonianism was a source of instruction to Whitman, it was also a source of warning. As we have seen, the movement was handicapped by well-publicized instances of backsliding. Though shocked by John B. Gough's apostasy, Whitman made a gesture toward defending temperance in an 1845 piece from the Brooklyn *Star*, declaring, "If the temperance doctrine fell whenever one of its converts became a backslider again, sad indeed would be its fate! . . . So long as the endless and overwhelming train of all fact and argument founds the great cause of temperance as a rock immovable, it matters not whether one, two, or twenty of its shining lights go out."[68]

This was bravely put, but by the time he wrote it, Washingtonianism had already fallen into disrepute. It is understandable, in light of the unrelenting assaults on Washingtonianism, that for Whitman all reform movements, temperance included, became suspect. The best alternative seemed to be poetry that encompassed reform but transcended it. Sometimes in his poetry he poked fun at ranting reformers, as in this line in "Respondez!":

> Let the reformers descend from the stands where they are forever bawling!
> let an idiot or insane person appear on each of the stands![69]

At other times, posing as the all-embracing "Me impeturbe, aplomb in the midst of irrational things" (*LGC*, 11), he claimed to be driven by both reform and its opposite:

What blurt is this about virtue and about vice?
Evil propels me and reform of evil propels me, I stand indifferent
(*LGC*, 50).

More characteristically, he sought positive alternatives to what he regarded
as tainted reform movements. In *Leaves of Grass* he constructed a poetic persona who embodied temperance, strength, and health but who had no direct
association with such movements. Some of his poems used the language of
dark temperance, associating drunkards with impure or disgusting things. "A
drunkard's breath," he wrote in "A Hand-Mirror"; "unwholesome eater's face,
venerealee's flesh, / Lungs rotting away piecemeal, stomach sour and can-
kerous, / Joints rheumatic, bowels clogged with abomination" (*LGC*, 268–69).
Similarly, in "Song of Prudence" he decried "Putridity of gluttons or rum-
drinkers," "privacy of the onanist," and "seduction, prostitution" (*LGC*, 374).
More often, however, he balanced his negative pictures of intemperate types
with more positive images, as when in "Song of the Open Road" he writes,
"Only those may come who come in sweet and determined bodies, / No
diseas'd person, no rum-drinker or venereal taint is permitted here" (*LGC*,
155).

Occasionally, his poetic versions of temperance were paralleled by his efforts to regulate his private behavior, as when he wrote in his notebook: "I
have resolv'd to inaugurate for myself a pure perfect sweet, cleanblooded
robust body by ignoring all drinks but water and pure milk—and all fat meats,
late suppers—a great body—a purged, cleansed, spiritualised and invigorated
body—."[70] But he remained a lifelong believer in convivial drinking, and his
main effort at temperance was the imaginative reconstruction of it in his
poetry, where he could advertise himself, as in the original version of "Song of
the Broad-Axe," as one "of reckless health, his body perfect, free from taint
from top to toe, free forever from headache and dyspepsia, clean-breathed."[71]

Whitman's promotion of physical and spiritual equilibrium, in accord with
the laws of the physical universe, reflected his determination to establish poetry, rather than reform or legislation, as the locus of health and temperance.
His persona announces himself as chaste, religious, and temperate, on the
one hand, and as erotic in every sense of the word. This fusion of the mystical
and the sexual was made possible, at least partly, by his transcendental re-
definition of temperance. Just as Thoreau declared that the highest ebrosity
was to breathe the common air, so the Whitman persona repeatedly becomes
intoxicated, both physically and spiritually, by ordinary things: a mouse, the

hair on the back of his hand, a morning-glory, a goose's honk, a spear of summer grass. In the transcendental version of temperance, alcohol was an unnecessary stimulant, since the everyday world, rightly perceived and experienced, was itself continuously intoxicating.

It is this sense of the intoxicating nature of common experience that Emily Dickinson often communicated in her poems, several of which share of the spirit of transcendental temperance. In particular, poems #214 ("I taste a liquor never brewed—") and #230 ("We—Bee and I—live by the quaffing") show Dickinson boasting about her capacities for consuming huge quantities of the kind of physical/spiritual alcohol Thoreau and Whitman had advertised.[72] By directing the notion of drunkenness toward the sensuous reveling in nature's beauty, Dickinson follows the lead of the transcendentalists by adopting and transforming images and themes of popular temperance reform.

This transforming process is visible in the opening verse of #214:

> I taste a liquor never brewed—
> From Tankards scooped in Pearl—
> Not all the Vats upon the Rhine
> Yield such an Alcohol!

This "I" is a wonderfully fresh avatar of the intemperate temperance advocate. She is both completely drunk and completely temperate. She can exult in her drunkenness because hers is a liquor "never brewed," filling tankards "scooped in Pearl," an image suggesting the pearllike whiteness of the air she loves and the extreme preciousness of her love of nature.

Having immediately revised the popular trope of the intemperate temperance advocate, in the next two verses Dickinson gambols with it, revising several other popular images in the process:

> Inebriate of Air—am I—
> And Debauchee of Dew—
> Reeling—thro endless summer days—
> From inns of Molten Blue—
>
> When "Landlords" turn the drunken Bee
> Out of Foxglove's door—
> When Butterflies—renounce their "drams"—
> I shall but drink the more!

This speaker is not the hypocritical intemperate temperance advocate, publicly sober but privately debauched, but the exultantly open one, proclaiming a debauchery that is allied with the highest form of temperance. Dickinson, who was fully aware of antebellum popular culture in all its dimensions, seems to be intentionally playing on well-known temperance images. A central sequence in T. S. Arthur's 1854 best-seller *Ten Nights in a Bar-room* involves a landlord, Simon Slade, who kicks out of his saloon the drunken Joe Morgan, who later renounces alcohol due to the ministrations of his dying daughter. Dickinson uses similar imagery in her references to " 'Landlords' " who turn drunks out their doors and in alcoholics who "renounce their 'drams' "; her use of quotation marks underscores the fact that she is "quoting," or borrowing, images from others—specifically, from temperance writers like Arthur. But she uses these images only to transform them. The drunkard being dismissed here is a bee that has extracted nectar from a flower. The renouncers of drams are butterflies that are leaving their resting places and fluttering through the air. And the "I" watching this beautiful spectacle only gets more and more drunk for having enjoyed it.

Dickinson has carried popular temperance images to a truly new, transcendent space, a fact she enforces in the final verse:

> Till Seraphs swing their snowy Hats—
> And Saints—to windows run—
> To see the little Tippler
> Leaning against the—Sun—

The conceit of seraphs and saints celebrating the "little Tippler" for her intoxication over nature's bounty emphasizes the poem's metaphysical dimension. The playful oddity of the hat-swinging angels, the gaping saints, and the girl leaning against the sun gives the poem a metaphysical energy that leaves the reader intoxicated, as it were, with the poet's imaginativeness.

Dickinson's creative toying with temperance images continues in poem #230, which begins:

> We—Bee and I—live by the quaffing—
> 'Tisn't *all Hock*—with us—
> Life has its *Ale*—
> But it's many a lay of the Dim Burgundy—
> We chant—for cheer—when the Wines—fail—

Once again, the "I" is the transformed intemperate temperance advocate, who can openly say that she lives "by quaffing" since her drinking companion is the bee and her "ale" and "burgundy" are beautiful things of nature. Dickinson again adopts a popular trope in the italicized "*all Hock*," a common phrase used at temperance meetings to urge all present to pledge ("hock") themselves to sobriety. When the "I" says that she and the bee don't use the "*all Hock*" prompt, she is saying that pledges against alcohol are unnecessary for those who understand that life itself "has its *Ale*."

Dickinson's adaptation of popular sources continues to the end of the poem:

> Do we "get drunk"?
> Ask the jolly Clovers!
> Do we "beat" our "Wife"?
> I—never wed—
> Bee—pledges *his*—in minute flagons—
> Dainty—as the tress—on her deft Head—
>
> While runs the Rhine—
> He and I—revel—
> First—at the vat—and latest at the Vine—
> Noon—our last Cup—
> "Found dead"—"of Nectar"—
> By a humming Coroner—
> In a By-Thyme!

The quotation marks used around several phrases are strategic, for Dickinson is quoting extensively from popular culture. The common dark-temperance trope of the drunken husband who brutalizes his wife is cited in the rhetorical questions "Do we 'get drunk'?" and "Do we 'beat' our 'Wife'?" The sensationalists' association of alcohol with death is repeated in the reference to the drunkard " 'found dead' " by a coroner. The taking of the temperance pledge is recalled in the phrase about one who "pledges *his*." But all of these standard temperance images are couched in paeans to ordinary natural phenomena—bees, clover, nectar, noontime—that redirect dark temperance toward an affirmation of life itself.

By manipulating popular temperance images, the major writers of the American Renaissance were transforming popular enthusiasms that had become highly problematic by the 1850s. While popular culture had gone full cycle through its evangelical, Washingtonian, and prohibitionist phases, virtually exhausting then-current theories about cures for alcoholism, some authors were demonstrating that imaginative writing itself had restorative value. Infusing originality into the desiccated temperance tropes of their age, these writers created literary "wine" that would improve with time.

Notes

1. Bayard Rust Hall, *Something for Every Body: Gleaned in the Old Purchase, from Fields Often Reaped* (New York: D. Appleton, 1846), 126.

2. New York *Genius of Temperance, Philanthropist and People's Advocate*, January 5, 1831.

3. *Genius of Temperance*, November 2, 1831. The next quotation in this paragraph is in the September 15, 1830, issue.

4. *Edmund and Margaret* (Cambridge, MA: Hilliard and Metcalf, 1822), 60.

5. *The Lottery Ticket* (Cambridge, MA: Hilliard and Metcalf, 1822), 30.

6. *Memoirs of a Water Drinker* (New York: Saunders and Otley, 1836), II:208.

7. *Genius of Temperance*, November 2, 1831.

8. *The Catastrophe, A Tale of the Nineteenth Century* (Lowell: Rand and Southmayd, 1833), 15.

9. *Poems of M'Donald Clark* (New York: J. W. Bell, 1836), 124.

10. *The Ramrod Broken; or, The Bible, History, and Common Sense in Favor of the Moderate Use of Good Spirituous Liquors* (Boston: Albert Colby, 1859), 141.

11. Hall, *Something for Every Body*, 126.

12. In *Social Classes in a Republic*, ed. Samuel A. Eliot (Boston: American Unitarian Association, n.d.), 122, 29.

13. Leonard Woolsey Bacon, *The Mistakes and Failures of the Temperance Reformation* (New York: Mason Brothers, 1864), 19.

14. John Bartholomew Gough, *Platform Echoes; or, Leaves from My Note-Book of Forty Years* (Hartford: A. D. Worthington, 1885), 154–55.

15. *Autobiography and Personal Recollections of John B. Gough* (Toronto: A. H. Hovey, 1870), 199–200.

16. *Letters from the Alms-House, on the Subject of Temperance* (Lowell: Brown and Colby, 1841), 10. The following quotation is on p. 37.

17. *The Confessions of a Rum-seller* (Boston: Lothrop and Bense, 1845), 20.

18. Maria Lamas, *The Glass* (Philadelphia: Martin E. Harmstead, 1849), 22.

19. *Confessions of a Reformed Inebriate* (New York: American Temperance Union, 1844), 142–43.

20. *Autobiography of a Reformed Drunkard; or Letters and Recollections by an inmate of the Alms-house* (Philadelphia: Griffith and Simon, 1845), 143.

21. Lamas, *The Glass*, 27.

22. *Beneath the American Renaissance: The Subversive Imagination in the Age of Emerson and Melville* (New York: Knopf, 1988), 86–88.

23. *Adventures of Huckleberry Finn* (1885; rpt., New York: Norton, 1977), 99.

24. Lippard, *The Quaker City; or, The Monks of Monk Hall*, ed. David S. Reynolds (1845; rpt., Amherst: U of Massachusetts P, 1995), 201. The following quotations in this paragraph are on pp. 291 and 269.

25. George Thompson, *New-York Life: The Mysteries of Upper-Tendom Revealed* (New York: Charles S. Atwood, 1849), 83. The following quotation is also on p. 83.

26. George Thompson, *City Crimes; or, Life in New York and Boston* (New York: William Berry, 1849), 121. The following quotation in this paragraph is on p. 138.

27. George Thompson, *Adventures of a Pickpocket; or, Life at a Fashionable Watering Place* (Boston: Berry, 1849), 33.

28. *Adventures of Huckleberry Finn*, 23.

29. See J. Cowen, *The First and Last Days of Alcohol the Great, in the Empire of Nationalia* (Providence: B. T. Albro, 1848), and [anon.], *An Account of the Marvelous Doings of Prince Alcohol, as Seen by One of His Enemies, in Dreams* (n.p., 1847).

30. Lamas, *The Glass*, 31.

31. J. K. Cornyn, *Dick Wilson, The Rumseller's Victim; or, Humanity Pleading for the "Maine Law"* (Auburn, ME: Derby and Miller, 1853), vii.

32. T. S. Arthur, *Ten Nights in a Bar-room* (1854; rpt., New York: Odyssey , 1966), 124.

33. *The Ramrod Broken*, 64.

34. See Francis P. Dedmond, " 'The Cask of Amontillado' and the War of the Literati," *Modern Language Quarterly* 15 (1954): 137–46, and David S. Reynolds, "Poe's Art of Transformation: 'The Cask of Amontillado' in Its Cultural Context," in *New Essays on Poe's Major Tales*, ed. Kenneth Silverman (New York: Cambridge UP, 1993), 93–112.

35. *Collected Works of Edgar Allan Poe*, ed. Thomas Olive Mabbott (Cambridge, MA: Harvard UP, 1978), III: 1257. The following quotations from "Cask" are on pp. 1259, 1260, and 1262.

36. Introductory notes to "The Cask of Amontillado," *Collected Works of . . . Poe*, III: 1252.

37. *Collected Works of . . . Poe*, III: 851. The following quotations from "The Black Cat" are on pp. 851, 858.

38. *Typee. A Peep at Polynesian Life* (1846; rpt., Evanston: Northwestern UP, 1970), 192.

39. *Mardi and a Voyage Thither* (1849; rpt., Evanston: Northwestern UP, 1970), 261. The subsequent quotations from *Mardi* in this paragraph are on pp. 224, 489, and 577.

40. *Redburn, His First Voyage. Being the Sailor-boy Confessions and Reminiscences of the Son-of-a-Gentleman, in the Merchant Service* (1849; rpt., Evanston: Northwestern UP, 1969), 12. The subsequent quotations in this paragraph are in *Redburn*, pp. 42, 44, and 245.

41. *White-Jacket, or The World in a Man-of-War* (1850; rpt., Evanston: Northwestern UP, 1970), 390. The subsequent quotations from *White-Jacket* in this paragraph are on p. 54.

42. *Moby-Dick; or, the Whale* (1851; rpt., New York: Norton, 1967), 31.

43. *Moby-Dick*, 367. Subsequent quotations from *Moby-Dick* will be included parenthetically in the text.

44. Nathaniel Hawthorne, *Twice-Told Tales* (1837; rpt., Ohio State UP, 1974), 146. The following quotations are on pp. 147–48.

45. *The American Notebooks. Centenary Edition* (Ohio State UP, 1932), 8: 10.

46. Nathaniel Hawthorne, *House of the Seven Gables* (1851; rpt., Ohio State UP, 1965), 84; *The Elixir of Life Manuscripts* (Ohio State UP, 1977), 13: 265; *Our Old Home: A Series of English Sketches* (f.p. 1861–62; rpt., Ohio State UP, 1970), 5: 2. The following quotation in this paragraph is on p. 279.

47. *Mosses from an Old Manse* (1856; rpt., Ohio State UP, 1974), 385, 402.

48. *The Snow-Image and Uncollected Tales* (Ohio State UP, 1974), 92.

49. *The Blithedale Romance* (1852; rpt., New York: Norton, 1978), 162.

50. *Twice-Told Tales*, 184.

51. *The Blithedale Romance*, 160–61.

52. Ralph Waldo Emerson, *Essays and Lectures* (New York: Library of America, 1983), 134. The next two quotations in this paragraph are on p. 159.

53. *Emerson in His Journals*, ed. Joel Porte (Cambridge, MA: Harvard UP, 1982), 178. The subsequent quotation in this paragraph is on p. 78. The first quotation in the next paragraph ("I wish to say . . .") is on p. 224.

54. *Essays and Lectures*, 128.

55. *The Early Lectures of Ralph Waldo Emerson*, ed. Stephen E. Whicher and Robert E. Spiller (Cambridge, MA: Harvard UP, 1972), III: 262.

56. *Essays and Lectures*, 162.

57. *The Complete Works of Ralph Waldo Emerson* (1904; rpt., New York: AMS Press, 1968), X: 163.

58. *Complete Works of R. W. Emerson*, X: 454.

59. *The Writings of Henry David Thoreau* (1906; rpt., New York: AMS Press, 1982), II: *Walden*, 285.

60. *The Writings of Henry David Thoreau. Reform Papers*, ed. Wendell Glick (Princeton: Princeton UP, 1973), IV: 182. The following quotations are on pp. 184 and 191.

61. *Reform Papers*, 184. The next two quotations in this paragraph are on p. 191.

62. *Writings of H. D. Thoreau*, II: *Walden*, 240.

63. *Walt Whitman of the New York Aurora*, ed. Joseph Jay Rubin and Charles H. Brown (State College, PA: Bald Eagle P, 1950), 35, 36.

64. Walt Whitman, *The Early Poems and the Fiction*, ed. Thomas L. Brasher (New York: New York UP, 1963), 237. This volume is subsequently cited in the text as *WEP*.

65. Horace Traubel, *With Walt Whitman in Camden* (1905; rpt., New York: Rowman and Littlefield, 1961), I: 93.

66. *Brooklyn Daily Eagle*, December 22, 1846.

67. *Prose Works, 1892*, ed. Floyd Stovall (New York: New York UP, 1962), III: 363.

68. Brooklyn *Star*, October 2, 1845.

69. Whitman, *Leaves of Grass, Comprehensive Reader's Edition*, ed. Harold Blodgett and Sculley Bradley (New York: New York UP, 1965), 593. This volume is subsequently cited in the text as *LGC*.

70. Whitman, *Notebooks and Unpublished Prose Manuscripts*, ed. Edward F. Grier (New York: New York UP, 1984), I: 438.

71. *Leaves of Grass, A Textual Variorum of the Printed Poems*, ed. Sculley Bradley et al. (New York: New York UP, 1980), I: 189.

72. Quotations from these poems are from *Final Harvest: Emily Dickinson's Poems*, ed. Thomas H. Johnson (1951; rpt., Boston: Little, Brown, 1961), 25 and 28–29, respectively.

Temperance in the Bed of a Child

Incest and Social Order in
Nineteenth-Century America

✒ Karen Sánchez-Eppler

> And now she saw that Joe had crept into the bed behind the sick child, and that her arm was drawn tightly around his neck.
>
> "You won't let them hurt me, will you, dear?" said the poor frightened victim of a terrible mania.
>
> "Nothing will hurt you, father," answered Mary, in a voice that showed her mind to be clear, and fully conscious of her parent's true condition.
>
> She had seen him thus before. Ah! What an experience for a child! . . .
>
> "I knew I would be safe where you were," he whispered back—"I knew it, and so I came. Kiss me, love."
>
> How pure and fervent was the kiss laid instantly upon his lips! . . . Now the sphere of his loving, innocent child seemed to have overcome, at least for the time, the evil influences that were getting possession even of his external senses.[1]

OVER AND OVER AGAIN, NINETEENTH-CENTURY TEMPERANCE FIC-tion tells this story of a drunken father creeping into bed with his young child.[2] This is not, of course, the only plot available to temperance fiction. Indeed, from my readings, the single most dominant temperance plot was one of degeneration from first misguided sip to destitution and death. Still, this scene of conversion wrought by the embraces of a young child appears at least as a vignette in fully one quarter of the over three hundred tales I have read; it is a favorite device in a literature generally characterized by formulaic writing.

Narrative formulas index cultural obsessions, and this scene is repeated as obsessively and fervently as the caresses with which—in another story—little Debby Colt greets her father with "eager lips . . . kissing him over and over again."[3] Just returned from the foundling hospital, Debby is newly healed of the broken bones caused by her father's frequent beatings; Mary may promise that nothing will hurt her father while he lies in her arms, but her sickness was caused by being hit on the head by a beer tumbler an angry tavern-keeper had thrown at her father. There is every reason to suspect that in nineteenth-century America, as now, the drunken father's demand for such caresses was— along with beatings and flying beer mugs—simply another, more secret, form of abuse. With those suspicions, so amply corroborated by twentieth-century analysis of childhood sexual abuse, it is hard not to read the insistence that Joe is only "safe" in Mary's bed, that "nothing will hurt" him there, as an inverted trace of how these embraces must have hurt her, how they strip her of all safety. "Ah! What an experience for a child!" the narrator exclaims. And yet what I find most startling about these scenes is the vehemence with which they define this hardly veiled erotic contact not as abuse but as the surest and best antidote to abuse. With their kisses, Debby and Mary ultimately convert their drunken fathers into good, temperate men.

These conversion stories are structured by their own logic of conversion; they make drunks temperate by transforming what we cannot help but recognize as scenes of pederasty and incest into loving mechanisms of redemption. In noting the double valence of these plots—at once culturally subversive and culturally conservative—my work runs counter to what meager literary analysis such texts have already received. Temperance fiction has been damned and (occasionally) praised along with other forms of nineteenth-century reform literature for its adherence to sentimental conventions, like that of the lovingly redemptive child, or for its grotesque fascination with such alcoholic effects as delirium tremens and spontaneous combustion.[4] My concern is not to choose between these reform rhetorics but to recognize the violence and sensuality embedded within even the most angelic and sentimental generic conceit, and so to explore the cultural and ideological implications of this strange redemption plot.

In this essay, I ask why temperance fiction locates its scenes of salvation in the bed of a child. My answers will suggest the erotic potential of the new stress on disciplining through love as the nineteenth century's chosen model of child rearing and how this emphasis on love rather than punishment works to ally domesticity both with self-control *and* with the fulfillment of desire. The easy conjunction of restraint and indulgence characteristic of this redemption plot will prove, moreover, integral to the structures of bourgeois capitalism. Thus, although this fiction depicts children successfully disciplining their fathers, the child's ability to domesticate and even feminize male desires does not fundamentally alter the structures of power. As the loving domestic scene is proffered as a replacement for the dissipation and excesses of drunkenness, the child's love works to enforce a bourgeois patriarchal order that leaves the child as vulnerable as ever.

Love and the Law

We tend to forget that "temperance was the most popular, influential and long-lived social reform movement of the late nineteenth and early twentieth centuries."[5] I will not detail this history here, but stretching between the 1810s and the passing of the Eighteenth Amendment in 1919, the evolving methods and goals of temperance reform indicate changing attitudes toward the social power of domesticity. In particular, the shifting strategies of the temperance movement reveal a fundamental tension between a belief in "moral suasion" (that the reform of individual sinners would precede and produce the salvific purification of society as a whole) and a reliance on prohibition (that only through state action—such as the "Maine law" of 1851, which forbade the manufacture or sale of intoxicating liquor—could the problems of drunkenness be alleviated for individual or state). This debate on tactics has an obvious gender bias, as arguments over the efficacy of moral suasion implicitly assess the social efficacy of the American family in the face of a problem that—as temperance workers were quick to remind—rendered woman and children particularly vulnerable.

Moral suasion is woman's work both because it depends upon women's presumed skill at nurturing the good and because it conforms to women's limited access to public power. "What then is the aid that woman can most fitly lend to the noble science of being 'temperate in all things'?" Lydia Sigourney asks in the introduction to her collection of temperance verse. "Not the assumption of masculine energies, not the applause of popular assemblies; but the still small voice singing at the cradle-side."[6] Describing the Washingtonians' goal of redeeming the drunkard through example and moral suasion, John Hawkins relies upon maternal metaphors: "we don't slight the drunkard; we love him, we nurse him, as a mother does her infant learning to walk."[7] Hawkins's manner of reclaiming individual drunkards presumes that maternal love wields social power; but though they claimed to work "as a mother," Washingtonian meetings, with their public and histrionic confessions, clearly breached domestic norms of privacy and decorum. All too aware of the limits of such maternal politics, the woman suffrage movement gained most of its early adherents among women who wished to vote for prohibition.[8]

This national ambivalence over the efficacy of moral suasion as a means of public reform coincides with its rising preeminence as a mechanism for internal domestic discipline.[9] Prohibition might deem the law, not familial love, to be the best way to rule the nation's drunkenness, but love was clearly the best way to rule the home. What Richard Brodhead insightfully labels "disciplinary intimacy" reorganized the order-inducing structures of the American home on the basis of affection rather than authority—with the result of an increasingly internalized and perfect domestic discipline: "love's beauty as a disciplinary force, is that it creates a more thorough order of subjugation."[10] Part of love's thoroughness, I would add, stems from its implicit reciprocity: love's new familial order figures children not only as objects of discipline but also, and more interestingly, as its agents. This essay focuses on the disciplinary possibilities of the child and demonstrates how children may effectively impose domestic order. Thus, although disciplinary intimacy provides a domestic configuration of the reform methods of moral suasion, it overlays the gender bias of moral suasion with issues of age and innocence. The salvific effects of children's love are a sentimental norm, but one that complicates normative adult models of social control. So, when in one temperance story "Phoebe's love had saved" her father, who pledging abstinence, "kissed her passionately and burst into tears," the narrator concludes that "what reason, persuasion, conscience, suffering, shame, could not do, the love of a little child had wrought. Oh! love is very strong."[11] These conclusions celebrate the power of a child's love; they distinguish it not only from the public and masculine purview of reason but also from such feminine tools of moral suasion as persuasion, conscience, and shame. As Phoebe's strong love suggests, differentiating the power of women from the power of even more vulnerable children reimagines moral suasion in a newly transcendent guise. Temperance authors know that the weaker the agent of reform the more spectacular is love's success.

Speaking about the family and about the state, temperance fiction assumes a mixed allegiance to the discourses of law and love and to masculine, feminine, and childlike strategies of reform. The demands of genre require that temperance fiction align itself with moral suasion—after all, it is the aim of these sentimental tales to touch their readers' hearts—and so insist that social change rests upon the loving regeneration of individual drunkards or readers. There is no narrative motive in prohibition; the law is its own last word. Thus, although many tales do endorse the closing of taverns, the rhetoric of temperance fiction runs counter to the increasing political preference for legislative solutions.[12] Temperance fiction does include stories that call for social and legislative—not individual—reform: in *The Sedley Family; or, The Effect of the Maine Liquor Law*, pledges and family love prove insufficient to redeem Mr. Sedley from intemperance, so the family moves to Maine where, Mrs. Sedley hopes, "the law might save her husband."[13] Yet though the reforming tactics advocated in such stories may have changed to reflect national interest in prohibition, the rhetoric remains grounded in emotional persuasion—and particularly in the strong love of a child. In the story of "The Red Frock," for example, Father, repentant after having thrown little Molly's new red dress into the fire in a fit of drunken temper, takes the pledge. But "the pledge alone wouldn't save him," and his bouts of drunkenness only end once "he had got us a new home in a place where no liquor was sold." "You will bless God, with me," Father writes, "that there are places to be found where no license can be had to send men to perdition." This prohibitionary tale ends, however, by celebrating not only the efficacious law but also the initiatory and invisible blessing of a drunkard's redeeming love for the little girl whose red dress—need I insist upon its erotic symbolism?—he burnt. Leaving off its praise of prohibition, the narrative's last sentence recalls Molly, now grown and a schoolteacher, but still innocent in her ignorance, "who does not know the story of the little red frock—the turning point of her life."[14]

Even when little girls explicitly choose public and political temperance strategies, these stories invariably locate their power in counterdistinction to prohibitionary laws. In the story "What Two Little Girls Did," Katy and Ellen bewail their powerlessness to combat intemperance:

> "O my! If we were men!" exclaimed Katy, her face flushed with excitement.
> "But we are only little girls," answered Ellen mournfully.
> "May be little girls could do something, if they tried," suggested Katy.

What they did was write a letter to the newspaper explaining that they are "puzzled" by "something very bad," the willingness of the town's leaders to sanction the selling of alcohol. Their letter does "rouse up a whole town," prompting action among the men Katy wished they were, and, within two weeks, every drinking-saloon has been closed. Yet even here, the letter succeeds because it is, as the newspaper's editor observes, "the artless, earnest appeal and protest of two children."[15] In short, it produces prohibition not with votes and laws, as men would, but with the sentimental appeal of moral suasion. Yet, no longer devoted to reforming individual drunkards, these tactics of sentimental persuasion work instead to prompt legislation. Though the story insists that these little girls derive their efficacy from the political innocence of their domestically circumscribed position, it nevertheless takes the logic of disciplinary intimacy full circle by presenting moral suasion not as merely enforcing, but as actually revising, the law of the father.

Relying on sentimental appeals, the genre of temperance fiction presumes the power of a domestically based campaign of moral suasion to transform the public soul. Temperance fiction's depiction of family discipline, however, destabilizes the family's alliance with the tactics of moral suasion. Instead, this fiction reveals the social inversions inherent in relying on domesticity to correct a failure internal to the domestic scene—a failure of patriarchy. Dedicated to maintaining conventional familial order, temperance fiction is conservative; nevertheless, in these tales disciplinary intimacy cannot simply uphold patriarchal rule since it is the wife, and even more the children, who must bring the erring man under discipline.

The campaign for "Home Protection" vividly portrays drink as perverting family order so that affection is replaced by violence. Working for the New York Temperance Society, Samuel Chipman attempted to document such claims by visiting jails, asylums, and poorhouses throughout the state in order to ascertain the correlation between domestic violence and inebriation. The society published the results in 1834:

> ALBANY COUNTY: Of the intemperate, at least twenty have been committed for abuse to their families.

> BROOME COUNTY: One of the intemperate was committed for whipping his wife; and two on charges of rape.

> NIAGARA COUNTY: Of the intemperate a considerable number have been committed repeatedly; one man has lain in jail for two-thirds of the time for three years past, for abuse of his family when intoxicated; when sober, is a kind husband and father.[16]

By 1850, Elizabeth Cady Stanton argued that alcoholism ought to be a valid grounds for divorce. As she saw it, the dissolution of the conventional family would be far better than to "come into daily contact, with a coarse, beastly, disgusting drunkard, and consent to be the partner of his misery and rage through a long weary life."[17] Or, as she put it to the New York State Legislature in February 1854 in an argument about custody laws, "Instead of your present laws, which make the mother and her children the victims of vice and license, you might pass laws prohibiting all drunkards, libertines and fools the rights of husbands and fathers."[18] Urging divorce, she warned the drunkard's wife, "be not misled by any pledges, resolves, promises, prayers or tears. You cannot rely on the word of a man who is, or has been the victim of such an overpowering appetite."[19] Temperance fiction was never so radical. After all, its moral goals rested upon the presumed efficacy of promises, prayers, tears, and—most of all—the appeal of the loving family. But, although this sentimental aesthetic was fundamentally committed to maintaining traditional domestic and patri-archal structures, its depiction of the drunkard's devastated home largely echoes Stanton's critique of patriarchy itself.

Like temperance fiction's relation to patriarchy, the incest discernible in the plots of these stories proves ambiguous; it serves both as the most extreme mark of familial disintegration and as the mechanism best able to produce family order and happiness. This redemption plot thus seems to be a cultural and narrative reaction-formation, as it reconfigures trauma into the possibility of moral triumph. In the last decades of the nineteenth century, there is ample historical evidence both that incest was a relatively frequent occurrence and that its dominant form—at least as reported to child-protection agencies—was coercive relations between fathers and their preadolescent daughters. Evidence from earlier periods, where we do not have the benefit of agency records, is more scanty. The case records of child-protection agencies, and the pain-ful testimony of diaries, provide a real but inadequate measure of incest's trauma.[20] That this history remains fragmented and partial—that there is much that has been silenced and much that we do not and cannot know, is in itself part of that trauma. It is clear, however, that child advocates and temperance reformers believed that such abuse was linked to, if not completely caused by, alcoholic excess and, thus, that they recognized scenes of a drunken father in bed with his child as all too real.[21] For us, in the absence of more historical data, the incestuous patterns suggested and disguised by these stories can provide at most only elusive access to actual behaviors.

In reimagining scenes of drunken sexual abuse as sites of moral redemption, temperance writers were engaged in an act that disavows actual behaviors and individual abuses. Yet this very denial works to reveal some of the contradic-tions that infuse familial order and affection. Incest is central to the confronta-tion between the disciplinary forces of law and love I am describing precisely because of its double role as what the family must prohibit and as what constitutes and maintains the family. Foucault asserts "that sexuality has its privileged point of development in the family; that for this reason sexuality is 'incestuous' from the start" and hence that, for the family, incest is both "a dreadful secret and an indispensable pivot."[22] Recent work on incest and pedophilia in Victorian culture, both American and British, provides these generalizing structures with literary and historical particulars, and suggests that a "monstrous" sexual attraction to children, however strenuously denied and demonized, nevertheless informs nineteenth-century conceptions of desire, of domesticity, and even of innocence itself.[23] The new regime of disciplinary intimacy illustrates these arguments by demonstrating how incestuous bonds actively function to hold the family together and to endow the home with affective meaning.

Foucault's focus on how incest functions in the maintenance of social order fails to acknowledge the pain of individual abuses. Conversely, therapeutic discussions only depict incest as the infliction of individual pain and as a mark of familial dysfunction—as if admitting the socializing effects of the circulation of incestuous desires would endanger the creation of "safe families" so integral to the recovery process.[24] The difference stems from a division between the symbolic and the enacted: the incest that structures the family is an incest more felt and disciplined than acted upon; the incest that destroys the family is one that has been acted out. The shock of these temperance plots lies in their conflation of such categories so that recognizably incestuous acts—however innocently portrayed—yield social order. In my readings of these stories, I purposefully imitate temperance fiction's own practice of fusing the real and the symbolic in order to uphold incest's individual and cultural meanings simultaneously: to acknowledge the child's vulnerability and incest's trauma while still recognizing the eroticized child as an effective disciplinary agent. By insisting on the individual and cultural significance of temperance's incestuous redemption plots, I find individual abuse to be not merely an evil ignored by patriarchy but one assimilated into—indeed necessary to—the construction and maintenance of patriarchal power.

If father/daughter incest has been found to be most prevalent in practice, erotic relations between mothers and sons have long dominated the symbolic discourse of incest. Myth, anthropology, and psychoanalysis may have labeled such relations as taboo—the prohibition that constitutes culture—but it is equally clear that this incest orders and "instructs" culture, and so permeates the rhetoric of the ideal nineteenth-century American family.

Every son, "Behold thy mother!" Make love to her, and her your first sweet-
heart. Be courteous, gallant, and her knight-errant, and your nearest friend
and bosom confident. Nestle yourself right into her heart, and her into yours.
Seek her "company" and advice, and imbibe her purifying influences. Learn
how to court by courting her. No other society will equally sanctify and
instruct.[25]

The gendered division of incest into violent, family-disabling relations between fathers and daughters and loving, family-propping relations between
sons and mothers suggests that incest serves patriarchy both as a sign of male
coercive power and as a promise of sexually satisfying domestic love. In their
stories of redemption through the love of a child, temperance writers have
actually crossed these two cultural versions of incest, and reimagined male
violence as domestic love.

Readers and Drinkers

We are left, however, with the question of who is served by such a reimagining
of familial abuse as familial redemption. This question has large social implications, but before it is possible to even begin postulating responses, we need to
know who in nineteenth-century America actually read these stories, for surely
this plot would carry different meanings for audiences of different class, age,
gender, and domestic status and for sober or drinking readers. Ascertaining
readership remains a largely speculative business, and what we do know suggests that reading patterns were far more eclectic and the structuring of knowledge far more chaotic than has been commonly assumed; men often prove, for
example, to be nearly as avid readers of sentimental fiction as women.[26] What
clues I have found for the readership of temperance tales do, however, imply a
division between authorial hopes that these stories would convert drunkards
and the realization that their primary readership lay in the already-temperate
home. Moreover, recognition that temperate men, women, and especially children comprised the major audience for these stories links the ability of temperance fiction to reform drunkards with the ability of domestic love to pass
on this saving lesson. Thus assertions of the genre's efficacy oddly echo the plot
of individual temperance tales: both genre and plot imagine the good child-
reader as the means of redeeming the drunken man.

The National Temperance Society founded a publication house in 1865 to publish and distribute temperance fiction, and, at that year's National Temperance Convention, James Black voiced the society's expectations for this proposed venture.

> We must have publications spread broadcast over the land, or many more thousands of drunkards' graves will be filled, many more families broken up, many more hearts, hopes, and joys crushed, many more children made orphans, to grow up a curse to themselves, a disgrace to friends, and a burden to society. . . .

As his talk progressed to goals for distribution, this "broadcast" proved more and more narrow in its reach: from the public "booksellers," the imagined site of distribution contracts first to "house-hold and Sabbath-School libraries" and then to the "sales of publications made at the close of an interesting [temperance] lecture" that, Black argues, would not only spread the word but also raise money to support the lecturers' travel.[27] Society advertisements selling collections of temperance books at a discount ("48 volumes specially adapted to Sunday-School Libraries, written by some of the best authors in the world"), the practice of selling pamphlets in batches of one thousand, and the financial reports of the Publication House all suggest that in practice distribution occurred mainly through Sabbath-Schools and local temperance organizations.[28] Nevertheless, the discussions of the Publication House that appear in the proceedings of all subsequent conventions continue to assert evangelical success; they boast the number of pages published and celebrate an immense and essential demand: "the demand of the present is *books*, BOOKS, BOOKS! Men *must* have books, women *will* have books, and children *should* have books" (1868).[29] The gradient of auxiliary verbs hints, however, at the gender imbalance of their actual audience, for while "will" confidently assumes a female readership and "should" implies the ease with which such moral lessons can be imposed on children, the fundamentally internal obligations of "must" are both most strongly desired and most difficult to impose. Indeed by 1873, the Society itself had begun to openly acknowledge that temperance literature rarely reached drunkards:

> Our mission is not merely nor mainly to rescue the drunkard, but to save every boy and girl from the drunkard's sin and shame. . . . Our literature is not to be the life-buoy flung out to the man already sinking in the death tide, but the baby-tender, if you will, to train and strengthen the least of the little ones.[30]

Temperance was in fact a familiar nineteenth-century "baby tender," even outside adamantly "cold water" circles. In the general moral pedagogy of *The Good Boy's and Girl's Alphabet*, for example, it is no surprise that "D was a Drunkard" or that "V was a Vintner, who drank all himself," or that these— along with a host of other sinful letters—should stand as warnings to Y, "a Youngster that loved not his school." [31] Temperance writers continued to claim, moreover, that thus producing protemperance children could itself save drunkards. If temperance stories could not reach the fathers directly, who was to say that they could not rescue them through their sons and daughters?

The juvenile temperance tale "The Snow Storm: Or, What Jennie Scott Did" is subtitled "a true story," but what it offers is a wishful emblem of how such juvenile fiction might work to reduce adult alcoholism. Given a copy of *The Youth's Temperance Banner* on a train, Jennie Scott reads about a middle-class family who aids the destitute children of a drunkard. In the *Banner* story,

> the tears began to flow from all the children's eyes, and from those of their dear Mama too. . . . Jennie also cried when she read this story, then she asked her father [who likes a glass of wine after dinner] to read it. . . . By and by putting her arms around her father's neck, and pulling his head down, so that she could whisper in his ear, she said in a most loving tone,—
>
> "O my dear papa, will you let anybody say [like the child of the story] that 'MY father drinks?' "
>
> . . . For a moment he made no reply, but little Jennie saw the tear-drops glistening in his eyes, and took courage. In another moment he brushed away the tears, and pressing his arm tighter around his child's waist, he said,—
>
> "No, Jennie, no!" [32]

As the tears spread from the *Banner* story, to Jennie, to her father, and presumably to her young reader and then—why not?—to her reader's father, this sentimental deluge—waters *mise en abîme*—promises to sweep all wine and liquor away. Jennie need not even write like Katy and Ellen, all she need do to end intemperance is read and cry.

This faith that temperance tales could reach drunkards through their children is not an isolated fantasy; [33] it may indeed be the inaugural fiction of the genre. Lucius Manlius Sargent wrote a series of "Temperance Tales" beginning in 1833 that, if not the earliest such stories, were certainly among the genre's first successes. In his preface to the first tale, Sargent urges his reader,

When you have read it, if, among all your connections and friends, you can think of none whom its perusal may possibly benefit—and it will be strange if you cannot—do me the favor to present it to the first little boy that you meet. He will no doubt take it home to his mother or father. If you will not do this, throw it in the street, as near to some dram-seller's door as you ever venture to go.[34]

Sargent himself gave a two-volume, elegantly bound copy of the *Temperance Tales* as a gift, inscribed to "David Eckley, Esq. from his old friend L. M. Sargent." David Eckley, however, left no mark in the books; it is "May Belle Eckley" (sister? wife? daughter?) who writes her name inside the covers of both volumes. Passing from parent to child and not—as Sargent wished—the other way around, another set of the tales is inscribed to "Freddie—from his mother E. C. Brown."[35] The tales' own images of transmission—through little boy or sidewalk—feel less convincing than even such anecdotal marks of readerly proprietorship. Indeed, the preface already figures the tale's dismal incapacity to reach an alcoholic readership, for if no little boy will carry it, Sargent's suggestion for how to circulate his pamphlets would leave them trampled in the gutter.

No doubt inadequate to their temperance goals, these fantasies of effective literary dissemination are striking for how closely they mirror the plot of redemption-through-a-child's-love that these stories so repeatedly tell. It seems to make remarkably little difference whether the child rescues a drunken father through the sharing of caresses or the sharing of temperance tales. Indeed, as is the case with Jennie Scott, caresses and stories are easily and frequently combined. In their insistence that children—and therefore fiction read by children—can save despite family violence and the threat of the gutter, these redemptive-love stories serve to buttress the genre's own claim to efficacy.[36] Thus, to return to the question with which this section began, the links temperance fiction draws between familial abuse and familial satisfaction serve to mask the inherent powerlessness of child and story to end social abuse—discursively endowing both abused child and temperance tale with a power they too often and too painfully lacked. But if these images of sentimental power rarely converted drunkards, it need not follow that the good child reading in a Sunday School library or an already-temperate home did not find such fictions compelling. Indeed, as a closer examination of these redemption scenes will show, much of the cultural importance of this fiction lies in the tightly enmeshed doubleness with which it figures the child as simultaneously victim of abuse and agent of discipline.

Restraint and Indulgence

Juvenile temperance fiction regularly asserts that its purpose is to teach children the ethos of self-denial, which will protect them from alcoholism and other sins—an ethos associated with the wise parent.

> My darling child, be thankful every day you live that you have parents wise enough to restrain you in your childhood . . . the time will come when you will be grateful that you learned self-denial when you were young.
>
> . . . For instance, when you awake on a cold morning, don't lie still in bed, thinking how warm and pleasant it is there, until you fall asleep, but jump up at once; don't indulge yourself. All these little victories will help you in fighting with greater temptations as you grow older.[37]

Yet the stories in this collection—the National Temperance Society's 1868 "special effort for the children"[38]—rarely tell of childhood self-restraint. Rather they tell of children's efforts to regenerate drunken men; their successes are often linked not with self-denial but with the indulgences of a warm and pleasant bed. In these stories the love of a child undeniably functions to enforce self-restraint and social order, but it does so through the promise not of delimiting, but rather of fulfilling desires.

Suggestively, *The History of a Threepenny Bit* ends with the reformed tavern-keeper setting up a new establishment "in the windows of which might be seen marbles, lollypops, toys, picturebooks, and other articles likely to tempt the youth of a country village."[39] The transformations wrought by little Peggy's love have altered the content of temptation, but they have not rejected its pleasures or its profits. Far from denouncing temptation, this fiction depends on it, since the love of a child becomes itself the most potent object of desire. More than toys or candy these stories offer the child's love as the one temptation stronger than the love of drink. When, at closing time, the tavern-keeper finds Peggy sleeping in front of his fire—where she hid cold, heartbroken, and exhausted after her father had taken her last "threepenny bit" to spend on drink—he experiences her purely as temptation, as something he tries but cannot resist.

> "I'm not going to be made a fool of like this. Don't I know them? . . . It's no use," he went on, shaking his fist at the unconscious Peggy; "you'll be as cruel

and as bad as the rest some day, for all yer soft little voice, and yer, 'Daddy, daddy!' You don't come over me like this, —d'ye hear?"

And he waited again for his answer. . . . She moaned in her sleep and repeated:—

"Daddy, please don't."

The little voice was so hopeless and appealing, that it reached again the hidden chord in the publican's heart, and he knelt down and whispered soothingly:—

"No—no—no, dearie, I won't."

The little sleeper was calmed for the moment; but directly he moved, she burst out again:—

"Daddy, please don't."

"Don't what?" whispered the publican bending over her.

"Don't spend it," said Peggy, with a sobbing sigh.

Closer and closer he bent, till his lips almost touched her cheek; and gently he repeated:—

"No—no—no, dearie, I won't."

Whether the answer penetrated through the mists and shadows of sleep, I know not; but the child stirred no more. But long after she was wrapped in her peaceful slumber did the old man remain with his cheek against hers, dreamily repeating:—

"No—no—no, dearie, I won't." (85–87)

The pleasure the publican cannot resist, the pleasure that will ultimately compel him to shut down his tavern, is the pleasure of whispering "no" into the cheek of a sleeping child. In Peggy's hopeless and appealing "No, Daddy don't," the spending of a daughter's pennies echoes against all the other things a father ought not to do to his little girl. Thus the refusal of profligacy has its own satisfactions; there is an erotic charge to abstention, to saying "no."

My reading of this passage may seem to eroticize a familiar sentimental scene, but it is my contention that an insistence on the sexual innocence of children and of the disciplinary intimacy they are enlisted to enforce is precisely what enables these erotics to function; the suppression gives these scenes their sexual charge. It is the refusal to acknowledge childhood sexuality—either as subject or as object of desire—that makes a Mary, Debby, Phoebe, or Peggy so irresistible, so sexually vulnerable, and, at the same time, so strategically capable (at least within the logic of juvenile fiction) of disciplining the father. I am suggesting not merely that the practice of disciplining through love has erotic content but indeed that this eroticism is essential to its functioning. This observation has far wider ramifications for our understanding of the social power of American domesticity; here, it is sufficient to note how a domestically confined juvenile sexuality is used to displace an antidomestic, dissipating alcoholism.

The alliance of domestic discipline with the fulfillment of desire would seem to function as a means of luring wayward men home—a promise that their own hearth could be as intensely pleasurable as any barroom. Yet, as we have seen, there is little reason to believe that such undomesticated men read these tales; this testimony to the seductions of home is finally better understood as a story domesticity tells about itself to itself. It is thus the already-domestic family that imagines the well-regulated home as an erotically saturated space. But if viewing home—and particularly the good child—as a temptation that can save proves a self-referential domestic fantasy, it does not serve merely domestic ends. In particular, the promise that the fulfillment of desires will yield not chaos but good order suggests provocative connections to the social and economic agenda of an industrializing nation. After all, the belief that there need be no tension between social discipline and consumerist indulgence underlies claims for the social and moral efficacy of consumer capitalism. Desire, both home and market agree, need not result in dissipation but in a domestic, economic, and even national good. Thus temperance fiction's assertion of the compatibility of restraint and indulgence is not an isolated freak of reformist discourse; rather, it is constitutive of the newly dominant American middle class.

Temperance fiction's obsession with the sexual dynamics of the family is matched only by its obsession with money. If there is one point on which all temperance writing agrees, it is that drink results in destitution. In this fiction, men are forever spending their last pennies on rum instead of on much-needed bread; there is no more evil spot than that commercial establishment, the dram-shop. This might suggest that the public sphere of economic exchange should be understood as a threat to domestic happiness, and, like all sentimental fiction, these stories voice anxiety about the moral taint of the marketplace.[40] Yet, as with the tavern-keeper's new shop of tempting toys, the drunkard's salvation invariably appears fully ensconced in capitalist structures of industry and exchange. Just as surely as a drunkard's sad end lies in poverty, the clearest mark of redemption is signaled in these tales by the attainment of an adequately prosperous home.

The centrality of money for temperance fiction is literalized in *The History of a Threepenny Bit* through a narrative trope (quite conventional in nineteenth-century juvenile fiction, however bizarre it may seem to twentieth-century readers), for this story is actually told by Peggy's cherished coin.[41] This narrative strategy requires that, throughout the novel's 216 pages, the coin circulate primarily among the small group of socially quite diverse characters with whom the story is concerned. The social mobility of a threepenny bit, capable of passing from a wealthy lady to a beggar girl, does not, however, work to suggest the dangerous promiscuity and volatility of market econo-mies. Instead, this sequence of financial transactions connects characters who, it not surprisingly turns out, already bear more intimate, if unrecognized, domestic relations: Peggy's invalid mother once worked as the wealthy Mrs. Ogilvie's maid, and this lady's present maid proves to be the tavern-keeper Timothy Craig's long-alienated daughter. The ties that link shopkeepers, ser-vants, and mistress, moreover, are consistently figured as loving and familial rather than economic. Thus the very structure of this novel—both in narrative technique and in plot—depends upon refusing to uphold distinctions between the economic and the domestic: virtually all the relations in the novel involve both the exchange of coin and the exchange of affection At the novel's end, Peggy's happy cottage-home, a short walk from Craig's new store and on Mrs. Ogilvie's land, is in a very real sense made out of the circulation of a three-penny bit. Indeed the coin is not a detached, economic narrator of these emotional scenes but is itself an object of affection; Peggy awakens in the tavern to find that Craig had "slipped me [our narrator-coin] into one of her little hands, . . . [Peggy] pressed the little coin to her lips, and hugged it close up to her, exclaiming, as she did so, 'It's come back—it's come back to me! Peggy's own—Peggy's very, very own!' "[42]

The confusion between the erotic and the economic that leads Peggy to kiss her coin appears completely benign, for both Peggy's ability to love and her money secure the domestic bliss of the novel's end. This can only happen because the novel has so fully succeeded in domesticating the economic realm; it is, after all, on the barroom floor that Peggy and Timothy Craig make their cozy and redemptive bed. Shorn of such domestic security, the links among barroom, sex, and money may be far less tidy or comfortable. In *Ten Nights in a Bar-room*, Mary tells her groaning father a dream that nearly bursts with the effort to encompass this complex mesh of connections:

> I thought it was night, and that I was still sick. You promised not to go out until I was well. But you did go out; and I thought you went over to Mr. Slade's tavern. When I knew this, I felt as strong as when I was well, and I got

up and dressed myself and started out after you. But I hadn't gone far before I met Mr. Slade's great bull-dog Nero, and he growled at me so dreadfully that I was frightened and ran back home. Then I started again and went away round by Mr. Mason's. But there was Nero in the road, and this time he caught my dress in his mouth and tore a great piece out of the skirt. . . . But I . . . kept right on until I came to the tavern and there you stood in the door. And you were dressed so nice. You had on a new hat and a new coat; and your boots were new and polished just like Judge Hammond's. I said—"O father! is this you?" And then you took me up in your arms and kissed me, and said "Yes, Mary, I am your real father. Not old Joe Morgan—but Mr. Morgan now." It seemed all so strange, that I looked into the bar-room to see who was there. But it wasn't a bar-room any longer; but a store full of goods.[43]

Mary's dream has soaked the tavern with images of sexual threat, sexual attraction, and the pleasures of bourgeois status and procurement. This passage is dense with meanings, convincingly like those of real dreams in that they are at once so overdetermined and so contradictory. Rather than attempt to create a coherent interpretive order out of this tangle of dog-torn skirts and shiny new boots, I want to focus on the tangle itself, on the ways in which the sexual and the financial, the frightening dog "Nero" and the desirable "real" father, the evil barroom and the "store full of goods," all seem surprisingly and yet inextricably bound up with one another. If this passages makes clear that what Mary wants most is the embrace of a father who is "dressed so nice" and the riches of the storeroom, it seems just as evident that these affluent, domestic rewards remain contingent upon the violent sexual initiation of barroom barter and ripped skirts. Not only are sex and money impossibly entangled in one another, but the moral valence of both also appears drastically unstable.

Social historians have convincingly argued that the temperance movement was an important agent in nineteenth-century articulations of class conflict: that the middle class attempted to use temperance rhetoric and laws as a means of disciplining the working class and particularly the leisure activities of Irish and German immigrants.[44] In noting the congruence between temperance fiction's depictions of family sexual and economic dynamics, I expand upon this sense of how temperance serves middle-class interests. The prevalent image of the temperate home as the place capable of reconciling restraint and indulgence installs and affirms as dominant the elasticity of the middle-class position (stretched to encompass both producers and consumers) within capitalism's new, swiftly industrializing, national order. Thus these images of the temperate home domesticate, and so naturalize, the strains that result from capitalism's double call to work and leisure, to save and spend, to be temperate and profligate.

Submissive Daughters, Absent Women, and Effeminate Men

That the middle-class, temperate home bolsters factory and marketplace should not surprise, despite the nineteenth century's insistent rhetoric of separate spheres—exclusively male or female, public or private, economic or sexual, disciplined by law or by love. But if, as the stories of Peggy and Mary suggest, such rhetorics of separation obscure the dynamics of identity and power in the American middle class, it nevertheless remains clear that the deconstruction of this divide remains fraught with anxiety—predominantly gender anxiety. For while the collusion of home and market are essential to the very existence of consumer capitalism in America, patriarchy has rested on the presumption of separate spheres.

The temperance stories of redemption through the love of a child are heavily gendered: Mary, Debby, Phoebe, Molly, Katy, Ellen, Jennie, and Peggy are all little girls. In a fundamental way, these stories of disciplinary intimacy offer the profoundly patriarchal promise that feminine sexual docility—the loving compliance with caresses, however drunken or aggressive—would be rewarded. The celebration of submissiveness at stake in this plot is, oddly enough, most transparent in a version of this familiar story line that occurs not in the guise of sentimental fiction but in that of biography. In writing *Hannah Hawkins: The Reformed Drunkard's Daughter*, Rev. John Marsh quotes from newspaper reports and John Hawkins's famous Washingtonian lectures in an effort to factually relate how this temperance hero attained "his rescue, from the fangs of the rumseller, through his own child." This is how John Hawkins describes Hannah's ministrations:

> I would come home, late at night, open the door, and fall prostrate on the floor, utterly unable to move. My daughter Hannah, sitting up for me . . . would come down with a pillow and a blanket, and there, as she could not raise me and get me upstairs, she would put the pillow under my head and cover me with the blanket, and then lie down beside me like a faithful dog.

What Marsh finds so admirable and efficacious about this scene is Hannah's doglike docility. Her loving submissiveness, he repeatedly explains, enables her to reform her father; if she acted differently—defiantly—John Hawkins would never have suffered her to say, "Father, don't send me for whisky to-day." She would have received a blow which would have felled her to the floor, and her father himself would have drank the more fiercely for it. But when his little Hannah, who had sat up late for him at night, and who had covered him with a blanket, put a pillow under his head and laid down by him, as he expressed it, like "a faithful dog," said, in tones of daughter-tenderness, "Father, don't send me for any whisky to-day," it was more than he could bear.[45]

The redemptive power of "daughter-tenderness" serves as a mark of the daughter's obedience. Her submissiveness protects the father from the "fierce" need to combat the threat of being disciplined by his child. Her submissiveness enables him to submit.

In his preface Marsh compares the "fancied" scenes of redemption in "My Mother's Gold Ring" with the actual salvation story he intends to share. The comparison is interesting because Sargent's tale enacts the blow Marsh hypothesized for a less perfectly docile child. I wonder, however, whether here the familiar redemptive scene of drunken paternal caresses can appear as a more probable moment of battering, precisely because the child—judgmental instead of submissively loving—is a boy. The scene is narrated by the mother, a voice domestically located at the kitchen sink:

> . . . while I was washing up the breakfast things, I heard our little Robert, who was only five years old, crying bitterly; and going to learn the cause, I met him running towards me with his face covered with blood. He said his father had taken him on his knee, and was playing with him, but had given him a blow in the face, only because he had said, when he kissed him, "Dear papa, you smell like old Isaac, the drunken fiddler."[46]

The concern here is more with little Robert's capacity for telling the truth than with the father's swift salvation. The juxtaposition of these two scenes postulates that it is feminine submissiveness, not masculine honesty, that can most effectively discipline the father.

In *A Million Too Much* (1871) an alcoholic young man defends his drinking with the assertion, "I don't intend to reform. . . . I am not domestic."[47] But such a reform into domesticity is precisely what this fiction intends. The discpline produced by sexually submissive little girls has the effect of creating submissive, domestic, and indeed feminized men; men who won't drink and won't hit. It was the same John Hawkins, we should recall, who would later describe his own efforts to save drunkards as the nurture "a mother [gives] her infant

learning to walk." These maternal men are, of course, a fundamentally feminine fantasy. One of the few little boys to voice the wish that his drunken father
"would let me lay my cheek to his, once more, as he used to do, when I was a
babe" can expect no male readers, since he speaks from the pages of Lydia
Sigourney's *Book for Girls*.[48] In the midst of this project of domesticating men,
traces of anxiety about emasculation can, of course, be found. The temperance
ballad "Learn to Say No," for example, strives, like the similarly named twentieth-century antidrug campaign, to represent domesticity and abstinence as
macho. The ballad concludes the story of John Brown's poverty-producing and
home-destroying drunkenness with this hopeful verse:

> John Brown took the pledge, and asked help from above
> That he still might provide for those he should love;
> He went back to work, determined to show
> That John Brown was a man when he learned to say NO.[49]

Yet, even here, *The Temperance Speaker*'s advertisement that the poems, dialogues, and addresses there collected were intended "for the use of temperance
organizations, schools, bands of hope, etc. . . ." and its publication in 1873 at the
advent of the "woman's campaign" (WCTU) suggests that John Brown's assertion of his maleness was often declaimed in the higher voices of women or
children—feminized once more.

Although temperance reform may emulate maternal nurture, it is rarely
mothers who do this feminine, redemptive work; this disciplinary task falls
instead to little girls. In a literature espousing "Home Protection," wives are
frequently absent or ineffective. Peggy's mother is ill, Debby's mother is dead,
Phoebe's mother can do nothing to match her daughter's "strong love." For
sentimental fiction, the appeal of these structurally motherless homes stems
both from the consequent increase in the vulnerability of the child and from
the therefore more pressing need to make the abusive father into a good,
loving, and effectively maternal parent. Indeed these two advantages prop one
another since in the absence of a mother, and countered only by a vulnerable
and submissive child, it becomes easier to imagine a genuinely domesticated
father as compatible with patriarchal power.

One problem with figuring adult women as disciplinary agents is that their
power within the domestic sphere, however circumscribed, remains relatively
real. Children, by comparison, can claim no arena of control. The reciprocal
structure of disciplinary intimacy may permit them to function as disciplinary
agents, but their efficacy in this role remains derivative, completely dependent

on an already constituted domestic order. For temperance fiction, it is this very powerlessness that makes children, not wives, the ideal agents of Home Protection. A suggestive counterexample, Sargent's tale of "Kitty Grafton" tells the story of a wife who actively opposes her husband's cider-drinking and child-battering ways. As Kitty's responses to her husband's behavior grow more aggressive—sharp words are gradually replaced by such violent acts as hitting him over the head with a poker, or pushing him down the basement stairs until the house becomes "a battleground"—Sargent's sympathy with his heroine wanes. By the tale's end Kitty's unwomanly violence, not her husband's drunkenness, stands as the most damning sign of domestic dysfunction. Better no woman at all, temperance fiction seems to propose, than one as threatening to patriarchal control as Kitty Grafton.

Along with their lack of power, another advantage children bring to these tales of disciplining the father is their supposed sexual innocence. The stories discussed in this essay may represent incest, but they do not acknowledge it. The historical record suggests that absent or ineffective mothers were characteristic of incest situations. One form of child sexual abuse especially prevalent in the nineteenth-century is what Linda Gordon calls "domestic incest," in which "girls became virtual housewives, taking over not only wifely sexual obligations but also housework, child care, and general family maintenance."[50] Within temperance fiction, where the incest plot remains masked by avowals of children's sexual innocence, domestic incest's penchant for replacing wives with daughters has the ostensible result of desexualizing disciplinary intimacy. It is the innocence of children—their supposed exclusion from the erotic—that permits the child to domestic adult sexuality, and so feminize the father.

In "The Baby in the Brown Cottage," after their mother's death two little girls take on responsibility for their home, including the redemption of their alcoholic father. But in their housekeeping role even these little girls, with their pledge to do "everything to make it comfortable for him," are too much like adult women to serve as a sufficiently strong—sufficiently vulnerable, sufficiently innocent—alternative to the allure of the barroom. Instead they proffer their baby brother as a more potent lure for paternal rectitude. As little Hetty explains:

> "Father loves baby, and . . . we'll always keep baby looking so sweet and clean that he'll love to come home just to see him, instead of going to the tavern when he shuts down the mill. If Mrs. Florence would give baby a nice white frock, and one with a pink or blue spot in it, and a pair of new shoes, I could keep him looking, oh! so lovely. Father couldn't help coming right home

from the mill to see him; and who knows, Mrs. Wilder," Hetty continued, growing warm and hopeful, "but father might stop drinking altogether."[51]

To further ensure that Father will indeed "love baby," his attractions must be propped by decidedly fine clothing—unaffordable for a drunkard's child.[52] With his new pink or blue spotted frock the gender of this baby boy appears as yet unmarked. I would submit that it is precisely because the indecipherable gender of baby-garments and babyhood would seem to bespeak the complete absence of sexuality that loving baby provides the perfect antidote to Father's intemperate desires.[53]

Regardless of dress, the story remains quite clear that baby is indeed a boy, so that the father's love for him feminizes not only because it removes the erring father from the tavern and the purportedly more sexual embraces of adulthood to relocate him in that most feminine of spots, the cradle-side, but also because it evokes that other threat to patriarchy: homosexuality. That, in this instance, the baby is a boy reminds us of how the merest suggestion of homoerotic desire underscores the feminization at stake in all these tales of salvific pederasty. I want to insist that, for this fiction, going to bed with little boys is not essentially more feminizing than going to bed with little girls; just as baby's genderless frock does not distinguish his sex, both scenes place the father in the same maternal, feminine role of loving a small child. For the purposes of these temperance tales, then, homosexuality functions predominantly as an index of feminization, not as a sign of distinct sexual desires. Nevertheless, such production of homosexual meanings does mark the possibility that the feminization of the father this fiction seeks may prove irreconcilable with the privileged heterosexual mythos of the domestic scene. In this fiction's essentially conservative model of domesticity, the desire to bring the man home conflicts with normative definitions both of the home as woman's sphere and of the man as, well, manly. The difficulty these stories have in positively representing such a feminized father—their reluctance to keep a wife alive and present and so consummate a fully domestic marriage (for what is heterosexual about the union of two such feminine figures?)—provides fictional markers of cultural contradictions. What these temperance writers want, and cannot unambivalently imagine, is a universalizing of domestic virtues—virtues the culture had coded feminine—that would not alter traditional gender roles or hierarchies. Temperance fiction's efforts to create a patriarchal home actively occupied by the father thus falters in the uncertainty of what it would mean to be a fully domesticated man. Might this domesticated man not be a man at all?

In his temperance story "The Child's Champion," Walt Whitman obviously cares about the homoerotic possibilities of staging the standard redemptive love scene between a man and a boy. Viewed in the context of temperance fiction's pedophilic conventions, the homoerotic energies of this story provide an insightful vantage on the genre's widespread concern with the creation of effeminate men. Especially in the earliest version of this story, Whitman is abundantly clear about the sexual urgency of the love the young man feels for little Charles.

> Why was it that from the first moment of seeing him, the young man's heart had moved with a strange feeling of kindness toward the boy? He felt anxious to know more of him—he felt that he should love him. O, it is passing wondrous how in the hurried walks of life and business, we meet with young beings, strangers, who seem to touch the fountains of our love, and draw forth their swelling waters.

The fountains and swelling waters of love have a rhapsodic quality familiar from the later poems. What is more surprising, especially for those who have not read much of Whitman's early prose, is this story's commitment to the structures of disciplinary intimacy I have been describing—the ways in which this sexual, and specifically homosexual, intensity is enlisted in a decidedly conservative and bourgeois project of reforming the profligate young man to a productive and apparently heterosexual domestic life: "head of a family of his own."

> It was now past midnight. The young man told Charles that on the morrow he would take steps to have him liberated from his servitude; for the present night, he said, it would be best for the boy to stay and share his bed at the inn; and little persuading did the child need to do so. As they retired to sleep, very pleasant thoughts filled the mind of the young man; thoughts of worthy action performed; of unsullied affection; thoughts too—newly awakened ones—of walking in a steadier and wiser path than formerly. All his imaginings seemed to be interwoven with the youth who lay by his side; he folded his arms around him, and, while he slept, the boy's cheek rested on his bosom."[54]

Whitman found these passages too open an expression of male-male desire and censored them from later versions of the story, although the basic erotic structure of the plot remains in place even as man and boy are safely tucked into separate but neighboring beds. Whitman's self-censoring here serves to acknowledge the sexuality of a scene temperance fiction as a whole avows as powerfully but not erotically sentimental.⁵⁵ As Whitman makes clear, however, the aim of these bedroom conversions is to domesticate men not simply by removing them from the bar to the bed, but by actually transforming their desires and replacing the dissipations of drink with the pleasurable containment of enfolding a child in one's arms. Such pleasures are at once sexual and feminizing. The young man's imaginings of a "steadier and wiser" life are "interwoven" with, indeed indistinguishable from, the pressure of the boy's cheek on—not his chest—but his "bosom."

The clear current of homosexual desire in Whitman's story lays bare both the sexual intensity of this conventional conversion scene and its feminizing potential. Thus, despite all its submissive daughters, temperance fiction's plot of redemption in a child's bed evokes a double threat to patriarchal norms: these are at once stories of male violence that would disable family structures and stories of an equally destabilizing homoerotic emasculation. Juxtaposing a world in which everyone has been feminized against one in which male power victimizes women and children, this fiction strives to imagine male consent to a domestication women have always and already undergone. This essay has argued, however, that, while such imaginings may reorganize and generalize patriarchal control, they do not dispense with it. That an explicitly feminine and feminizing love serves to cover fundamentally patriarchal practices of sexual abuse makes clear the relation between erotically based patterns of disciplinary intimacy and patriarchal power. In these stories children may prove effective disciplinary agents but, in reforming their fathers, they do not empower themselves.

I end with a pair of images that stunningly codify temperance fiction's reorganization of patriarchal norms—how the child remains as vulnerable as ever, even as he or she takes on the work of enforcing a new bourgeois order. The "Home of the Intemperate" and the "Home of the Temperate" appeared as paired frontispieces to Jane Stebbins's *Fifty Years History of the Temperance Cause.*⁵⁶ In the home of the intemperate, Father is there breaking tables, knocking out daughters, and threatening the wife and son who would confine him. In the home of the temperate, there is no father at all, though the luxury of the room implies that he is out producing wealth, not out consuming gin. Still, the fully domesticated male proves unrepresented and unrepresentable. In his place, it is his children who embody the mechanisms of middle-class domestic order. While the daughter, a benign and enabling presence, stands behind the chair, one son reads (intellect), one pulls a wagon (industry), and baby holds the whip.

"Home of the Temperate"

"Home of the Intemperate"

Paired frontispieces to Jane E. Stebbins, *Fifty Years History of the Temperance Cause* (Hartford, CT, 1876). Courtesy, American Antiquarian Society.

Notes

An earlier version of this chapter appeared in *American Quarterly* 47, 1 (March 1995) and is reprinted with permission.

1. Timothy Shay Arthur, *Ten Nights in a Bar-Room, and What I Saw There* (1854; facsimile reprint, Cambridge: Harvard UP, Belknap Press, 1964), 78–79.

2. On August 4, 1836, at the annual convention of the American Temperance Union held in Saratoga, New York, the members voted to endorse the use of fiction and "the products of fancy" in their campaign against intemperance; and by the 1850s fiction had clearly become the favored form for temperance propaganda. See Herbert Ross Brown, *The Sentimental Novel in America, 1789–1860* (Durham, NC: Duke UP, 1940), 201–3. Joan Silverman reports that the National Temperance Society's Publication House, founded in 1865, alone produced "over two billion pages of temperance literature." " 'I'll Never Touch Another Drop': Images of Alcoholism and Temperance in American Popular Culture, 1874–1918" (Ph.D. diss., New York University, 1979), 1. My own coverage of this voluminous material has relied simply on those temperance tales that have found their way into the collections of the American Antiquarian Society and the Amherst College, Mount Holyoke College, and Forbes libraries—312 in all.

3. "Debby Colt: What She Did, And How She Did It," in *The Old Brown Pitcher and Other Tales* (New York, 1863), 169.

4. David Reynolds's *Beneath the American Renaissance: The Subversive Imagination in the Age of Emerson and Melville* (New York: Knopf, 1988), chapter 2, contains the most comprehensive discussion of temperance fiction to date. Reynolds would decidedly exclude the stories I discuss here from the category of the subversive, and castigate them as do Brown and others as simplistically and conservatively maudlin.

5. Jed Dannenbaum, "The Social History of Alcohol," *Drinking and Drug Practices Surveyor* 19 (1984), 11.

6. Lydia Sigourney, *Water Drops* (New York, 1850), v.

7. Quoted in Jed Dannenbaum, *Drink and Disorder: Temperance Reform in Cincinnati from the Washingtonian Revival to the WCTU* (Urbana: U. of Illinois Press, 1984), 38. Hawkins, a former hatmaker and reformed drunkard, was one of the national leaders of the Washingtonians. Founded in 1841, the Washingtonians relied heavily on the example of their already reformed members; their open meetings consisted of "reformed drunkards" telling the highly dramatic stories of their past dissipation and the happiness and prosperity total abstinence had brought to their lives. Although public events, Washingtonian meetings bear a striking resemblance to the "twelve step" program of today's Alcoholics Anonymous. In terms of the relation between temperance and pederasty, it is worth noting that contemporary groups working with either the victims or perpetrators of childhood sexual abuse frequently employ similar therapeutic procedures.

8. For a historical account of the temperance movement's gradual abandonment of moral suasion sensitive to these gender issues, see Lori D. Ginzberg's chapter

" 'Moral Suasion is Moral Balderdash' " in her *Women and the Work of Benev-olence: Morality, Politics and Class in the Nineteenth-Century United States* (New Haven: Yale UP, 1990). Ruth Bordin, *Woman and Temperance: The Quest for Power and Liberty, 1873–1900* (Philadelphia: Temple UP, 1981) describes the complex of goals, activities, and political philosophies developed by the Women's Christian Temperance Union (WCTU) in the later part of the century: "women used the WCTU as a base for their participation in reformist causes, as a sophisticated avenue for political action, as a support for demanding the ballot, and as a vehicle for supporting a wide range of charitable activities" (xvi). This range of activities continues to work both for legislative prohibitions and for individual reform.

9. The passing of the Maine law in 1851 marks the initial upsurge of support for prohibition. It is harder to provide a precise date for the adoption of disciplinary intimacy as the favored mode of child rearing; still, domestic manuals of the 1830s–50s become increasingly consistent and assured in their preference for affec-tionate persuasion over punitive coercion. Moreover, during this period, mothers, not fathers, were increasingly represented as the parent primarily responsible for child rearing and child discipline. For discussion of this transition in American culture see Bernard Wishy, *The Child and the Republic* (Philadelphia: U of Pennsyl-vania P, 1968); Mary Ryan, *The Cradle of the Middle Class: The Family in Oneida County, New York, 1790–1865* (Cambridge: Harvard UP, 1981) and *The Empire of the Mother: American Writing About Domesticity 1830–1860* (New York: Institute for Research in History, 1982); Steven Mintz, *A Prison of Expectations: The Family in Victorian Culture* (New York: New York UP, 1983); and Richard Brodhead, "Spar-ing the Rod: Discipline and Fiction in Antebellum America," *Representations* 21 (Winter 1988): 67–96. The writings of John Locke and Jean-Jacques Rousseau provide the Enlightenment foundations for this shift, so that Philippe Ariès can argue that the West's reorganization of the family around love rather than author-ity began as early as 1700. See his *Centuries of Childhood: A Social History of Family Life,* trans. Robert Baldick (New York: Vintage, 1962).

10. Brodhead, "Sparing the Rod," 87. Though my work is largely inspired by Brod-head's essay, I want to mark how our understandings of "disciplinary intimacy" diverge. Taking the "intimacy" of Brodhead's term literally, I am interested in the erotic dimensions of thus producing domestic order. I therefore construe the disciplinary forces evoked by love as more complexly multidirectional than those he describes.

11. T. S. Arthur, "Phoebe Grey," in *The Pitcher of Cool Water and Other Stories* (New York, 1873), 131–32.

12. Reading this fiction I was struck by the persistence of scenes of redemptive child-love from the height of moral suasion in the 1830s, through the prohibitionary successes of the 1850s, and into the founding of the WCTU in the 1870s. Both in style and in professed political goals, temperance fiction changed a great deal during this half-century, yet this formulaic plot device remained similarly present and powerful throughout. My discussion of this fiction ranges widely through

these decades in an effort to demonstrate this continuity, both as an instance of the recalcitrance of narrative convention and as an index of the persistence of the familial structures that link love and abuse—regardless of shifts in political methodology.

13. *The Sedley Family; or, The Effect of the Maine Liquor Law* (Boston, 1853); note that the publication date is only two years after the passing of the Maine liquor law. Quoted by Ginzberg, who discusses this novel on 117–18.

14. Kruna, "The Red Frock," in *The Drinking Fountain Stories* (New York, 1873), 177, 178.

15. T. S. Arthur, "What Two Little Girls Did," in *The Pitcher of Cool Water*, 77, 82, 79, and 88.

16. Samuel Chipman, *The Temperance Lecturer* (Albany, 1834). In *The Politics of Domesticity: Women, Evangelism and Temperance in Nineteenth Century America* (Middletown, CT: Wesleyan UP, 1981), Barbara Leslie Epstein quotes this material but cautions that "Chipman's reports do not, of course, tell us how many sober men were incarcerated for beating their wives or children, nor do they give us any hint of how many men beat their wives or children without being incarcerated" (109–10).

17. Published in *The Lily* 2, no. 4 (April 1850): 31. The piece is signed simply "S.F." for "Sunflower," one of Stanton's frequent pseudonyms during this period.

18. Stanton's speech was reprinted in *The Una* 2, no. 5 (May 1854): 260.

19. Quoted in Elizabeth Pleck, *Domestic Tyranny: The Making of Social Policy Against Family Violence from Colonial Times to the Present* (New York: Oxford UP, 1987), 57.

20. Linda Gordon's research into the records of three Boston child-protection agencies confirms the prevalence of coercive incest within nineteenth-century families and the predominance of sibling and father/daughter relations. Although child-protection agencies were first organized in the 1870s, Gordon's discussion suggests that these patterns of family violence have a far longer history. *Heroes of Their Own Lives: The Politics and History of Family Violence, Boston 1880–1960* (New York: Viking, 1988) and Linda Gordon and Paul O'Keefe, "Incest as a Form of Family Violence: Evidence from Historical Case Records," *Journal of Marriage and the Family* 46 (February 1984): 27–34. The earliest autobiographical account of incest I have found, *Memoirs of Mrs. Abigail Bailey, Who had been the Wife of Major ASA Bailey* (Boston, 1815), alludes to Major Bailey's sexual abuse of their daughter. For a record of family violence in the 1860s, including sexual relations between the diarist's husband and a series of young nieces, see *A Private War: Letters and Diaries of Madge Preston, 1862–1867*, ed. Virginia Walcott Beauchamp (New Brunswick, NJ: Rutgers UP, 1987).

21. In terms of the relation between incest and alcoholism, Linda Gordon convincingly observes that "familial sexual abuse was rarely a crime of uncontrolled, momentary passion to which the lowering of inhibitions by alcohol might contribute; but a longer-term, calculated relationship perpetuated during sober as

well as drunken moments." Nevertheless, her correlation of stress factors for family violence reveals alcoholism to be by far the most significant stress factor for incest. In all events, it is clear from her readings of case reports that late-nineteenth-century child-protection agents considered drunkenness to be a prime cause of child sexual abuse, and there is every reason to believe that temperance writers shared this view. *Heroes of their Own Lives*, 218 and Table 6, 174.

22. Michel Foucault, *The History of Sexuality, Volume I: An Introduction* (New York: Vintage, 1978), 108–9.

23. See James Kincaid, *Child-Loving: The Erotic Child and Victorian Culture* (New York: Routledge, 1992) and G. M. Goshgarian, *To Kiss the Chastening Rod: Domestic Fiction and Sexual Ideology in the American Renaissance* (Ithaca: Cornell UP, 1992).

24. In *Trauma and Recovery* (New York: Basic, 1992), Judith Lewis Herman argues that the willingness of societies to acknowledge trauma, including childhood abuse and incest, is contingent on political conditions: "To hold traumatic reality in consciousness requires a social context that affirms and protects the victim and that joins victim and witness in a common alliance.... For the larger society, the social context is created by political movements that give voice to the disempowered" (9). Yet, although her discussion of the ability to acknowledge trauma is thus highly conscious of the import of social context, her discussion of trauma itself and the process of recovery effaces this context. Consequently, though she describes how discourse about sexual trauma can have a social function, she does not admit that incestuous desires are in any way integral to family order. See, for example, her description of how a therapeutic group ritually "welcomed [an incest survivor] into a 'new family' of survivors" (228–29). In pointing out this gap, I do not mean to criticize Herman's powerful book but to demonstrate how, even in what I consider to be the most socially engaged discussion of incest's trauma, such silences hold.

25. O. S. Fowler, *Perfect Men, Women, and Children, in Happy Families* (Boston, 1878), 170, one of many paeans to mothers by the famed phrenologist and temperance advocate. This passage is quoted in Bryan Strong, "Toward a History of the Experiential Family: Sex and Incest in the Nineteenth-Century Family," *Journal of Marriage and the Family* 35 (August 1973), 462. Although I find Strong's conclusions about the sexual anxieties of nineteenth-century men reductive and unconvincing, I do concur with him in discerning a sexual "undercurrent flowing beneath the sentimental cult of motherhood."

26. Ronald J. Zboray's "Gender and Boundlessness in Reading Patterns," in *A Fictive People: Antebellum Economic Development and the American Reading Public* (New York: Oxford UP, 1993) supports these findings through an analysis of the charge records of the New York Society Library.

27. "National Temperance and Tract Publication House, paper read by James Black," *Proceedings of the Fifth National Temperance Convention, Saratoga Springs, New York, August 1, 2 and 3 1865* (New York, 1865), 51, 52.

28. All of these materials can be found in the National Temperance Society and Publication House files of the American Antiquarian Society.

29. J. R. Syper, "Temperance Literature," *Proceedings of the Sixth National Temperance Convention, Cleveland, Ohio, July 29, 1868* (New York, 1868), 113.

30. A. G. Lawson, "Temperance Literature," *Proceedings of the Seventh National Temperance Convention, Saratoga Springs, New York, August 26 and 27, 1873* (New York, 1873), 140.

31. *The Good Boy's and Girl's Alphabet* (Philadelphia, 1841).

32. Peter Carter, "The Snow Storm; or, What Jennie Scott Did," in *The Old Brown Pitcher*, 178, 180, and 181.

33. For a novella-length version of this fantasy see Jenny Marsh Parker, *The Story of a Story-Book* (New York, 1858), which traces the moral influence of a book from a Sunday-School library as it is read by a series of sinners young and old.

34. Lucius Manlius Sargent, "My Mother's Gold Ring; Founded on Fact" (Boston, 1833), iii–iv.

35. The Eckley copy is in the collection of the American Antiquarian Society. The Brown copy is in the collection of the University of Virginia. For an illuminating discussion of what we can learn about past readers from the signatures and marginalia they leave behind see Cathy N. Davidson, *Revolution and the Word: The Rise of the Novel in America* (New York: Oxford UP, 1986), chaps. 1–4.

The temperance movement's own claims for Sargent's tales presume a very different readership. Charles Jewett asserts, for example, that "thousands of men before the year 1840 had been converted to the doctrine and practice of abstinence by their perusal—many of them by the perusal of a single number of the series." *Forty Years Fight with the Drink Demon; or a History of the Temperance Reform as I Have Seen It and of My Labor in Connection Therewith* (New York, 1872), 217. Whether or not thousands were converted, there is no question that these tales were extremely popular in temperance circles. The first tale had sold 114,000 copies by 1843, and there are multiple editions both of individual tales and of collected volumes. Yet, in a "Prefatory Sketch of their Origin and History" that Sargent wrote for a complete edition of his twenty-one tales, *Temperance Tales* (Boston, 1863), he draws all his evidence for their emotional power, and every testimony to their efficacy, from responses garnered within temperance circles, which suggests once again the limits of distribution, even for such popular tales. One quoted testimony begins:

"I write you from the office of the New York State Temperance Society. Mr. Delavan informs me that you have recently prepared a tract, entitled the 'Gold Ring,' which he thinks better calculated to promote the cause than anything he has yet seen. Several of his friends, as well as himself, had read it, with the deepest emotion; but, afraid of trusting entirely their own judgements on a subject where their feelings had been so deeply enlisted, they resolved to have it read in a very crowded temperance convention. The effect produced upon the audience he described as overwhelming. They were not simply in tears, they were convulsed with emotion." (4–5)

36. Interestingly, a frequent contemporary criticism of temperance fiction was that it might corrupt innocent young readers rather than permit them to purify the world.

> [many temperance novelists] of refined sentiments and delicate nerves are employing their talents in describing minutely the scenes of drunkenness which are said to occur at public hotels, and in bringing to light the secret sins of individuals, which, for all the good that can be anticipated from their exposure, might well be left in the darkness and privacy in which they were committed. The object which these good and gifted ladies have in view, as understood, is to teach morality. But would it be safe, think you, for a prudent mother, in order to impress upon the still pure heart of her daughter a warmer regard for the beauty and dignity of virtue to introduce her to the companionship of the vulgar, the obscene and the vicious, even admitting that she kept her guarded by the presentation of the most vivid contrasts? Would not the experiment be dangerous, we ask, the end and good effect doubtful to say the least?

    Quoted from a review in *Godey's Lady's Book* (September 1854) in Nina Baym, *Novels, Readers and Reviewers: Responses to Fiction in Antebellum America* (Ithaca: Cornell UP, 1984), 180. For a discussion of this immoral or "subversive" potential in reform fiction more generally see David Reynolds, *Beneath the American Renaissance: The Subversive Imagination in the Age of Emerson and Melville* (New York: Knopf, 1988) especially chapter 2, "The Reform Impulse and the Paradox of Immoral Didacticism"; and R. Laurence Moore, "Religion, Secularization, and the Shaping of the Culture Industry in Antebellum America," *American Quarterly* 41 (June 1989): 216–42.

37. "The Sleigh Ride," in *The Old Brown Pitcher*, 75, 77.

38. Introductory "Note," *The Old Brown Pitcher*.

39. *The History of a Threepenny Bit* (New York, 1873), 211. In this story too, the tavern-keeper's reform and a host of other reconciliations are all brought about by the love of little Peggy. She is not, however, completely omnipotent—her father dies of delirium tremens.

40. See Gillian Brown, *Domestic Individualism: Imagining Self in Nineteenth-Century America* (Berkeley: U of California P, 1990) for a brilliant discussion of how, despite the pervasive rhetoric of separate spheres, American domesticity actively organizes the possessive individualism of American capitalism.

41. For another example of a narrating object see *The Biography of a Bottle, By a Friend of Temperance* (Boston, 1835).

42. *The History of a Threepenny Bit*, 87, 94–95.

43. T. S. Arthur, *Ten Nights in a Bar-Room*, 92–93.

44. Paul E. Johnson discusses the authority Rochester's leading families evoked to repress workplace drinking, and the fervor evangelical revivals wielded against

alcohol—a fervor Johnson describes as "very much like class violence." *A Shop-keeper's Millennium: Society and Revivals in Rochester, New York, 1815–1837* (New York: Hill and Wang, 1978), 79–83 and 113–15. Roy Rosenzweig's ethnically differentiated account of the politics of leisure in nineteenth-century Worcester explores these issues in terms of working-class resistance, *Eight Hours for What We Will: Workers and Leisure in an Industrial City, 1870–1920* (New York: Cambridge UP, 1983), chapter 2. For antebellum accounts of similar dynamics in Philadelphia and Boston see Bruce Laurie, *Working People of Philadelphia, 1800–1850* (Philadelphia: Temple UP, 1980), and Jill Seigel Dodd, "The Working Classes and the Temperance Movement in Ante-Bellum Boston," *Labor History* 19 (Fall 1978): 510–31.

45. Rev. John Marsh, *Hannah Hawkins: The Reformed Drunkard's Daughter* (New York, 1848), vi, 21, and 45.

46. Sargent, "My Mother's Gold Ring," 6–7.

47. Julia McNair Wright, *A Million Too Much, A Temperance Tale* (Philadelphia, 1871), 257. Indeed this novel blames the youth's alcoholism, dissipation, and eventual death on his lack of a properly domestic upbringing: not only is he orphaned at birth, but from infancy his nurse pours gin in his milk. Such stories suggest some of the ways in which the temperance plots of youthful temptation and those of paternal redemption may intersect.

48. Lydia H. Sigourney, "Wife of the Intemperate," in *A Book for Girls in Prose and Poetry* (New York, 1843), 131.

49. "Learn to Say No," in *The Temperance Speaker: A Collection of Original and Selected Dialogues, Addresses and Recitations, for the Use of Temperance Organizations, Schools, Bands of Hope, Anniversaries Etc.*, ed. J. N. Stearns (New York, 1873), 67.

50. Gordon, *Heroes in Their Own Lives*, 212, 225. Gordon describes domestic incest as being far more common before 1930 and the changes in the norms of childhood household labor that followed from mandatory secondary education.

51. T. S. Arthur, "The Baby in the Brown Cottage," in *The Pitcher of Cool Water and Other Stories*, 60–61.

52. Boston child-saving agencies understood the effect of putting fine middle-class garb on their "waifs": a standard feature of their fund-raising brochures were before and after photographs with the children dressed first as they had been found and then in elegant, lace-trimmed clothes. Gordon, *Heroes of Their Own Lives*, 36; a sample photograph is opposite p. 51.

53. In nineteenth- and early twentieth-century America, red and pink were considered stronger, more masculine colors, while blue was thought to be feminine; even this color-coding, the inverse of our present practices, was not thought to hold for young children. Clothing for children under the age of five was entirely genderless, an absence of sex-markers that implied the child's sexual innocence. See Jo B. Paoletti and Carol L. Kregloh, "The Children's Department," in *Men and Women: Dressing the Part*, ed. Claudia Brush Kidwell and Valerie Steel (Washington, DC: Smithsonian Institution, 1989), 22–41.

54. "The Child's Champion," in *Walt Whitman: The Early Poems and Fiction*, ed. Thomas L. Brasher (New York: New York UP, 1963), 74n, 79, 76n. Whitman published a total of four versions of this story. While the suggestion of a heterosexual happy ending appears in all versions, the two longer passages appear only in the original *New World* (1841) version.

55. In *Disseminating Whitman: Revision and Corporeality in Leaves of Grass* (Cambridge: Harvard UP, 1991), 26–36, Michael Moon treats the self-censorship evident in Whitman's revisions of "The Child's Champion" as a model for the strategies that both here and in the later *Leaves of Grass* would permit Whitman to voice culturally proscribed sexual and power relations. While Moon's discussion of this story richly explores its coding of homosexual desire, he does not situate this plot in relation to the pedophilic conventions of the temperance genre.

56. Frontispiece to Jane E. Stebbins, *Fifty Years History of the Temperance Cause*, published in the same volume with T.A.H. Brown, *A Full Description of the Origin and Progress of the New Plan of Labor by the Women Up to the Present Time* (Hartford, CT, 1876).

"Whiskey, Blacking, and All"

Temperance and Race in William Wells Brown's *Clotel*

📧 Robert S. Levine

In the March 18, 1852 issue of *Frederick Douglass' Paper*, Douglass printed an editorial supporting legislation intended to bring the 1851 Maine law, which banned the liquor trade, to New York state. At around the same time he began printing numerous articles championing Harriet Beecher Stowe's *Uncle Tom's Cabin*. By 1853 Stowe's antislavery novel and temperance emerged as dominant, even linked, concerns of his newspaper, and these interrelated interests were addressed in a letter from William Wells Brown printed in the issue of August 26, 1853. Writing from London on August 2, 1853, Brown declares that " 'Uncle Tom's Cabin' is still doing a great work; its popularity and its wide circulation is not only arousing the dormant feeling of that generous love of freedom and lofty enthusiasm which, a few years ago, burst from the limbs of the beaten and outraged slaves of the West Indies, but will do much to create a desire for the elevation of the laboring classes in Europe, and especially in Great Britain." Brown's rhetoric initially suggests that the "laboring classes," like the slaves of the West Indies, are the victims of brute exploitation and arbitrary authority, but as the letter develops he increasingly places the burden for the "elevation" of the working poor on the poor themselves, whom he portrays less as "wage slaves" than as "slaves" of the bottle:

> It is true that much can be said of the sad position in which a large portion of the people are placed, but very much of their degradation is brought upon by themselves.—The amount of drunkenness is frightful. . . . It is enough to horrify any one to go amongst these people, who seem abandoned to the varied evils that neglect, ignorance, and vice have produced. . . . Many of

these appear so worn in countenance, form, feature, and expression, that one is almost led to doubt whether they are of the same species with the well-organized and the noble of the race.—Through the vice of intemperance and its degrading influences, the lofty lineaments of their better nature gradually wear away, until nothing is left but the attributes of the idiot or the fiend.[1]

In this anxious meditation on the corporeal and moral degradation brought about by intemperance, Brown suggests that "drunkenness," a form of self-enslavement, transforms the white working classes into a different sort of "species" from the human race.

Brown also develops connections between temperance, slavery, and race in his 1853 *Clotel; or The President's Daughter: A Narrative of Slave Life in the United States*, generally regarded as the first novel published by an African American. In a revealing scene on a stagecoach late in the novel, a Connecticut minister, who "went the whole length of the 'Maine law,'" tells the passengers of how he used to keep "spirits about the house" before he became a "tee-totaller."[2] He did so in part because his servant, "who was much addicted to strong drink" (200), insisted that he needed whiskey on hand to mix with the boot blacking. Suspicious of the servant's demands, the minister one morning himself pours the whiskey into the boot blacking. He triumphantly describes the servant's response to his experiment: "He took the blacking out, and I watched him, and he drank down the whiskey, blacking, and all" (200). More explicitly than in Brown's letter on English poverty, the rhetoric of this account suggests with an uncomfortable literalism that to drink intemperately is to transform oneself into a "black" slave to the bottle. The fact that the servant's race is never mentioned only underscores the "universality" of the lesson encoded in this anecdote.

From the mid-1830s to the time of his death in 1884, Brown participated in a number of temperance organizations that were committed to the belief that the free blacks could elevate themselves in the United States by liberating them-selves from liquor. At his most optimistic, Brown argued that if blacks could overcome "the enslaving appetite" for drink, as he termed intemperance in *The American Fugitive in Europe* (1855), they could even overcome slavery.[3] Yet as Brown knew full well, black elevation was extraordinarily difficult to achieve in a racist slave culture. Aware that a progressive model of temperance risked absolving white racist culture for its role in enslaving and dominating blacks, Brown and other black temperance reformers sought to expand their concerns beyond the problem of controlling blacks' drinking habits in order to portray whites' antiblack racism and desires for mastery as themselves forms of intemperance. In *Clotel*, as I will be elaborating below, many of the most intemperate figures are whites, not blacks. Over the course of the novel Brown shows how the lack of restraints on whites' "enslaving appetite" for drink, power, and sexual gratification helps to perpetuate the enslavement of blacks in the South and the marginalization of free blacks in the North. The novel's fragmentary collage technique, with its dislocating shifts back and forth among various characters and scenes, allows Brown to display a wide range of intemperate actions among a wide range of characters, thereby challenging easy dichotomies of temperance and intemperance along racial lines. The result is a novel that, despite its problematic metaphor of "blacking," destabilizes notions of temperance and race and (perhaps unwittingly) challenges idealistic conceptions of the transformative power of temperance. That said, progressive models of temperance reform have an important place in the novel, and it is with Brown's optimistic belief that temperance could help put an end to slavery and racism that I want to begin.

In the "Narrative of the Life and Escape of William Wells Brown," which prefaces the 1853 London first printing of *Clotel*, the third-person biographer (probably Brown) comments on Brown's temperance work in Buffalo several years after escaping from slavery in 1834:

> In proportion as his mind expanded under the more favourable circumstances in which Brown was placed, he became anxious, not merely for the redemption of his race from personal slavery, but for the moral and religious elevation of those who were free. Finding that habits of intoxication were too prevalent among his coloured brethren, he, in conjunction with others, commenced a temperance reformation in their body. Such was the success of their efforts that, in three years, in the city of Buffalo alone, a society of upwards of 500 members was raised out of a coloured population of less than 700. (42–3)

As the three-time president of this society, Brown sought to help the free blacks to assume "a position," as Josephine Brown notes in her 1856 biography of her father, "where they could give a practical refutation to the common belief, that the negro cannot attain to the high stand of the Anglo-Saxon."[4] In this respect, his goals were of a piece with those of the black temperance movement of the period. Numerous black reformers argued that the free blacks should make a concerted effort to control their drinking so that they could elevate themselves in U.S. society and thereby convince whites of the errors of proslavery ideology.[5] For example, the Report of the Committee on Temperance delivered at the 1833 "Third Annual Convention, For the Improvement of the Free People of Colour in These United States" warned that whites could say blacks were better off in slavery when they observed "degraded men, clustering around those fatal corners, where *'liquid fire'* is dispensed"; and the Report went on to blame black intemperance, not white racism, for "*four fifths* of the pauperism known among us." Though William Whipper, the founder of the American Moral Reform Society, contested the notion that blacks were "more intemperate than whites," he nonetheless argued, in his 1834 presidential address to the Colored Temperance Society of Philadelphia, "that we must be more pure than they, before we can be duly respected." Martin Delany, who in 1834 helped to organize a black temperance society in Pittsburgh, drafted a resolution at the 1841 State Convention of the Colored Freemen of Pennsylvania calling on blacks to adopt "TOTAL ABSTINENCE" as a way of gaining "the esteem of all wise and virtuous men." For, as Stephen Meyers put it in the February 10, 1842 issue of his temperance/abolitionist newspaper, *Northern Star and Freeman's Advocate*, "[W]henever it can be said (and not gainsayed) that the free blacks are a sober, industrious and intelligent people, capable of self government, the only argument in favor of slavery falls to the ground."[6]

In their writings, Brown and other black temperance reformers of the period can appear to be placing undue emphasis on the ways in which, as Douglass remarks in his 1845 "Intemperance and Slavery," a "large class of free people of color in America . . . has, through the influence of intemperance, done much to retard the progress of the anti-slavery movement." But by the 1840s, it is worth underscoring, these temperance reformers had also taken up the more radical agenda of highlighting abuses of white power. In "Intemperance and Slavery," for example, Douglass, after seeming to "blame" intemperate free blacks for their degraded status in the United States, quickly shifts his attention to racist whites of the North and South, whom he presents as exhibiting analogous forms of intemperance far more insidious than the putative drunkenness of northern blacks. He lambastes the white racist mob that attacked 1,200 black members of Philadelphia's Moyamensing Temperance Society during the August 1, 1842 celebration of West Indies emancipation. And by insisting that prior to his escape from slavery "I was not a slave to intemperance, but a slave to my fellow-men," he makes clear, through analogy and metaphor, that for the most part it was the slaveowners, not this particular former slave, who evinced intemperance.[7] Commenting on slavery's tendency to promote "intemperance," the white abolitionist Theodore Weld writes in his influential *American Slavery As It Is* (1839): "Arbitrary power is to the mind what alcohol is to the body; it intoxicates. Man loves power. It is perhaps the strongest human passion; and the more absolute the power, the stronger the desire for it." Brown similarly remarks in an 1847 lecture delivered to the Female Anti-Slavery Society of Salem: "Give one man power *ad infinitum* over another, and he will abuse that power; no matter if there be law; no matter if there be public sentiment in favor of the oppressed." "Drunk" on unlimited power, the individual enslaver, like the alcoholic, becomes a "slave" of appetite.[8]

As the Female Anti-Slavery Society setting of Brown's 1847 lecture suggests, the discourse of intemperate appetite was often specifically gendered as an attack on patriarchal power. Josephine Brown points to the pronounced vulnerability of the female slaves: "If there is one evil connected with the abominable system of slavery which should be loathed more than another, it is taking from woman the right of self-defence, and making her subject to the control of any licentious villain who may be able to purchase her person."[9] In his writings, Brown repeatedly represents such violations, in large part because a trauma that he experienced as a slave and mourned throughout his life was the sexual violation of his mother and sister (Brown barely mentions his three brothers in his autobiographical narratives). As he remarks in the "Narrative" prefacing *Clotel*: "nothing could be more heart-rending than to see a dear and beloved mother or sister tortured by unfeeling men" (18). The violation of his mother was a particularly traumatic source of guilt for Brown because without that violation he would not have been born; his very existence thus depends upon the intemperate patriarchal violation that is the focus of his social critique. In the "Narrative" the innkeeper Mr. Freeland, to whom Brown is briefly hired out, assumes representative status as the "tyrannical and inhuman" (18) slaveholder par excellence: "he was a horse-racer, cock-fighter, gambler, and, to crown the whole, an inveterate drunkard. What else but bad treatment could be expected from such a character?" (18). That large question becomes a haunting one when Brown's mother is sold to the New Orleans slave market and his sister, having been purchased "for the master's own use" (25), is put in a slave pen with four other women. Similar questions about the "enslaving appetite" of the masters haunt the opening chapters of *Clotel*.

The narrator asserts at the beginning of *Clotel* that the relative lack of existence of "the real Negro, or clear black" provides the "best evidence of the degraded and immoral condition of the relation of master and slave in the United States of America" (59). Brown writes in his 1853 *Three Years in Europe*, published the same year as *Clotel*, that the increasingly white complexion of the slaves "is attributable, solely to the unlimited power which the white slave owner exercises over his victim."[10] It is attributable, in short, to the sexual domination that slavery vouchsafes the patriarch, a power which is depicted in *Clotel*'s opening chapters as a form of intemperance that corrupts master and slave alike. The forever offstage (because dead) Thomas Jefferson emerges as the ur-intemperate master for having fathered two daughters by Currer, the slave woman who formerly "kept house" (64) for him.[11] As a sign of the corruption resulting from such hypocritical exploitation, Currer in effect prostitutes her daughters, Clotel and Althesa, by sending them to balls in the misguided hope that they might become, as their mother once was, "the finely-dressed mistress of some white man" (63). By depicting the daughters first at the "Negro ball" (64) and then (with their mother) at the slave sale after they have been legally defined as "property," Brown suggests that there is little difference between the two institutions, insofar as both put slave women at the mercy of white men. Brown presents the slave sale as an occasion in which grossly physical masters, "joking, swearing, smoking, spitting" (67), compete to purchase female bodies for sexual purposes. While Currer and Althesa are sold to a slave speculator and sent downriver to New Orleans, Clotel is purchased by Horatio Green, the son of a wealthy Richmond gentleman, who seems to have fallen in love with her. As the novel develops, however, it becomes clear that the seemingly "fortunate" Clotel is in fact also at the mercy of a master's intemperate appetite.

As is well known, Brown, in telling Clotel's story, drew on Lydia Maria Child's "The Quadroons" (1842), breaking Child's narrative into several sections, changing names, but otherwise adhering so closely to the story as to lift numerous passages word for word.[12] What appealed to Brown about Child's story, I think, was the way in which it conjoined antislavery and feminist discourses to suggest that from the very start, intemperate desires govern a white master's decision to make a slave woman into his mistress. Green initially rents a country cottage for Clotel, where she gives birth to a daughter, Mary. But increasingly he spends his time with his male friends in the city, and though Brown (Child) never comments on the obvious—that he would have been drinking with these friends—he portrays Green as "drunk" with ambition in eventually choosing to marry Gertrude, the daughter of "a very popular and wealthy man" (85). In the widely read antebellum temperance fictions of T. S. Arthur, economic desires and political ambition are presented as intoxicants that "enslave" mind and body.[13] Brown similarly presents Green's ambition as analogous to moments in temperance tracts when the young man takes the first drink that precipitates the inevitable decline: "this new impulse to ambition, combined with the strong temptation of variety in love, met the ardent young man weakened in moral principle, and unfettered by laws of the land" (85). Green's initial "taste" of power and unrestrained sexuality stimulates desires for more; lacking in "the idea of restraint" (85), he succumbs to appetite. His metaphorically intemperate ambition and carnality are literalized in his actual descent into alcoholism: "While [Clotel] was passing lonely and dreary hours with none but her darling child, Horatio Green was trying to find relief in that insidious enemy of man, the intoxicating cup" (149).

Through his appropriation of Child's story, Brown develops in the novel a damning portrayal of slavery as a patriarchal institution that stimulates, rather than restrains, the intemperate desires of the white male masters. Because the masters become "enslaved" to these desires, even a man with some moral potential—like the Reverend John Peck, who purchases Currer—can find himself succumbing to the temptations of the South. Originally from Connecticut, Peck, invited by his uncle to Natchez, Mississippi, marries a woman with a slave plantation and becomes a proslavery advocate who uses the Bible to justify his mastery. That such mastery makes him into a beast of sorts is made clear by his daughter Georgiana, who tells the story of how her father joined in the pursuit of fugitive slaves with "those nasty Negro-dogs" (143), and eventually did the work of the dogs in killing one of the fugitive slaves. The depiction of the parson's descent into doglike bestiality is consistent with Brown's depiction throughout the novel of the results of governing "by decrees and laws emanating from . . . uncontrolled will" (183).

Given Brown's gendered focus on patriarchal exploitation and domination, and his admiration for Harriet Beecher Stowe, it is not surprising that the white woman Georgiana should emerge as one of the more exemplary characters of the novel. Like her father, Georgiana has been educated in the North, but having moved back to the South after completing her education, she has "had the opportunity of contrasting the spirit of Christianity and liberty in New England with that of slavery in her native state, and had learned to feel deeply for the injured Negro" (94). In some respects she has recovered the lost spirituality of her fallen father.

Following the death of her father to cholera, Georgiana, in alliance with Carlton, the northern "free-thinker" whom she converts and marries, adopts a plan of "gradual emancipation" (165) for the slaves of her plantation. Consistent with arguments made by Frederick Douglass, W. C. Nell, and other black leaders of the period (including Brown), Georgiana rejects Carlton's initial suggestion that she ship her approximately one hundred slaves to Liberia, insisting that blacks have earned the right to regard the United States as "their native land" (163).[14] (She later remarks that it would be better to deport "the vicious among the whites" [191].) In an effort to set an example to her southern neighbors, she thus resolves to demonstrate blacks' capacities for temperate industry by paying them for their labors and allowing them to use their earnings to purchase their freedom. Georgiana's belief that it is the slaves' responsibility to display their industry places an enormous burden of proof on the slaves. However, the rhetorical and political dimensions of her plan are quite similar to what I noted in the rhetoric and politics of black temperance reformers of the period, and there is every sense that Georgiana is viewed quite positively by Brown as "The Liberator" (161). (Brown is so taken by Georgiana that in the same chapter in which he describes her gradual emancipation plan he mentions only in passing Currer's death by yellow fever.) In fact, Georgiana's plan produces the kind of changes in her slaves that black temperance reformers like William Whipper argued would contribute to black elevation: "They became temperate, moral, religious, setting an example of innocent, unoffending lives to the world around them, which was seen and admired by all" (166).

The need for the slaves to demonstrate their capacities for temperate industry assumes even greater urgency when Georgiana, suffering from consumption, decides to liberate her slaves before she dies. Summoning them before her as a group, she delivers her emancipation proclamation:

> From this hour, . . . you are free, and all eyes will be fixed upon you. I dare not predict how far your example may affect the welfare of your brethren yet in bondage. If you are temperate, industrious, peaceable, and pious, you will show to the world that slaves can be emancipated without danger. Remember what a singular relation you sustain to society. The necessities of the case require not only that you should behave as well as the whites, but better than the whites. . . . Get as much education as possible for yourselves and your children. An ignorant people can never occupy any other than a degraded station in society; they can never be truly free until they are intelligent. (189–90)

In order to help her former slaves elevate themselves in the United States, she has purchased land for them in Ohio, "where I hope you will all prosper" (190). On that purchased land, to pick up on the John Winthrop–like rhetoric of her speech, the liberated blacks would be a "city upon a hill" where "all eyes" will be watching their progress. With her implicit suggestion that should the liberated slaves fail to prosper, they will only reconfirm whites' racist notions of blacks' unsuitability for freedom, Georgiana, in the disciplinary mode of Winthrop, places the large burden of black elevation squarely on the blacks themselves.

Georgiana's emancipation program thus raises a number of questions. One might ask, for example, how far the former slaves' adoption of temperate industry will take them in light of the existence of Ohio's "Black Codes." Surely Brown would have been aware of the fate met by the slaves of the Virginian John Randolph, who similarly bequeathed land in Ohio for his liberated slaves, who were then unable to claim the land because of the opposition of racist white farmers.[15] One might also ask what would keep the industrious slaves from succumbing to the lure of the market and becoming "slaves" to their speculative ambition for material gain. Relatedly, one might ask whether it is so easy to dismiss Southerners' critiques of market capitalism as a form of "wage slavery."[16] It is notable, for example, that the moment Georgiana's slaves adopt their temperate, industrous habits, the surrounding slaveowners, rather than becoming convinced of the slaves' capacities for freedom, want to purchase them to work on their plantations (167). In this respect, Georgiana's experiment implicitly suggests that the more industrious are the black workers, the more those with power and capital will want to exploit them.

Brown attempts to elide such questions and contradictions by inserting into the novel, just before Georgiana announces her emancipation plan, a Manichaean mythic account of the origins of regional differences in which the good Puritans are presented as begetting the temperate ideals of free labor in the North and the bad colonizers at Jamestown are presented as begetting the intemperate practice of slavery in the South. Despite the fact that the Puritans slaughtered Indians and bought and sold slaves, Brown memorializes the *Mayflower* as the "parent" of the "labour-honouring, law-sustaining institutions of the North" (188), while anathematizing the "low rakish ship hastening from the tropics" (188) to Jamestown as the "parent" of "idleness, lynch-law, ignorance, unpaid labour, poverty . . . and the peculiar institutions of the South" (188).[17] According to this myth, the differences between the regions' founders created in the nation's social institutions "parallel lines" (188). As an advocate of free labor, Georgiana works to bring these lines together by reforming the South, but she can only succeed if the North is as committed to free labor as the Pilgrims of this mythic account. Brown would like to think that such is the case—hence his commitment to black elevation and self-help—but when, later in *Clotel*, he casts a critical eye on actual social practices in the North, the regions don't seem so very different after all. Northern prejudice against blacks, Brown writes in an account of Jim Crow practices on a train, is "another form of slavery" (176). In a concession that relieves blacks of the burden of demonstrating their abilities to rise in a "free labor" economy, Brown likewise notes, following the death of Georgiana, that racists throughout the United States are making efforts "to retard the work of emancipation for which she laboured and so wished to see brought about" (193). That such efforts may be regarded as forms of intemperance is made clear in the episode immediately following Georgiana's liberation of her slaves: Clotel's ride in the stagecoach where she hears the Connecticut minister's account of how his servant "drank down the whiskey, blacking, and all."

Clotel, who has been sold to a slave trader by the vengeful Gertrude, eventually escapes from slavery by disguising herself as a gentleman accompanied by a black servant, the intelligent and industrious slave William.[18] While William continues on to Canada after the escape, Clotel, still dressed as an "Italian or Spanish gentleman" (194), takes a stagecoach to Richmond in pursuit of her daughter, Mary. In an anachronistic moment typical of the ironies generated by Brown's use of historical collage, those aboard the stage discuss the "contemporaneous" politics of the election of 1839–40 and the Maine law of 1851 (the irony is that the Whig "Old Tip" William Harrison wins his "log cabin" campaign for the presidency by freely distributing hard cider and whiskey to his supporters). With reference to his home state, the Connecticut minister who supports the Maine law argues a point similar to what Brown argued in his 1853 letter to *Frederick Douglass' Paper*: that social prosperity is "attributable to the disuse of intoxicating drinks" (196). The linkage between temperance and prosperity set forth by the minister reinforces Brown's mythic notion of regional origins and differences; Connecticut, in this account, keeps alive the putative freedom-loving spirit of the Puritans. And yet Brown, through the response of a proliquor Southerner aboard the stage, suggests that the North's commitment to temperance is little more than a self-aggrandizing myth. For the Southerner tells a hilarious story of visiting his "teetotaling" relatives in Vermont and discovering a secret world of rampant drinking. Though when among the family group the Southerner hears "nothing but talk about the 'Juvinal Temperance Army,' the 'Band of Hope,' the 'Rising Generation,' the 'Female Dorcas Temperance Society'" (197), as soon as he is alone with one or two members of his family he is offered drinks from their hidden stashes of rum and brandy. As a result, the Southerner proclaims, "during the fortnight that I was in Vermont, with my teetotal relations, I was kept about as well corned as if I had been among my hot water friends in Tennessee" (199).

Though most of the stage's passengers applaud the story, Brown is hardly sympathetic to the Southerner's moral position. If anything, the tale, rather than turning the tables on temperance, underscores the need for the restraints of Maine law legislation. Thus Brown gives the final word to the Connecticut minister, who in addition to sharing his account of his servant's "blacking," offers a follow-up disquisition on intemperance and slavery. He proclaims to the group (to extract just a portion of his long speech): "Look at society in the states where temperance views prevail, and you will see there real happiness. The people are taxed less, the poor houses are shut up for want of occupants, and extreme destitution is unknown. Every one who drinks at all is liable to become an habitual drunkard. . . . *I have known* many young men of the finest promise, led by the drinking habit into vice, ruin and early death. *I have known* many tradesmen whom it has made bankrupt . . . *I have known* . . . kind husbands and fathers whom it has turned into monsters" (199–200). The litany of intemperate "husbands and fathers" reinforces Brown's focus on the ways in which men, by succumbing to their desires for mastery, sexuality, and money, become slaves of appetite. And it suggests, against the grain of Brown's mythic account of regional origins and differences, that such "slavery" exists in the North as well as in the South. That said, the minister's warnings on social and moral decline speak most specifically to the life trajectory of the Southerner Horatio Green, whose intemperate actions generate much of the plot of the novel.

Green, in this respect, may be viewed as a stand-in for Thomas Jefferson, whose role in the production of the Declaration of Independence and Currer's children makes him the ultimate patriarchal originator not only of the plot of the novel but also of the plot of the nation. Persisting as a perpetual challenge to this national "plot" is a counterplot, black rage and rebellion. In a famous passage in his 1785 *Notes on the State of Virginia*, Jefferson offered a nightmare vision of the enactment of that plot, describing how "ten thousand recollections, by the blacks, of the injuries they have sustained; new provocations; the real distinctions which nature has made; and many other circumstances, will divide us into parties, and produce convulsions, which will probably never end but in the extermination of the one or the other of the race."[19] Though Brown's political perspective is quite different from Jefferson's, insofar as he rejects essentialist notions of racial difference and believes that African Americans have earned their rights to citizenship, he presents in *Clotel* a similarly anxious vision, in an account late in the novel, of the aftermath of Nat Turner's rebellion: "Without scruple and without pity, the whites massacred all blacks found beyond their owners' plantations: the Negroes, in return, set fire to houses, and put those to death who attempted to escape from the flames. Thus carnage was added to carnage, and the blood of the whites flowed to avenge the blood of the blacks. These were the ravages of slavery" (215). Such violence may be regarded as the well-deserved "ravages" of Jeffersonian (national) hypocrisy and expediency. And yet as sympathetic as Brown may be to black rebels, his emphasis on the "full-blooded" (213) blackness of Turner and his swamp-dwelling coconspirator Picquilo, who "imbrued his hands in the blood of all the whites he could meet" (214), conveys his anxieties that revolutionary violence is a form of intemperate "blacking" in which "low and vindictive passions" (212) in effect enslave the individual who succumbs to them.[20]

Concerns that revolutionism, however legitimate and necessary, can lead to a loss of self-government inform Brown's writings from the 1840s to the 1870s. Commenting on the French revolutions of the 1790s and 1840s in *The American Fugitive in Europe*, for example, Brown attacks Marat as "that bloodthirsty demon in human form" and praises Lamartine as a more temperate leader who, "by the power of his eloquence, succeeded in keeping the people quiet" and under control. Along the same lines, he celebrates the black revolutionaries Toussaint L'Ouverture and Madison Washington as models of self-restraint. Indicative of Toussaint's self-control and "humanity," as Brown points out in a lecture of 1854, was his decision to help "his master's family to escape from the impending danger." Brown similarly praises Madison Washington for throwing himself between the rebellious slaves and "their victims, exclaiming 'Stop! no more blood,'" when the blacks of the *Creole* had clearly gained control over the white enslavers. As Brown remarks in *The Black Man, His Antecedents, His Genius, and His Achievements* (1863), Madison Washington's "act of humanity raised the uncouth son of Africa far above his Anglo-Saxon oppressors." As for Nat Turner, Brown made an especially vigorous effort in two texts of the 1860s to present him as a temperate revolutionary whose "acts, and his heroism live in the hearts of his race." Indicative of his clear-headed response to his white oppressors, Turner, Brown informs his readers, was a teetotaler who "never tasted a drop of ardent spirits in his life." Appropriately, he was hung by a "poor old white man, long besotted by drink."[21]

To return to *Clotel*, it is noteworthy that however much Brown may be concerned about the "intemperate" rage of Turner and Picquilo, he presents their violence as a direct response to forms of white intemperance. For example, just prior to the account of the Turner rebellion, Brown tells the story of how Althesa's daughters (Jefferson's granddaughters), Ellen and Jane, become objects of the sexual desires of male enslavers after the death of their mother and "stepfather" Morton. (Though the white Morton, who purchased Althesa in New Orleans, is presented as a more positive figure than Green, he nonetheless fails as a husband and father by not moving North to legalize their "marriage.") Depicted at the slave market as "shrinking from the rude hands that examined the graceful proportions of their beautiful frames" (207), Ellen poisons herself after being purchased by an old man, while Jane, purchased by "an unprincipled profligate" (208), witnesses her lover killed by her "master" and subsequently dies of grief. The conjunction in the novel of the cholera epidemic, which kills off many of the slaveholders, and Nat Turner's rebellion, which similarly "seizes persons who were in health, without any premonition" (205), suggests that Brown is participating in Turner's and Picquilo's rage against white enslavers in the account of their rebellion.[22] Sharing in that rage, Brown also wants to suggest ways of making that rage more temperate. He does so, in part, by describing Picquilo as an African who fights to protect his wife from the kinds of imprecations black women face throughout the novel by making a home in the Dismal Swamp: "He had met a Negro woman who was also a runaway; and, after the fashion of his native land, had gone through the process of oiling her as the marriage ceremony. They had built a cave on a rising mound in the swamp; this was their home" (213).

Anticipating that his white readers may feel threatened by the celebration of the swamp-dwelling revolutionary Picquilo, Brown in the concluding chapters of *Clotel* attempts to transmute black rebellion into a more progressive vision of black elevation through his characterization of the slave George Green. Despite the fact that he participated in Turner's rebellion, Green emerges as a model of temperate industry and fidelity, and is "as white as most white persons" (224). With the notable exception of his skin's complexion, George resembles the temperate and intelligent slave William, a "full-bodied Negro" (171) who had helped Clotel to escape from her slave master and then temperately (through rational confutation) refused to abide by northern Jim Crow laws aboard a train (176–78). Suggestive of his link with William, George is introduced into the novel immediately following the account of Clotel's heroic escape from a District of Columbia slave prison and her suicidal dive into the Potomac River. Her suicide can be viewed as an act of temperate revolutionism that preserves her body from the bestiality of the "profane and ribald crew"

(219) of the pursuing bloodhounds and slave catchers, and from her own intemperate rage. George too is presented as a temperate revolutionary. Though sentenced to hang for participating in Turner's rebellion, he chooses to risk his life during a fire to save "valuable deeds belonging to the city" (224), thus prompting the "humane" city authorities to postpone for a year his scheduled execution. George's control over his body, evidenced by his seemingly contradictory actions of joining with Turner and then later risking his life to save whites' deeds, emerges as his most praiseworthy trait and that which ensures his success.

George eventually escapes from slavery when his beloved Mary, Clotel's white-skinned daughter whom Gertrude earlier had tried "blacking" in the hot sun, dresses him in her clothes and takes his place in jail. In a novel that so insistently focuses on male intemperance, as manifested in sexual domination and exploitation, it is oddly appropriate that Mary's cross-dressing strategy makes Brown's hero George into a white-skinned woman. Though George reassumes his male identity after making his way to Canada, for the rest of the novel he evinces an androgynous disposition that only further develops his heroic status. A model of Franklin-like industry, he works by day, studies by night, and when it becomes clear that he cannot help Mary, who is sold South, he journeys to Liverpool, takes a job in a Manchester mercantile house, and after ten years becomes "a partner in the firm that employed him, and . . . [is] on the road to wealth" (232). Though "African blood course[s] through his veins" (224), George keeps this fact a secret.

George thus is regarded as white by his partners and, given the book's racializing of intemperance in relation to "blacking" (to the point that most of the white characters of the novel, ironically enough, can seem themselves to have undergone a "blacking"), he can seem "white" as well. In the improbable happy ending of the novel, George, during a vacation in France, is reunited with Mary, now Mrs. Devenant. She had escaped from slavery with the help of the Frenchman Devenant, who fell in love with her because she resembled his dead sister. As in Susan Warner's best-selling *The Wide, Wide World* (1850), the brother-sister aspect of the marriage spiritualizes it into a nonsexual one; Devenant dies a few years after a marriage that resulted in no children. In the course of his upward rise, George had also apparently lived a nonsexual existence. Brown celebrates him at the end of the novel, then, not for his "manly" linkage with Nat Turner, nor for his "manly" rise in the free market, but for his womanly fidelity: "the adherence of George Green to the resolution never to marry, unless to his Mary, is, indeed, a rare instance of the fidelity of man in the matter of love" (244).

In terms of the novel's presentation of numerous sexual violations of (slave) women as indicative of men's "enslavement" to sexual appetite, George's sexual continence and fidelity, his adherence to the conventional values of a "true woman" (112), emerges as the novel's ultimate act of temperance, contributing significantly to what black reformers regularly argued temperance would bring about: his economic, social, and moral elevation.[23] And yet because his particular rise occurs not in the United States but in Britain, Brown conveys some skepticism about the ability of temperance to bring forth blacks' moral and social elevation in the United States. In this sense, the novel, even as it is informed by the discourse of black elevation so central to the black temperance movement, at the same time challenges the movement's progressive ideals. Lurking in the Dismal Swamp, the vengeful Picquilo, Nat Turner's coconspirator and "heir," suggests an alternative route to black elevation in the United States through the unleashing of revolutionary violence.[24]

Temperance would remain central to Brown's antebellum and postbellum writings, both as a metaphor for unrestrained patriarchal power and as a program for black elevation. In the late 1850s he regularly lectured with Frances Ellen Watkins Harper on the interrelated topics of "slavery, temperance, and the elevation of colored Americans." Though he championed black emigration to Haiti in the early 1860s, Brown embraced the Union cause after Lincoln issued the Emancipation Proclamation, and in his revised versions of *Clotel* transformed the figure of the "white" and womanly George into the full-blooded black Jerome, who vindicates his manhood and rights to citizenship by fighting in the Civil War. Following the Civil War, as Alonzo D. Moore writes in the "Memoir of the Author" prefacing Brown's *The Rising Son; or, The Antecedents and Advancement of the Colored Race* (1874), Brown renewed his "efforts, in connection with his estimable wife, for the spread of temperance among the colored people of Boston." As part of his commitment to Reconstruction, Brown in 1868 created the "National Association for the Spread of Temperance and Night-schools among the Freed People of the South," and soon after became one of the first blacks initiated into the Massachusetts Grand Division of the Sons of Temperance. He participated in the 1870 State Convention for the Promotion of a Prohibitory Political Party in Massachusetts, and for the rest of the decade campaigned for prohibition. His commitment to temperance influenced Pauline Hopkins, who in 1880 won an essay contest sponsored by Brown for blacks at Boston high schools on the topic of "The Evils of Intemperance and Their Remedies."[25] Soon after Brown's death in 1884, his wife was elected president of the local branch of the Women's Christian Temperance Organization.

Given the failure of Reconstruction in the South by the late 1870s, however, we might question the value of black temperance in the face of white "intemperance." Brown addresses this issue in his last major work, *My Southern Home; Or, the South and Its People* (1880). In 1867 Brown remarked that the southern secessionists who fomented the Civil War were "[d]runk with power";[26] and in *My Southern Home* he depicts power-crazed Southerners as suffering an extended hangover. In response to white Southerners' continued demands for mastery, Brown urges blacks to be more temperate than whites, warning black waiters, for instance, against following the "bad example" of the heavy drinking they view "in white society of the 'Upper Ten.'" Like his white heroine Georgiana in *Clotel*, he places an extraordinary responsibility on the blacks themselves to achieve their elevation by adopting temperate, industrious behavior. "The time for colored men and women to organize for self-improvement has arrived," he states near the end of the book, and he offers this recipe for black elevation: "[W]e must cultivate self-denial. Repress our appetites for luxuries and be content with clothing ourselves in garments becoming our means and our incomes. The adaptation and the deep inculcation of the principles of total abstinence from all intoxicants. The latter is a pre-requisite for success in all the relations of life."[27] As in the phrase "whiskey, blacking and all," Brown's use of the word "all" here extends temperance beyond the literal act of drinking to encompass various aspects of corporeal self-control. Among the intoxicants suggested in "all intoxicants" are desires for vengeance, inordinate wealth, power, and sexual gratification.

But in a troubling revision of the gender politics of *Clotel*, where black women are often the victims of white male intemperance, Brown in *My Southern Home* suggests that it is black women who most often exhibit intemperate behavior, blaming them for becoming intemperate consumers rather than responsible (re)producers. Under the influence of the alcohol that white merchants freely distribute to blacks who visit their stores, the women in particular succumb to an appetite for consumption that "amounts almost to madness," refusing to "stop buying until their money is exhausted." Brown's image of intemperate consumption expands to a gendered image of intemperate drinking: "a drunken girl—a drunken wife—a drunken mother—is there for women a greater depth? Home made hideous—children disgraced, neglected, and maltreated" In terms of Brown's metaphorics of color and intemperance in *Clotel*, such a mother would be contributing to the "blacking" of her children, and a similarly disturbing use of color imagery is used in the concluding chapter of *My Southern Home*. For despite the fact that he urges his black male readers to take pride in their color ("Black men, don't be ashamed to show your colors, and to own them"), Brown's utopian hope in the book, similar to Frederick Douglass's in the 1880s, is for an end to color. Calling upon blacks to consider emigrating to the North, where they will "come in contact with educated and enterprising whites, [which] will do them much good," he proclaims that "history demonstrates the truth that amalgamation is the great civilizer of the races of men."[28] In order to encourage such amalgamation, Brown suggests, black women need to create temperate homes wherein would be raised children that the best sort of whites would want to marry. This appeal for "civilizing" marriages between blacks and whites allows us retrospectively to view the relationships between Jefferson and Currer (Sally Hemings), Horatio and Clotel, and Morton and Althesa, however exploitative they may have been in the antebellum discursive context of *Clotel*, as predictors and rehearsals of the deracialized union between blacks and whites that Brown envisions as the ultimate fruit of temperance.

Notes

1. Letter from William Wells Brown, *Frederick Douglass' Paper*, August 26, 1853, 2. For the editorial in support of the Maine law, see *Frederick Douglass' Paper*, March 18, 1852, 2. The Maine law of 1851 banned the sale and manufacture of alcoholic beverages within the state. By 1855, thirteen states had adopted their own versions of the law, though by the Civil War most such laws had been repealed. For a sampling of Douglass's varied efforts to support a "Maine law" for New York state, in part by reprinting key temperance speeches and transcripts of temperance conventions, see the following issues of *Frederick Douglass' Paper*: December 25, 1851, 1; April 1, 1852, 1; May 13, 1852, 2; June 24, 1852, 2; June 10, 1853, 1–2; September 9, 1853, 1; April 14, 1854, 1; August 11, 1854, 1; April 30, 1855, 1; and May 1, 1855, which celebrates the passage of "The Maine Law in New York" (1). For a good discussion of the politics of the Maine law, see Ian R. Tyrrell, *Sobering Up: From Temperance to Prohibition in Antebellum America, 1800–1860* (Westport, CT: Greenwood P, 1979), chapter 10. On Douglass and Stowe, see Robert S. Levine, "*Uncle Tom's Cabin* in *Frederick Douglass' Paper*: An Analysis of Reception," *American Literature* 64 (1992): 71–93; on Brown and Stowe, see Peter A. Dorsey, "De-authorizing Slavery: Realism in Stowe's *Uncle Tom's Cabin* and Brown's *Clotel*," *ESQ* 41 (1995): 257–88.

2. William Wells Brown, *Clotel; or, The President's Daughter: A Narrative of Slave Life in the United States*, ed. William Edward Farrison (New York: Carol Publishing Group, 1989), 196, 200. Subsequent citations from the novel will be noted parenthetically.

3. Willliam Wells Brown, *The American Fugitive in Europe. Sketches of Places and*

People Abroad (Boston: John P. Jewett and Company, 1855), 189. While abroad from 1849 to 1854, Brown attended numerous temperance conventions and was voted a life member of the Edinburgh Temperance Society. See William Edward Farrison's excellent *William Wells Brown: Author and Reformer* (Chicago: U of Chicago P, 1969), 180.

4. Josephine Brown, *Biography of an American Bondman, by His Daughter* (Boston: R. F. Wallcut, 1856), 52. She notes about her father: "As one of the pioneers in the Temperance cause, among the colored people in Buffalo [circa 1840–43], he did good service. He regarded temperance and education as the means best calculated to elevate the free people of color" (52). In 1843 Brown resigned from the presidency of the Buffalo temperance organization he helped to establish. For Brown's first-person account of his temperance work in Buffalo, see his 1848 *Narrative of William W. Brown, A Fugitive Slave. Written by Himself*, in *From Fugitive Slave to Free Man: The Autobiographies of William Wells Brown*, ed. William L. Andrews (New York: Mentor, 1993), 80. Brown, or an editor, drew on the first-person 1848 *Narrative* for the third-person "Narrative" prefacing *Clotel*. On Brown's self-authorizing strategies in *Clotel*, see Robert B. Stepto, *From Behind the Veil: A Study of Afro-American Narrative* (Urbana: U of Illinois P, 1979), 27–31. Given that whites tended to write the prefaces that authorized black texts, Brown in authoring the "Narrative" would have been putting on "whiteface." On this point I am indebted to a conversation with Leonard Cassuto.

5. As Donald Yacovone and others have documented, temperance groups were formed by free blacks in the late eighteenth century; by the late 1820s temperance was central to the emergent black press and black convention movement of the period. At the 1831 First Annual Convention of the People of Colour, held in Philadelphia, for example, it was resolved that "*Education, Temperance,* and *Economy* are best calculated to promote the elevation of mankind to a proper rank and standing among men" (rpt. in *Minutes of the Proceedings of the National Negro Conventions, 1830–1864*, ed. Howard Holman Bell [New York: Arno P, 1969], 5). That "universalist" view of temperance dominated black writings until the mid-1830s, when, as Yacovone notes, "temperance became viewed more narrowly, but more effectively, as a survival strategy and as an antislavery tactic." See Yacovone's excellent "The Transformation of the Black Temperance Movement, 1827–1854: An Interpretation," *Journal of the Early Republic* 8 (1988): 285, et passim. On black temperance see also Benjamin Quarles, *Black Abolitionists* (New York: Oxford UP, 1969), 91–100; Frederick Cooper, "Elevating the Race: The Social Thought of Black Leaders, 1827–50," *American Quarterly* 24 (1972): 604–25; Jane H. Pease and William H. Pease, *They Who Would Be Free: Blacks' Search for Freedom, 1830–1861* (New York: Atheneum, 1974), 56–57, 124–26; and Denise Herd, "Ambiguity in Black Drinking Norms: An Ethnohistorical Interpretation," in *The American Experience with Alcohol: Contrasting Cultural Perspectives*, ed. Linda A. Bennett and Genevieve M. Ames (New York: Plenum P, 1985), 149–70.

6. "Minutes and Proceedings of the Third Annual Convention, For the Improvement of the Free People of Colour in These United States, Held by Adjournments in the

City of Philadelphia" (1833), rpt. in *Minutes and Proceedings*, ed. Bell, 18; William Whipper, "Presidential Address to the Colored Temperance Society of Philadelphia," rpt. in *The Black Abolitionist Papers: The United States, 1830–1846*, ed. C. Peter Ripley, et al. (Chapel Hill: U of North Carolina P, 1991), 125–26; "Proceedings of the State Convention of the Colored Freemen of Pennsylvania, Held in Pittsburgh, on the 23d, 24th, and 25th of August, 1841, for the Purpose of Considering Their Condition, and Means of Its Improvement," in *Proceedings of the Black State Conventions, 1840–1865*, ed. Philip S. Foner and George E. Walker (Philadelphia: Temple UP, 1979), I: 109; *Northern Star and Freeman's Advocate* 1 (1842), 18. On Delany's interest in temperance in the 1830s, see Victor Ullman, *Martin R. Delany: The Beginnings of Black Nationalism* (Boston: Beacon, 1971), 25–30.

7. Frederick Douglass, "Intemperance and Slavery: An Address Delivered in Cork, Ireland, on 20 October 1845," *The Frederick Douglass Papers: Series One: Speeches, Debates, and Interviews*, ed. John W. Blassingame, et al. (New Haven: Yale UP, 1979), I: 56. By the 1840s, according to Yacovone, "temperance and abolitionism had become virtually synonymous" ("Transformation of the Black Temperance Movement," 290). For a fuller discussion of Douglass and temperance, see, in addition to John Crowley's essay in this volume, Robert S. Levine, *Martin Delany, Frederick Douglass, and the Politics of Representative Identity* (Chapel Hill: U of North Carolina P, 1997), chapter 3.

8. Theodore Weld, *American Slavery As It Is: Testimony of a Thousand Witnesses* (New York: American Anti-Slavery Society, 1839), 115; William Wells Brown, *A Lecture Delivered Before the Female Anti-Slavery Society of Salem, at Lyceum Hall, Nov. 14, 1847* (Boston: Massachusetts Anti-Slavery Society, 1847), 4. As a historian of antebellum temperance observes, central to the liberationist agenda of the movement was the belief that to "be free, it was necessary to curb appetites, to subordinate passions to reason, to control animalistic impulses through the development of moral ideas" (W. J. Rorabaugh, *The Alcoholic Republic: An American Tradition* [New York: Oxford UP, 1979], 200). On temperance in the larger context of antebellum reform, see Ronald G. Walters, *American Reformers: 1815–1860* (New York: Hill and Wang, 1978), especially chapter 6.

9. Josephine Brown, *Biography*, 11. For good discussions of Brown's concerns about the sexual exploitation of slave women, see *Violence in the Black Imagination: Essays and Documents*, ed. Ronald T. Takaki (New York: Oxford UP, 1993), 215–30; and Ann duCille, *The Coupling Convention: Sex, Text, and Tradition in Black Women's Fiction* (New York: Oxford UP, 1993), 17–29. On women's participation in temperance see Barbara Leslie Epstein, *The Politics of Domesticity: Women, Evangelism, and Temperance in Nineteenth-Century America* (Middletown, CT: Wesleyan UP, 1981). On the (sometimes problematic) alliance between feminist reform and antislavery reform, see Blanche Glassman Hersh, *The Slavery of Sex: Feminist-Abolitionists in America* (Urbana: U of Illinois P, 1978); Karen Sánchez-Eppler, "Bodily Bonds: The Intersecting Rhetorics of Feminism and Abolition," *Representations* 24 (1988): 28–59; and Jean Fagan Yellin, *Women and Sisters: The Antislavery Feminists in American Culture* (New Haven: Yale UP, 1989).

10. W. Wells Brown, *Three Years in Europe; or, Places I Have Seen and People I Have Met* (London: Charles Gilpin, 1852), 274.

11. On Brown's use of "rumors" of the relationship between Jefferson and his slave Sally Hemings, see William Edward Farrison, "Clotel, Thomas Jefferson, and Sally Hemings," *CLA Journal* 17 (1973): 147–74. On the significance of Brown's historical and cultural sources, see also Russ Castronovo, *Fathering the Nation: American Genealogies of Slavery and Freedom* (Berkeley: U of California P, 1995), 162–70, and John Ernest, *Resistance and Reformation in Nineteenth-Century African-American Literature: Brown, Wilson, Jacobs, Delany, Douglass, and Harper* (Jackson: U of Mississippi P, 1995), chapter 1.

12. See Lydia Maria Child, "The Quadroons," in *Fact and Fiction: A Collection of Stories* (New York: C. S. Francis, 1847), 61–76. For a good discussion of Child's antislavery fiction, see Carolyn L. Karcher, "Rape, Murder and Revenge in 'Slavery's Pleasant Homes': Lydia Maria Child's Antislavery Fiction and the Limits of Genre," *Women's Studies International Forum* 9 (1986): 323–32.

13. See, for example, T. S. Arthur, *Temperance Tales; or, Six Nights with the Washingtonians*, 2 vols. (Philadelphia: W. A. Leary & Co., 1848), especially "The Broken Merchant" and "The Tavern Keeper"; and Arthur, *Riches Have Wings; or, A Tale for the Rich and Poor* (New York: Charles Scribner, 1851).

14. See William C. Nell, *Services of Colored Americans in the Wars of 1776 and 1812* (1851; rpt. New York: AMS Press, 1976); Frederick Douglass, "What to the Slave is the Fourth of July?: An Address Delivered in Rochester, New York, on 5 July 1852," in *The Frederick Douglass Papers*, II: 359–87; and Martin Delany, *The Condition, Elevation, Emigration and Destiny of the Colored People of the United States* (1852; rpt. New York: Arno P, 1969), chapter 8.

15. On John Randolph and the fate of the approximately five hundred slaves emancipated at his death in 1833, see William H. Pease and Jane H. Pease, *Black Utopia: Negro Communal Experiments in America* (Madison: State Historical Society of Wisconsin, 1963), 26–27.

16. See, for example, George Fitzhugh, *Slavery Justified, by a Southerner* (Fredericksburg, VA: Recorder Printing Office, 1850).

17. For a good discussion of this scene, see Christopher Mulvey, "The Fugitive Slave and the New World of the North: William Wells Brown's Discovery of America," in *The Black Columbiad: Defining Moments in African American Literature and Culture* (Cambridge: Harvard UP, 1994), especially 99–102. This myth of origins would continue to speak to Brown's post–Civil War concerns as well. In *The Rising Son; or, The Antecedents and Advancement of the Colored Race* (1874; rpt. New York: Negro Universities P, 1970), he refers to the founders of Jamestown, now representative of the white racists opposing Reconstruction, as intemperate drinkers who "had with them their 'native beverage,' which, though not like the lager of the present time, was a drink over which they smoked and talked of 'Faderland,' and traded for the negroes they brought" (265). On temperance and northern "free labor" rhetoric, see Eric Foner, *Free Soil, Free Labor, Free Men: The Ideology of the*

Republican Party Before the Civil War (New York: Oxford UP, 1971), especially 230–42. Consistent with his own commitment to free labor ideals, Brown in *Clotel* calls attention to the ways in which slavery "reflects discredit on industry" (110), thus leading poor southern whites to become, in the words of the New York missionary Hontz Snyder, "worthless, drunken, good-for-nothing[s]" (107).

18. In December 1848 the light-skinned Ellen Craft escaped from slavery in Georgia with the dark-skinned William Craft by masquerading as a slave master accompanied by her valet. Brown befriended the Crafts in 1849, lectured with them on numerous occasions in Great Britain, and modeled *Clotel's* cross-dressing escape with William on the Crafts' escape. For Brown on the Crafts, see his letter to William Lloyd Garrison in the *Liberator*, January 12, 1849, 7. According to R. J. M. Blackett, when Brown and the Crafts lectured together, one of their large topics was the importance of temperance to black elevation (*Beating Against the Barriers: Biographical Essays in Nineteenth-Century Afro-American History* [Baton Rouge: Louisiana State UP, 1986], especially 97).

19. Thomas Jefferson, *Notes on the State of Virginia* (New York: Harper Torchbooks, 1964), 124, 132–33.

20. On black writers' hesitations in representing black violence, see Raymond Hedin, "The Structuring of Emotion in Black American Fiction," *Novel* 16 (1982): 35–54. Even in a text like James Holly's 1857 account of the black revolution in San Domingue, *A Vindication of the Capacity of the Negro Race for Self-Government, and Civilized Progress*, Holly found it necessary to emphasize the "judicious self-control" and, as his title suggests, self-government of the black rebels (rpt. in *Black Separatism and the Caribbean 1860*, ed. Howard H. Bell [Ann Arbor: U of Michigan P, 1970], 30).

21. Brown, *American Fugitive*, 83–86; Brown, *St. Domingo: Its Revolution and Its Patriots. A Lecture, Delivered Before the Metropolitan Athenaeum, London, March 16, and at St. Thomas' Church, Philadelphia, December 20, 1854* (Boston: Bela Marsh, 1855), 13; Brown, *The Black Man, His Antecedents, His Genius, and His Achievements* (1863; rpt. New York: Arno P, 1969), 85, 71, 61, 72; see also the discussion of Nat Turner in Brown, *The Negro in the American Rebellion: His Heroism and His Fidelity* (1867; rpt. New York: Kraus Reprint Co., 1969), 20–24. As William L. Andrews notes, for many antislavery whites Madison Washington was the more appealing figure than Turner because Washington was seen "as singularly reasonable, self-controlled, and humane" ("The Novelization of Voice in Early African American Narrative," *PMLA* 105 [1990]: 28). Douglass, of course, presented just such a portrayal of Madison Washington in his 1853 "The Heroic Slave." On the admiration of many American writers of the period for Lamartine's ability to control the masses, see Larry J. Reynolds, *European Revolutions and the American Literary Renaissance* (New Haven: Yale UP, 1988), especially 18–24.

22. An anticipation of Turner's (and Picquilo's) rage comes earlier in the novel in an account by the minister Snyder of an unnamed slave, who, after witnessing the flogging of his wife, kills the perpetrator and then flees into the swamps. Snyder

describes what happens when the pursuing whites finally catch up with him: "He was then shot three times with a revolving pistol, and once with a rifle, and after having his throat cut, he still kept the knife firmly grasped in his hand, and tried to cut their legs when they approached to put an end to his life" (109).

23. It is noteworthy that when Brown reworks the novel in 1864, he creates what can be taken as an amalgam of William and George in the character of the industrious and "perfectly black" Jerome. Like George, Jerome at the end of the novel rises in the Manchester manufacturing house through temperate Franklin-like industry: "The drinking, smoking, and other expensive habits, which the clerks usually obliged in, he carefully avoided." See Brown, *Clotelle: A Tale of the Slave States*, rpt. in Takaki, ed., *Violence in the Black Imagination*, 289, 322. In the 1867 *Clotelle: or, The Colored Heroine. A Tale of the Southern States*, which is available in J. Noel Heermance, *William Wells Brown and Clotelle: A Portrait of the Artist in the First Negro Novel* (Hamden, CT: Archon, 1969), Brown depicts Jerome enlisting in the Union army and dying when he tries to retrieve the body of a white officer. Though Brown exhibits racial pride in his "blacking" of the George character, he nonetheless portrays Jerome as committed to what M. Giulia Fabi perceptively terms a "proto-nationalist self-help philosophy" ("The 'Unguarded Expressions of the Feelings of the Negroes': Gender, Slave Resistance, and William Wells Brown's Revisions of *Clotel*," *African American Review* 27 [1993]: 651). For an insightful discussion of Brown's endings to the 1853, 1864, and 1867 versions of his novel, see Richard Yarborough, "Race, Violence, and Manhood: The Masculine Ideal in Frederick Douglass's 'The Heroic Slave,'" in *Frederick Douglass: New Literary and Historical Essays*, ed. Eric J. Sundquist (New York: Cambridge UP, 1990), 169–72.

24. Picquilo's presence, to my mind, makes this first version of the novel the most subversive of the three versions published as books. The subsequent versions eliminate Picquilo. For an excellent discussion of Brown's tendency to gender resistance as the province of his male characters (while keeping his female characters circumscribed by a sentimental plot that seems to demand their deaths), see Fabi, "The 'Unguarded Expressions of the Feelings of the Negroes.'"

25. The comments on Brown and Harper were made by W. C. Nell in the *Liberator* of July 31, 1857, cited in Farrison, *William Wells Brown*, 288; Alonzo D. Moore, "Memoir of the Author," in Brown, *The Rising Son*, 25; on Brown and Hopkins, see Farrison, *William Wells Brown*, 436. Harper's "The Two Offers" (1859), of course, can be read as a temperance fiction.

26. Brown, *The Negro in the American Rebellion*, 52. Brown similarly uses temperance to address white racism in the North, blaming the 1863 Draft Riots on an "infuriated band of drunken men, women, and children" (193).

27. Brown, *My Southern Home: Or, The South and Its People*, in *From Fugitive Slave to Free Man*, ed. Andrews, 287, 281. The book first appeared in 1880; Andrews reprinted the 1882 edition.

28. Brown, *My Southern Home*, 236, 287, 296, 294, 293.

Slaves to the Bottle

Gough's *Autobiography* and Douglass's *Narrative*

John W. Crowley

Aᴌᴛʜᴏᴜɢʜ ᴛᴇᴍᴘᴇʀᴀɴᴄᴇ ᴡᴀs ᴀ ᴍᴀᴊᴏʀ sᴏᴄɪᴀʟ ᴍᴏᴠᴇᴍᴇɴᴛ ᴏꜰ ᴛʜᴇ American nineteenth century, the literature of temperance has long since been written off. In the most recent extended discussion—from over half a century ago—Herbert Ross Brown wittily weaves through "Ten Thousand and One Nights in a Barroom" (his chapter title) to the so-far definitive conclusion that "the temperance novel is dead; and, unlike John Barleycorn, whose demise they so confidently anticipated, these doubly dry pages are quite without that lusty gentleman's surprising power of resurrection."[1] But if the 1990s have ushered in "The New Temperance Movement,"[2] as some assert, then the writings of the old one may yet recover some currency. Even the temperance novel may rise again![3]

My present concern is with another type of temperance literature: the genre, located on the boundary between the novel and autobiography, in which inebriates recounted their enslavement to, and subsequent emancipation from, King Alcohol. Such first-person alcoholic confessions—or *temperance narratives*, as I will call them—began to appear during the 1840s as an outgrowth of the Washington Temperance Society. Some examples of the genre, such as Walt Whitman's relatively well-known *Franklin Evans; or, The Inebriate* (1842), were obviously fictional. Others, such as *Narrative of Charles T. Woodman, A Reformed Inebriate* (1843), were probably factual. But all of them had elements in common with novels in the sentimental and sensational veins, and they borrowed as well from spiritual autobiographies, especially the theme of conversion.

Most strikingly, however, the temperance narrative resembles the slave narrative, another genre that was flourishing during the 1840s. Although temperance narratives did not commonly invoke the rhetoric of abolition, they did portray slaves to the bottle whose bondage seemed comparable to that of plantation chattel. It so happens that the most significant temperance narrative, John Bartholomew Gough's *Autobiography*, appeared exactly the same year, 1845, as the most important slave narrative, *Narrative of the Life of Frederick Douglass*. This coincidence prompts the focal question of this essay: What, if anything, do these texts reveal about the interrelationship of temperance and abolition?

I

Like other temperance narratives of the 1840s, Gough's *Autobiography* sprang from the Washington Temperance Society's revolutionizing of antidrink reform.[4] From its start at the turn of the nineteenth century, the temperance movement had always been dominated by its respectable elements: the Protestant clergy, the legal and medical establishments, the rising mercantile class. Temperance reformers were "disinterested,"[5] in the sense that they did not ordinarily belong to the group targeted for reform—or, rather, for extinction, since full-fledged drunkards, held to be irredeemable, were expected obligingly to deplete their own ranks by drinking themselves to death. As the movement became more national and as the new pledge (teetotalism) gained adherents throughout the 1820s and 1830s, more hope was pinned to prevention than to rehabilitation. Emphasis fell on rescuing "moderate" drinkers from the brink of self-destruction.[6]

When the Washington Temperance Society was founded in April 1840 by six rum-soaked Baltimore artisans who pledged total abstinence, vowed mutual assistance, and recruited other besotted men to their weekly meetings, the focus suddenly shifted to drunkards themselves. What the Washingtonians demonstrated so dramatically was that even those mired in an alcoholic Slough of Despond could achieve sobriety through the compassionate aid of fellow inebriates.[7] Such support was expressed most powerfully in the confessional narratives that were the heart of Washingtonian meetings. Although the society eschewed appeals to organized religion—one source of friction with temperance traditionalists—its "citings of personal experience were like the 'testimony' that those 'getting religion' at camp meeting were supposed to give at subsequent 'experience meetings.'"[8] Bearing witness to their suffering and deliverance, Washingtonian speakers galvanized their audiences. As Abraham Lincoln, then a rising politician in Illinois, observed in 1842:

The *preacher*, it is said, advocates temperance because he is a fanatic, and desires a union of Church and State; the *lawyer*, from his pride and vanity of hearing himself speak; and the *hired agent* for his salary. But when one, who has long been known as a victim of intemperance, bursts open the fetters that bound him and appears before his neighbors "clothed, and in his right mind," a redeemed specimen of long lost humanity, and stands up with tears of joy trembling in his eyes, to tell of the miseries *once* endured, *now* to be endured no more forever; of his once naked and starving children, now clad and fed comfortably; of a wife, long weighed down with woe, weeping, and a broken heart, now restored to health, happiness and a renewed affection; and how easily all is done, once it is resolved to be done; how simple his language, there is a logic, and an eloquence in it, that few with human feelings, can resist.[9]

This, as Lincoln suggested, was a populist movement, infused by a radically democratic spirit; and the Washingtonians favored homespun eloquence over refined erudition in their speakers, the most successful of whom—John Gough and John H. W. Hawkins—had little polish or education. As these apostles of cold water tramped the lecture trail, harvesting pledges by the thousands, the meetings they led were fervidly raucous affairs, with plenty of singing and shouting. "In their evangelical techniques, indifference to theology, and vulgar identification with the manners and language of the masses," Gough and Hawkins were, in fact, "anathema to the more conservative and sedate leaders of the earlier movement."[10]

Gough, who has been dubbed the "poet of the d.t.'s" and the "Demosthenes of total abstinence,"[11] soon surpassed Hawkins (in part by outliving him) and became "the cause's champion pitchman and pledge seller," "the foremost platform performer of the century," "unquestionably the most popular orator in America."[12] Gough's renown was so great—on the order of Billy Graham's in our own day—that his present obscurity is all the more sobering a reminder of the transience of fame. His *Autobiography*, which first appeared in a privately published edition of a thousand copies, went through thirty-one reprintings between 1845 and 1853, as well as several issues in England, where Gough was also immensely popular. The revised and expanded version, first published in 1869 as *Autobiography and Personal Recollections*, was widely circulated as a subscription book[13]—as were Gough's later collections of lecture material, *Sunlight and Shadow* (1881) and *Platform Echoes* (1887). Much to the chagrin of his initial Washingtonian sponsors, Gough soon prospered from his lecture fees; and long after he had broken with the Society and ingratiated himself with the mainstream temperance movement, his career was marked by controversy over the rectitude and magnitude of his earnings.

Although Gough's lectures may now seem insipid on the page, they were spellbinding from the platform. An erstwhile actor, a gifted singer, a master of mimicry who once had cadged his drinks with barroom burlesque, Gough blended tearful testimony with oratorical thunder and dialect humor into a brew so potent that scores of listeners at every stop were driven to their feet and swept down the aisles to sign the pledge. After hearing Gough speak in upstate New York in 1849, Susan B. Anthony exclaimed to her mother: "What a lecture, what arguments, how can a man or woman remain neutral or be a moderate drinker." When he arrived in Cincinnati in 1851, "the hoopla and excitement rivaled that accompanying the visit of the famous singer Jenny Lind." Gough was "creating a tremendous sensation," one local paper reported. "He is comic, tragic, melo-dramatic, statesmanlike, and everything that is rare, in his manner and speech."[14]

Because the reform movements of the nineteenth century overlapped, many of those addressed by Gough and other Washingtonians had also attended abolitionist lectures by former slaves. Just as these oral slave narratives came to be written down, with or without editorial assistance,[15] and published in support of the cause, so temperance narratives began to appear as books, some of which were explicitly identified with Washingtonianism.

Like Gough and Woodman, several other ex-drunkards published their autobiographies during the 1840s: James Gale, *Long Voyage in a Leaky Ship; or A Forty Years' Cruise on the Sea of Intemperance* (1842); Joseph Gatchell, *The Disenthralled* (1843); *The Life and Adventures of the Reformed Inebriate, D. G. Robinson, M. D.* (1846); *Incidents in the Life of George Haydock, Ex-Professional Wood-Sawyer* (1847); Jacob Carter, *My Drunken Life* (1847); *The Life and Experience of A. V. Green, The Celebrated Ohio Temperance Sledge Hammer* (1848); *The Life and Sketches of James Campbell, Paper Maker* (1850).

The pseudonymous *Autobiography of a Reformed Drunkard* (1845), authored by "John Cotton Mather," supposed scion of a distinguished New England family, reads like fiction; but it also seems to incorporate personal experience. T. S. Arthur's *Six Nights with the Washingtonians* (1842) was a series of tales based closely on his 1840 reports for the *Baltimore Merchant* on early Washingtonian "experience" meetings.

Like *Franklin Evans*, which Whitman wrote on commission from the Washingtonians, other temperance narratives that purported to be autobiographical were novels cast in the form of anonymous alcoholic confessions. These included *Confessions of a Female Inebriate* (1842), likely written by a male temperance advocate (Isaac F. Shepard),[16] as well as *Confessions of a Reformed Inebriate* (1844) and *The Confession of a Rum-Seller* (1845).

The proliferation of such books suggests that a large and responsive readership existed for tales of reformed drunkards, whether fictional or not. This audience was likely divided between those attracted to uplifting didacticism and those allured by gothic titillation. As David S. Reynolds points out, the literature inspired by nineteenth-century reform movements transformed a "culture of morality" into a "culture of ambiguity." The work of "dark" or "immoral" reformers, which was subversive of dominant cultural values, often "deemphasized the remedies for vice while probing the grisly, sometimes perverse results of vice." Reynolds reads *Franklin Evans* as Whitman's attempt to capitalize on the lurid aspects of what was ostensibly wholesome. The book, "which pretended to be a Washingtonian temperance tract," was actually "a sensational novel unusual only for the sheer variety of dark-reform images it brought together."[17]

II

Although many of the same dark elements are found in Gough's *Autobiography*, it would be misleading to characterize this book as subversive. On the contrary, what pretended to be a sensational novel was truly a Washingtonian temperance tract, in which the central character follows a Dantean path from Inferno (drunken damnation) to Purgatorio (redemption by the Washingtonians) to Paradiso (apotheosis as a temperance speaker).[18]

Like Dante (and also Milton), the authors of temperance narratives struggled with the artistic problem of rendering Divine light without allowing it to be eclipsed by Satanic darkness; inebriation, after all, was more dramatic than reformation. Not surprisingly, then, the first two parts of Gough's *Autobiography*, those devoted to his drunken extremity, are far more gripping than the third part, which tediously details his sober success.

The story of Gough's descent into hell begins with the idyllic evocation of Sandgate, the coastal English village where his strict father and doting mother raised him up to value reading and righteousness. In 1829, at the age of twelve, Gough was placed in the care of a family emigrating to America. After two years on a farm in upstate New York, the boy struck out on his own. Gough moved to New York City and learned the bookbinding trade. His mother and sister soon joined him—his father stayed behind so as not to jeopardize his military pension—and despite hard times and harder winters, the reunited family endured until Mrs. Gough suddenly died in 1834. Gough drifted apart from his sister and strayed from the straight and narrow; drawn to the spiritous fellowship of city life, he ran with a fast crowd and lapsed into "habits of dissipation" (29).

Gough was seduced, in particular, by the glare of the footlights, and for several years he vainly pursued a career on the stage. Often left destitute by theatrical flops, he wandered about New England, working irregularly as a bookbinder, sailor, or fireman. All the while he was hurtling toward intemperance—but denying it.

> And yet, at this time, I did not consider myself to be what in reality I was—a drunkard. Well enough did I know, from bitter experience, that character, situations, and health, had been periled, in consequence of my love of ardent spirits. I felt, too, an aching void in my breast, and conscience frequently told me that I was on the broad road to ruin; but that I was what all men despised, and I, among them, detested, I could not bring myself to believe. I would frame many excuses for myself—plead my own cause before myself, as judge and jury, until I obtained, at my own hands, a willing acquittal. (33–34)

Gough spiraled down and down, losing everything along the way: jobs, friends, family (a wife and child)—and also decency, dignity, and all claim to human society: "I was debased in my own eyes, and, having lost my self-respect, became a poor, abject being, scarcely worth attempting to reform" (41). A failure even at suicide, Gough lived now only to drink.

What finally saved him was the kindness of a waiter in a temperance hotel, who offered Gough the hand of fellowship and begged him to take the pledge. With the support of the Washingtonians in Worcester, Massachusetts, Gough managed to stop drinking in October 1842; and despite a couple of backsliding binges a few months later, he was soon in tremendous demand as a temperance speaker. He claimed to have traveled over twelve thousand miles in his first two years on the platform and to have obtained nearly thirty-two thousand signatures to the total abstinence pledge.

In the last section of the *Autobiography*, which covers Gough's emergence as a public figure, he attributes his individual triumph over alcohol to the ascension of "the Genius of Temperance" (92) in America at large. Amid a chronicle of his lecture engagements, Gough commemorates two major events in which he was involved: the huge Washingtonian jubilee of May 30, 1844, in which many thousands of marchers, including a Cold Water Army of children, paraded through Boston ("Such a day I never, in my most sanguine dreams, imagined would have dawned on earth" [94]); and a temperance rally on New Year's Eve, 1844, in Faneuil Hall:

> The old "Cradle of Liberty" contained a vast assemblage, and hundreds who were present felt that, since the dying year commenced, they had thrown off fetters which had long galled them, and were now blessed with freedom, in its noblest sense. Minds which had long bowed down in blind idolatry to the monster—rum, had been emancipated from its tyrannic rule, and now saw the old year, as it passed away, bearing with it the record of their liberty. (112)

As he contemplated the miracle of his own deliverance, Gough was filled with awe. "What had I been, two or three years before? Why a houseless, homeless, inebriate! Penniless, friendless, and almost hopeless." Now he was "a humble monument" of Divine mercy, "feeling, as I trust I ever shall feel, that out of my utter weakness He had in me perfected strength to stand up and be privileged to warn others of the dangers of indulging in that which intoxicates" (114–15).

III

In celebrating his emancipation from the fetters of drunkenness, Gough does not remark what seems an inescapable analogy between slavery to the bottle and chattel slavery. After all, commerce in alcohol and slaves had long been intertwined in the colonial triangular trade, one leg of which was the exchange of rum for captive Africans.[19] There was also an ideological congruence between temperance and abolition; and it would not have been surprising had antidrink advocates appropriated the rhetoric of antislavery to their own purposes—in a way similar to that of antebellum feminists who conflated "the figures of woman and slave, and of the institutions of marriage and bondage."[20]

Gough does, in fact, write of becoming "the slave of a habit which had become completely my master, and which fastened its remorseless fangs in my very vitals" (38); and he adds: "Such a slave was I to the bottle, that I resorted to it continually, and in vain was every effort, which I occasionally made, to conquer the debasing habit" (40). But like other writers of temperance narratives, Gough does not suggest any strong linkage between temperance and abolition. At one point he refers to drunkards as being redeemed from "a worse than Egyptian thraldom" (99), allying them with ancient Israelites rather than contemporary Negroes.

Charles Woodman, who expresses aversion to Negroes, compares the bonds of inebriation not to southern slavery, but rather to colonial oppression under British rule. He recalls how veterans of the American Revolution used to gather on the Fourth of July to get drunk and swap war stories: "as young as I was, it was curious to me that . . . they who scorned to submit to the tyranny of the mother country, despising their ease and comfort, for liberty and independence, should, while they were talking over their conquests, suffer a greater enemy than ever oppressed our sires, to hold in the strong chains of habit, these otherwise free and independent sons of liberty."[21] "John Cotton Mather" also invokes the American Revolution, pointing out that "the poor, enslaved drunkard" who has shed his chains "feels the warm glow of freedom in his bosom" and "stands up like a man and proclaims his freedom, and holds his pledge aloft as his 'declaration of independence.' "[22]

This trope was, in fact, a Washingtonian commonplace. In naming their Society for the revolutionary hero who had led his countrymen "to independence from King George," the Baltimore founders hoped that he now might lead them symbolically "to independence from King Alcohol!"[23] One Washingtonian leader went as far as to recast the Declaration of Independence into temperance terms:

> When from the depths of human misery, it becomes possible for a portion of the infatuated victims to arise, and dissolve the vicious and habitual bands which have connected them with *inebriety* and degradation . . . an anxious regard for the safety of their former companions, and the welfare of society requires, that they should declare the causes that impel them to such a *Reformation*!
>
> We hold these truths to be self-evident;—that all men are created *temperate*;—that they are endowed by their Creator with certain natural and innocent desires;—that among these are the appetites for COLD WATER and the pursuit of happiness! . . .[24]

Abraham Lincoln also adopted this rhetoric, drawing a parallel between the American Revolution and the equally glorious "temperance revolution": "In *it*, we shall find a stronger bondage broken; a viler slavery manumitted; a greater tyrant deposed." The logical trajectory of Lincoln's remarks led to an argument for abolition, and he went on to extol temperance as a "noble ally . . . to the cause of political freedom":

> With such an aid, its march cannot fail to be on and on, till every son of earth shall drink in rich fruition the sorrow-quenching draughts of perfect liberty. . . .

And when the victory shall be complete—when there shall be neither a slave nor a drunkard on the earth—how proud the title of that *Land*, which may truly claim to be the birth place and the cradle of both those revolutions, that shall have ended in that victory. How nobly distinguished that People, who shall have planted, and nurtured to maturity, both political and moral freedom of their species.[25]

Lincoln's triumphant moral vision—in which "all men are created temperate" became subtly inseparable from "all men are created equal"—was not, however, widely shared either by the Washingtonians or by those in the temperance mainstream. On the contrary, the trope of "revolution" usually served to *elide* all reference to chattel slavery.

There were political reasons for this silence. Regional tensions entered early into the movement as southerners grew suspicious of "radical" northern reformers. Relations were "not entirely cordial after 1836," when the American Temperance Union supplanted the American Temperance Society as the chief national organization; and despite northern efforts at appeasement, including the suppression of abolitionist sentiment in temperance newspapers, the identification of antidrink with antislavery was still "strong enough to stifle completely the organization of the Temperance movement in the South."[26]

Even when they did compare intemperance with enslavement, northern reformers, including those deeply committed to abolition, did not believe necessarily that the slave's suffering exceeded the inebriate's. Indeed, the view was occasionally advanced that temperance was "the more crucial reform" because "while slavery encouraged the master to idleness and vice and the slave to ignorance and religious indifference, the effect of drink was worse: a slave had only lost control of his body, a drunkard lost mastery of his soul."[27]

Thus in an 1821 sermon, Eliphalet Gillet argued that while slavery "is an evil not to be endured," the evil of intemperance is ultimately more devastating:

> *That* enslaves the body, *this* the mind; *that* seizes upon and subjects the outward man, *this* prostrates also the more noble powers and faculties of the soul; *that* deprives a man of his just rank among his fellow creatures, *this* brutalizes him; *that* in its operations is restricted to the present life, *this* extends its deleterious influence through an unlimited futurity.[28]

A few years later in a Fourth of July oration, the president of Amherst College, Heman Humphrey, who was to become a partisan of John Brown, ingeniously argued the contention that "however cruel and debasing and portentous African servitude may be, beyond the Potomac, there exists, even in

New-England, a far sorer bondage, from which the slaves of the South are happily free." This, the bondage of intemperance, "is intellectual and moral as well as physical. It chains and scourges the soul, as well as the body. It is a servitude from which death itself has no power to release the captive." Appealing to the spirit of the American Revolution, Humphrey warned that nothing less than national independence was at stake; for intemperance threatened to extinguish freedom. "A sober people may possibly be enslaved," he declared, "but an intemperate people cannot long remain free." [29]

Although John Gough did not go to such extremes in his public statements, he too distinguished between what he regarded as the limited bondage of slavery and the total enslavement of intemperance. In the revised *Autobiography*, he relates an incident from 1846, when he addressed a large Negro audience in a Richmond Baptist church. At one point during his speech, a man spontaneously stood up and declaimed:

> "Bredren, jist look at me. Here's a nigger dat doesn't own his-self. I belong to Massa Carr, bless de Lord! Yes, bredren, Massa Carr owns me. Yes, bredren, dis poor old body belongs to Massa Carr; but my soul is de freeman of de Lord Jesus!"
>
> The effect was electrical, and the whole audience shouted: "Amen!" "Glory!" "Bless de Lord!"
>
> I took the opportunity of saying, "There is not a drunkard in this city can say that!" [30]

"Ah, yes, physical slavery is an awful thing," Gough avers in one of his later books, but a "man may be bought and sold in the market and yet be a freer man than he who sells him." He recalls having witnessed a slave auction at which a man given hope he would not be torn away from his wife and child was cruelly betrayed. Despite his agony, the slave was not broken:

> But from his blood-shot eyes, as he looked at the group around him, there flashed a light that told of a wild, free spirit,—a soul that could not be enslaved; and then, black as he was, bought and sold as he was, he loomed up before me in the glorious attitude of a free man compared with the tobacco-chewing, whiskey-drinking, blaspheming slaves to evil passions who were selling a brother into slavery. [31]

Whereas slaves to evil passions, including slaves to the bottle, fall below a threshold of human dignity that even chattel slaves may attain, the drunkard, according to Gough, "brings himself to the level of the slavering idiot, or the gibbering, raving madman." Intemperance, moreover, honors no class distinctions; inebriates of the middle and upper classes are finally no different from any wretch on the street:

> I consider a man as much a drunkard if he lies upon his bed of down, and rolls from it upon his magnificent carpet in a sumptuous apartment, with mirrors all around him showing him his own bestiality—as much a debased, degraded, and imbruted sot as the man who lies in the kennel, his hair soaking in the filth of the gutter. . . . The drunkard, in whatever station he may be, who stupefies his intellect, dethrones his reason, beclouds his mind, puts an extinguisher on the light that God has given him, commits as grievous a sin against God and his own soul as the man who wallows in the lowest kennel.[32]

By reducing himself to an animal, the man in servitude to alcohol forfeits any claim to being "de free-man of de Lord Jesus!"

IV

The idea that intemperance was worse than bondage might have served, in effect, to mitigate the horrors of slavery. To counter this idea, slave narratives— insofar as they were written in light of temperance narratives—might have insisted all the more that the "bestiality" enforced by slavery was unsurpassed by any degree of alcoholic degradation. In his *Narrative*, Frederick Douglass did, in fact, stress how profoundly debased, degraded, and imbruted he had become under the lash of Covey, the slave-breaker. "I was broken in body, soul, and spirit," he says in a crucial passage. "My natural elasticity was crushed, my intellect languished, the disposition to read departed, the cheerful spark that lingered about my eye died; the dark night of slavery closed in upon me; and behold a man transformed into a brute!"[33]

Douglass could have been describing his "beast-like stupor" (105) without any reference to the depiction of drunkards in contemporary temperance narratives, but there *is* evidence of his familiarity with the genre. In an 1848 speech on temperance, his first such address to an American audience, Douglass, like Lincoln in 1842, contrasted the "eloquent streams" of antidrink commentary from the "bench, bar, and pulpit" to a rougher—and, to his mind, all the more effective—sort of testimony:

> [A] mightier and more thrilling eloquence is that which has come up from the dram-shop and gutter. The simple, straightforward, unvarnished narra-

tion of individual suffering—the graphic pictures of family distress and
ruin—the painful exhibitions of shattered and broken constitutions—the
powerful exposures of the subtle schemes and alluring charms of rum-
venders, have nearly all come from this class of persons; men who have seen,
heard, and felt, the workings of the prison-house.[34]

From his own sufferance of bondage, Douglass felt a kinship with those who
had risen from the depths to tell their tales of alcoholic enslavement; and he
also understood how the subtle schemes of rum sellers resembled those of the
slave masters, who used intemperance as an instrument for tightening their
control.

During the holidays between Christmas and New Year's Day, Douglass reports, slaves were induced to get drunk and stay drunk. Douglass treats this
practice as a ploy by slaveholders to suppress insurrection: "These holidays
serve as conductors, or safety-valves, to carry off the rebellious spirit of enslaved humanity" (115). The object is to "disgust the slave with freedom, by
allowing him to see only the abuse of it":

> Thus, when the slave asks for virtuous freedom, the cunning slaveholder,
> knowing his ignorance, cheats him with a dose of vicious dissipation, art-
> fully labelled with the name of liberty. The most of us used to drink it down,
> and the result was just what might be supposed: many of us were led to think
> that there was little to choose between liberty and slavery. We felt, and very
> properly too, that we had almost as well be slaves to man as to rum. (115–16)

This last sentence quietly refutes—in the qualifying use of "almost"—the notion that bondage to rum is worse than bondage to man.[35] But Douglass does
acknowledge the enslaving power of alcohol, and he also seems to count himself among the "most" who "used to drink it down."

Douglass's own drinking experience went unstated in the 1845 *Narrative*, but
speeches he gave abroad the following year suggest that he had been decidedly
intemperate at one stage of his enslavement. Douglass's lecture tour of the
British Isles began in Dublin, where Father Theobald Mathew, founder of the
Irish temperance movement, invited the American visitor to address several
large meetings. It was at Father Mathew's home that Douglass, who had been a
staunch teetotaler for several years, officially took the pledge on October 22,
1845. Four months later, during a speech in Scotland, he confessed: "I used to
love drink—That's a fact. . . . I found in me all those characteristics leading to
drunkenness—and it would be an interesting experience if I should tell you
how I was cured of intemperance, but I will not go into that matter now."[36]

Douglass did pursue the matter in subsequent appearances, however. "I knew once what it was to drink with all the ardour of *old soker*," he divulged to another Scottish audience. "I lived with a Mr. Freeland who used to give his slaves apple brandy. Some of the slaves were not able to drink their own share, but I was able to drink my own and theirs too. I took it because it made me feel I was a great man. I used to think I was a president." Douglass explained himself with an anecdote about a tipsy man who once staggered into a temporarily vacant pig sty. When the residents returned, the man, who was too drunk to notice what species of creature he was dealing with, began to call for order, as if he were president of a meeting.[37] Perhaps Douglass was telling this tale on himself. In any event, when he later addressed the National Temperance Society in London, he repeated his admission that "I was once fond of a little drop occasionally." He did "not continue long in these practices," he hastened to add, "and I have been able, by the blessing of God, for the last seven years, to steer entirely clear of them.[38]

That Douglass considered himself to have been an "old soker" bears on the account in his *Narrative* of his two years' servitude under William Freeland. It is ironic that Douglass apparently became a slave to the bottle under the relatively benign regime of Mr. Freeland, whose treatment of him "was heavenly, compared with what I experienced at the hands of Mr. Edward Covey" (119). Although Freeland had "many of the faults peculiar to slaveholders" (117), Douglass gives him "the credit of being the best master I ever had, *till I became my own master*" (121). Unlike Covey, whose deviousness seemed demonic, Freeland was "open and frank, and we always knew where to find him" (117).

It would appear, then, that Freeland was *not* among those slaveholders who successfully used liquor to control their slaves and to forestall revolt. Indeed, Douglass was never more resistant to bondage than during the period when he was working for Freeland and—although the *Narrative* is silent on this point—drinking intemperately. "I began to want to live *upon free land* as well as *with Freeland*" (122), he punningly recalls. Douglass soon led his fellow slaves in a daring but aborted escape attempt: "In coming to a fixed determination to run away, we did more than Patrick Henry, when he resolved upon liberty or death. With us it was a doubtful liberty at most, and almost certain death if we failed. For my part, I should prefer death to hopeless bondage" (124).

As Douglass was later to acknowledge, his "hopeless bondage," at least in part, had been to alcohol. In laying claim to the Spirit of '76—as in his reference here to Patrick Henry—Douglass adopted the trope of the American

Revolution.[39] Like Lincoln, but unlike the Washingtonians, he also fused the revolutionary rhetoric of abolition with that of temperance, embracing the twin propositions that all men are created equal and that all men are created equally vulnerable to inebriation. As Douglass asserted in one of his speeches, "the same spirits which make a white man drunk make a black man drunk too. Indeed, in this I can find proof of my identity with the family of man."[40]

Douglass could even agree with those who argued that bondage to alcohol was an especially virulent form of slavery:

> In order to make a man a slave, it is necessary to silence or drown his mind. It is not the flesh that objects to being bound—it is the spirit. It is not the mere animal part—it is the immortal mind which distinguishes man from the brute creation. To blind his affections, it is necessary to bedim and bedizzy his understanding. In no other way can this be so well accomplished as by using ardent spirits![41]

What Douglass could *not* abide was the racism of the temperance movement itself.

Although he firmly believed that sobriety was essential "to promote black dignity and respectability as well as to illustrate black moral integrity,"[42] he was bitterly forced to accept that white reformers wanted no part of him and his people. Not only were blacks largely excluded from white temperance organizations; their own groups were subjected to attack. Whereas the Washingtonians were free to troop by the thousands through the streets of Boston in 1844, two years earlier, a small parade by the Negro temperance societies of Philadelphia had been assaulted by a mob of Irish immigrants.[43] When, during his 1846 tour, Douglass brought these bitter facts to the attention of the World's Temperance Convention in London, he infuriated the American delegates, who resented, as one of them said, his having "lugged in antislavery, or abolition, no doubt prompted to it by some of the politic ones who can use him to do what they would not themselves adventure to do in person."[44]

Douglass was minion to no man, and he continued to denounce the bigotry of the temperance movement even as he faithfully advanced its goals, eventually joining with feminist leaders in New York to promote the election of a "dry" governor in 1854, and the passage a year later of a law forbidding the sale of alcoholic beverages.[45] Prohibition in New York, as in most other states during the 1850s, was short-lived—a "wet" political coalition soon undid the damage to their interests—and Douglass's public commitment to temperance waned thereafter.

The Washington Society, meanwhile, had disbanded: torn apart by dissension within temperance ranks over the influence of organized religion and the tactics of moral suasion versus prohibition. John Gough, perceived by some Washingtonians to be a hypocrite and a traitor to their principles,[46] had survived a barrage of bad publicity and ensconced himself in the public's favor, in part by avoiding controversy and keeping his antislavery sentiments to himself. As Douglass himself later observed, "Delivering lectures under various names, John B. Gough says, 'Whatever may be the title, my lecture is always on Temperance.' "[47]

By adhering so single-mindedly to this cause, Gough unwittingly ensured his future obscurity; for anything and everything related to temperance was to become unmentionable in the wake of Prohibition's failure during the 1930s. There is, at present, no satisfactory biography of Gough and virtually no other published research.[48] Should the literature of temperance ever properly be reconsidered, Gough's *Autobiography* deserves recognition as, perhaps, *the* classic text of the movement. Among temperance narratives from the 1840s, Gough's is by far the best-written and most fully imagined; its shrewd delineation of the drunkard's psychology still rings true.

Although the *Autobiography* was more widely circulated in its day than Douglass's popular *Narrative*, and although temperance narratives continued to appear throughout the nineteenth century, the genre has vanished from literary-historical view. These accounts of slaves to the bottle seem, however, to have had a subtle bearing on the representation of bondage by Douglass and, it may well be, by other writers of slave narratives.

Notes

1. Herbert Ross Brown, *The Sentimental Novel in America 1789–1860* (Durham, NC: Duke UP, 1940), 240. On temperance literature, see also Alice Felt Tyler, *Freedom's Ferment: Phases of American Social History to 1860* (Minneapolis: U of Minnesota P, 1944). During the last five decades, while a few social historians have actively explored temperance, the silence of literary scholars has been nearly unbroken. Even advocates of New Historicism, whose thirst for contextualizing seems unslakable, have abstained from any traffic with Demon Rum. One notable exception is David S. Reynolds, who connects temperance fiction to canonical American literature in *Beneath the American Renaissance: The Subversive Imagination in the Age of Emerson and Melville* (New York: Knopf, 1988).

2. The phrase is attributed to David Pittman in Norman K. Denzin, *The Alcoholic Society: Addiction and Recovery of the Self* (New Brunswick, NJ: Transaction, 1993), xvi.

3. To some extent, the temperance novel *has* already been revived—in the guise of what I have elsewhere called the *recovery narrative*. See *The White Logic: Alcoholism and Gender in American Modernist Fiction* (Amherst: U of Massachusetts P, 1994), 155–56.

4. On the history of the Washingtonians see: Milton A. Maxwell, "The Washingtonian Movement," *Quarterly Journal of Studies on Alcohol* 11 (September 1950): 410–51; Leonard U. Blumberg (with William L. Pittman), *Beware the First Drink!: The Washington Temperance Movement and Alcoholics Anonymous* (Seattle: Glen Abbey, 1991).

5. The term derives from Joseph R. Gusfield, *Symbolic Crusade: Status Politics and the American Temperance Movement* (Urbana: U of Illinois P, 1963), 61.

6. In an 1825 letter, Justin Edwards, a founder of the American Temperance Society, expressed his hopes for the movement in terms that unite its utopian and macabre elements: "We are at present fast hold of a project for making all people in this country, and in all other countries, temperate; or rather, a plan to induce those who are now temperate to continue so. Then, as all who are intemperate will soon be dead, the earth will be eased of an amazing evil." Quoted in Jed Dannenbaum, *Drink and Disorder: Temperance Reform in Cincinnati from the Washingtonian Revival to the WCTU* (Urbana: U of Illinois P, 1984), 38.

   As Stuart Berg Flexner points out, the word *temperance*, which had connoted "moderation, self-restraint" since the fourteenth century, was radically redefined by the antidrink movement: "by 1830 the American Temperance Society defined *temperance* as 'the moderate . . . use of things beneficial and abstinence from things harmful,' going on to call hard liquor 'poison.' Thus, in regard to liquor, the American Temperance Society changed the meaning of *temperance* to *abstinence.*" *I Hear America Talking: An Illustrated Treasury of American Words and Phrases* (New York: Van Nostrand Reinhold, 1976), 355.

7. Washingtonian membership was never restricted solely to inebriates. On the contrary, the Society's goal was to create "a support network that would link drunkards and moderate drinkers with long-standing abstainers, drawing those who wished to give up alcohol into a social milieu that would reinforce rather than denigrate those intentions." Typically, the proportion of actual drunkards in Washingtonian groups "appears to have been about 10 percent or less of the total membership." Dannenbaum, *Drink and Disorder*, 38–39.

8. J. C. Furnas, *The Life and Times of the Late Demon Rum* (London: Allen, 1965), 89. In an early history of the Washingtonian movement, John Zug commended the efficacy of "experience" narratives: "How much more influence then has the man, who stands before an audience to persuade them to abandon the use of strong drink, when he can himself tell them of its ruinous and blasting effects on his own life and character—trace the progress of his own habits of intemperance,—and warn others to avoid the rock on which he split. A reformed man has the best access to a drunkard's mind and heart, because he best knows, and can enter into all a drunkard's feelings. And such appeals from such sources, properly directed,

can rarely fail of entire success." *The Foundation, Progress and Principles of the Washington Temperance Society of Baltimore* (Baltimore: John D. Toy, 1842), 42–43.

9. Abraham Lincoln, "An Address, Delivered before the Springfield Washington Temperance Society, on the 22nd February, 1842," rpt. in Blumberg, *Beware the First Drink!*, 105. Blumberg explains that although Lincoln probably took the Washingtonian pledge at the height of the movement's success, it is doubtful that he was ever "a constitutional member" of the Society (103).

10. Gusfield, *Symbolic Crusade*, 49.

11. Reynolds, *Beneath the American Renaissance*, 67; Furnas, *The Life and Times of the Late Demon Rum*, 150.

12. John Lardner, "Drinking in America: An Unfinished History," in *The World of John Lardner*, ed. Roger Kahn (New York: Simon, 1961), 217; John Kobler, *Ardent Spirits: The Rise and Fall of Prohibition* (New York: Putnam, 1973), 66; Lyman Abbott, "Introduction" to John B. Gough, *Platform Echoes; or, Living Truths for Head and Heart* (Hartford, CT: Worthington, 1887), 65. Gough, who kept meticulous records throughout his career, boasted that he had delivered 6,064 lectures and traveled 272,235 miles between May 14, 1843, and June 1, 1869. *Autobiography and Personal Recollections of John B. Gough* (Springfield, MA: Bill, Nichols, 1869), 544. Gough was no less active during the remaining seventeen years of his life.

13. Although the 1869 revision incorporated the 1845 *Autobiography*, the latter is far more powerful and direct. As Gough gained prominence, he became more protective of his public image, and his life story became more guarded, garrulous, and genteel. Much the same is true of other nineteenth-century American autobiographies that appeared in one or more revised versions, including those of P. T. Barnum and Frederick Douglass.

14. Dannenbaum, *Drink and Disorder*, 18.

15. Charges of forgery were routinely leveled at slave narratives, the authorship of which was, in fact, complexly collaborative in some instances. As Robin W. Winks observes, many such texts were "ghost written, or taken from dictation, or were almost wholly the work of another person, and thus more nearly biography than autobiography." "The Making of a Fugitive Slave Narrative: Josiah Henson and Uncle Tom—A Case Study," in *The Slave's Narrative*, ed. Charles T. Davis and Henry Louis Gates, Jr. (New York: Oxford UP, 1985), 113. Even Douglass's *Narrative* was not spared accusations of fraudulence.

In this regard, it is notable that the foremost temperance narrative was likewise suspect. Under assault by his enemies, Gough was forced to admit that he had, indeed, had some help in the writing of his 1845 *Autobiography*. But he insisted that the book was nonetheless his own: "John Ross Dix, then calling himself John Dix Ross, was an inmate of my family, and I, pacing the room, dictated to him, he being a good shorthand writer. When he had copied it out, we read it together and made alterations, and I wish to say that, excepting only three, or, at most, four instances, *my* language, not his, was used." *Autobiography and Personal Recollections*, 545.

16. That all the known temperance narratives, including *Confessions of a Female Inebriate*, were written by men is not surprising. The Washington Society, like other nineteenth-century temperance groups that focused on the reformation of drunkards, admitted women only in an auxiliary role. Although women may have been no less vulnerable than men to inebriety, the Victorian ideology of intemperance perceived it as a male problem in which women (except for drunken harlots) figured only as bystanders and victims. See Crowley, *The White Logic*, 116–18.

17. Reynolds, *Beneath the American Renaissance*, 59, 106. Blumberg also recognizes that "Washingtonian speakers were a part of the popular entertainment of the period, moralistic though it might be." *Beware the First Drink!*, 154.

18. In describing his "almost unmitigated woe," Gough cites the gateway to Dante's Inferno: "Over every door of admission into the society of my fellow-men, the words, 'No Hope,' seemed to be inscribed. Despair was my companion, and perpetual degradation appeared to be my allotted doom." When he recalls the horrors of delirium tremens, he claims that he "endured more agony than pen could describe, even were it guided by the mind of a Danté." *An Autobiography by John B. Gough* (Boston, 1845), 61–62, 45. Other quotations are taken from this (first) edition and are identified in the text.

19. Lardner notes that in the eighteenth century "one hogshead of rum bought an African or one healthy African woman." *The World of John Lardner*, 207.

20. Karen Sánchez-Eppler, "Bodily Bonds: The Intersecting Rhetorics of Feminism and Abolition," *Representations*, no. 24 (Fall 1988), 29. Sánchez-Eppler's purpose is to "interrogate" this "intersection of feminist and abolitionist discourses" in order to expose its tendency toward "asymmetry and exploitation." David R. Roediger points out that "concern over 'slavery' was very much in the air in Jacksonian America, whose citizens worried variously that Catholics, Mormons, Masons, monopolists, fashion, alcohol and the national bank were about to enslave the republic." *The Wages of Whiteness: Race and the Making of the American Working Class* (London: Verso, 1991), 67.

21. *Narrative of Charles T. Woodman, A Reformed Inebriate* (Boston: Abbot, 1843), 24.

22. *Autobiography of a Reformed Drunkard; or Letters and Recollections by an Inmate of the Alms-House* (Philadelphia: Griffith and Simon, 1845), 146.

23. Blumberg, *Beware the First Drink!*, 59.

24. Jesse W. Goodrich, *A Second Declaration of Independence; or the Manifesto of all the Washington Total Abstinence Societies of the United States*, 2d ed. (1841), rpt. in Blumberg, *Beware the First Drink!*, 95–96. Goodrich was to become a mentor and close friend to John Gough.

25. Lincoln, "An Address," in Blumberg, *Beware the First Drink!*, 114.

26. John Allen Krout, *The Origins of Prohibition* (New York: Knopf, 1925), 177; Gusfield, *Symbolic Crusade*, 54.

27. W. J. Rorabaugh, *The Alcoholic Republic: An American Tradition* (New York: Oxford UP, 1979), 214.

28. Eliphalet Gillet, *Evils of Intemperance: A Sermon Preached at Hallowell, on the Day*

of the Annual Fast in Maine, April 12, 1821 (Hallowell, ME: Goodale, Glazier, 1821), 13.

29. Heman Humphrey, *Parallel Between Intemperance and the Slave Trade: An Address Delivered at Amherst College, July 4, 1828* (Amherst, MA: Adams, 1828), 4, 28.

30. Gough, *Autobiography and Personal Recollections*, 219. This story is typical of those scattered throughout Gough's writings. He prided himself on his actor's mastery of accents, and he delighted in telling dialect stories from the platform. The ones about Negroes, as well as those about Irish, Germans, and other groups, rely on racialist stereotypes that were commonplace in the nineteenth century. As Gough himself acknowledged, at least one African American leader, William Wells Brown, had little use for his histrionics: "no one can sit for a hour, and hear John B. Gough, without coming to the conclusion that he is nothing more than a theatrical mountebank" (quoted in *Autobiography and Personal Recollections*, 301).

31. Gough, *Platform Echoes*, 550–51.

32. Ibid., 428, 485–86.

33. *Narrative of the Life of Frederick Douglass, An American Slave*, ed. Houston A. Baker, Jr. (New York: Penguin, 1982), 105. Other quotations are taken from this edition and are identified in the text.

34. "Principles of Temperance Reform: An Address Delivered in Rochester, New York, on 5 March 1848," in *The Frederick Douglass Papers; Series One: Speeches, Debates, and Interviews*, ed. John W. Blassingame and John R. McKivigan, 5 vols. (New Haven, CT: Yale UP, 1979–92), 2:106–7. Later in the same speech, Douglass showed a familiarity with Washingtonian principles. I have discovered no conclusive evidence that he read Gough's *Autobiography* in its original (1845) form. In an 1872 speech, however, Douglass borrowed a joke (which was garbled but also improved in the retelling) from the revised (1869) edition: "You know, when Gough presented himself at the door of the Tabernacle in New York, he said to the door-keeper: 'Let me in; I am Gough.' 'I'll be d——d if I do,' said the door-keeper; 'there are no less than seven Goughs gone in here already.' " Ibid., 3:310. For Gough's own version of this anecdote, see *Autobiography and Personal Recollections*, 237–38.

35. In the final revision of his autobiography, Douglass slightly changed the phrasing of the last sentence: "It was about as well to be a slave to master, as to be a slave to whiskey and rum." *Life and Times of Frederick Douglass* (1892; rpt. New York: Collier, 1962), 148. The passage was also echoed in an 1846 temperance address: "The holidays are days of liberty to the slave, but instead of making them days of pure and undefiled freedom the slaveholder makes them days of disgusting vice, disgusting debauchery, disgusting intemperance, and thus when the slave passes through his holidays, he feels that liberty, after all, is not of so much consequence, he might as well be enslaved to a man as enslaved to whiskey." "Intemperance Viewed in Connection with Slavery: An Address Delivered in Glasgow, Scotland, on 18 February 1846," in *The Frederick Douglass Papers*, 1:166–67.

36. "Intemperance Viewed in Connection with Slavery," *The Frederick Douglass Papers*, 1:170.

37. "Temperance and Anti-Slavery: An Address Delivered in Paisley, Scotland, on 30 March 1846," in *The Frederick Douglass Papers*, 1:207–8.

38. "The Temperance Cause in America and Britain: An Address Delivered in London, England, on 21 May 1846," in *The Frederick Douglass Papers*, 1:267. Douglass complained that it had been difficult at times for him to avoid temptation during his travels about Scotland, where he had encountered prominent clergymen given to disgracefully heavy drinking.

39. On Douglass's *Narrative* as "a revolutionary document," an African American equivalent of the Declaration of Independence, see James Olney, "The Founding Fathers—Frederick Douglass and Booker T. Washington," in *Slavery and the Literary Imagination*, ed. Deborah E. McDowell and Arnold Rampersad (Baltimore: Johns Hopkins UP, 1989).

40. "Temperance and Anti-Slavery," in *The Frederick Douglass Papers*, 1:206. Douglass conceded that intemperance among northern blacks had "done much to retard the progress of the anti-slavery movement" by furnishing arguments to the oppressors: "they have pointed to the drunkards among the free colored population, and asked us the question, tauntingly—'What better would you be if you were in their situation?' " "Intemperance and Slavery," *The Frederick Douglass Papers*, 1:56.

41. Ibid., 1:207.

42. Waldo E. Martin, Jr., *The Mind of Frederick Douglass* (Chapel Hill: U of North Carolina P, 1984), 190. As Martin suggests, "upwardly mobile and respectable" blacks had been among the earliest advocates of temperance. For them, as for many white reformers, sobriety "symbolized a willing and faithful acceptance of middle-class values." Douglass, too, "consistently identified intemperance as a manifestation of bad values, social disorder, and immorality," and he believed that "temperance constituted a natural extension of black liberation" (189).

43. In describing this incident, Blumberg notes, as Douglass did not, that although "the procession had been planned by black temperance people, the specific day [1 August] had been suggested by white abolitionists: it was the anniversary of freedom for over a million slaves in the West Indies." *Beware the First Drink!*, 144. Thus the Philadelphia riot of 1842 illustrated both the racial intolerance of the temperance movement and its aversion to abolitionism in any guise. See also Roediger, *The Wages of Whiteness*, 135.

44. Samuel Hanson Cox, quoted in *Life and Times*, 247. Douglass's most stinging remarks came at the beginning of his brief address, when he regretted that he could not "fully unite with the American delegates in their patriotic eulogies of America and American temperance societies" because "three million slaves are completely excluded by slavery, and four hundred thousand free colored people are almost completely excluded by an inveterate prejudice against them on account of their color." Ibid., 249.

45. See Benjamin Quarles, *Frederick Douglass* (Washington, DC: Associated, 1948), 139.

46. Washingtonians came to distrust Gough for consorting with the temperance establishment and for preaching prohibition. (The Society, with its emphasis on

individual reform, refused to countenance any measures stronger than moral suasion.) Gough was also pilloried for a notorious relapse in September 1845, when, after disappearing for a week in New York, he was discovered in a brothel, evidently recovering from a bender. Gough swore he had been drugged by his enemies and tricked into taking the fatal first drink that had triggered his binge; he had unknowingly fallen among prostitutes, he explained, in an alcoholic daze. Although Gough was officially exonerated by his church and defended by prominent temperance leaders, his story was widely disbelieved. For details of the scandal, see Gough's own statement, added as a "Supplement" to later editions of his 1845 *Autobiography*. The anti-Gough position is outlined in *Goffiana: A Review of the Life and Writings of John B. Gough* (Boston: Ruggles, 1846).

47. Douglass, *Life and Times*, 374.

48. Because all three of the extant biographies (one of which is intended for children) rely uncritically on Gough's own accounts of his life, they are, in effect, hagiographies. See: Edward A. Rand, *A Knight That Smote the Dragon: or, The Young People's Gough* (New York: Hunt & Eaton, 1892); Carlos Martyn, *John B. Gough: The Apostle of Cold Water* (New York: Funk, 1894); Honore W. Morrow, *Tiger! Tiger!: The Life Story of John B. Gough* (New York: Morrow, 1930). Gough's papers, on which more rigorous study might be based, are held by the American Antiquarian Society, Worcester, Massachusetts.

Temperance, Morality, and Medicine in the Fiction of Harriet Beecher Stowe

✍ Nicholas O. Warner

IN ADDITION TO HER LONG-STANDING REPUTATION AS THE CREATOR of what James Baldwin called "everybody's protest novel," Harriet Beecher Stowe has gained increasing attention as a writer and social leader whose works provide a rich ground for exploring issues other than the obviously crucial one of abolition. Her works encompass such concerns as race relations, the changing roles of women in nineteenth-century American society, and that peculiar blend of progressive idealism, sentimentalism, and religious zeal that Stowe herself embodied.[1] My focus here is on Stowe's literary understanding of drinking and temperance, with specific reference to the nineteenth-century debate over alcoholism as vice or disease.

In her earliest works, Stowe characterized the drunkard as a sinner, albeit one often to be pitied, and drunkenness as the result of a weak moral temperament. Her treatment of drink follows conventional temperance lines in her first stories and novels which, among their other concerns, seek to demonstrate the evils of alcoholic excess, and to expose even moderate drinking as an insidious prelude to addiction. Eventually, however, without rejecting religion's beneficent influence on the drunkard, Stowe turned to a more medical model of alcoholism and to a more sympathetic view of the alcoholic as an individual, thereby challenging the growing negative moral stereotype of the heavy drinker within both the temperance movement and society at large. Even more surprisingly, in some of Stowe's late work alcoholism becomes a grandly tragic affliction, involving profound questions of destiny, self-determination, and personal identity. These changes are most apparent in the complex character of Bolton, who appears in two novels of the 1870s, *My Wife and I* and *We and Our Neighbors*. Although many temperance workers also called alcoholism a disease, Stowe's depiction of the alcoholic in these late novels stands out for its opposition to the increasing tendency of the times toward negative moral stereotypes of the drunkard, and for its unusual treatment of alcoholism not as contemptible moral blemish but as tragic fate, fully worthy of the complexity and moral high seriousness of classical tragedy. In order to understand the complexity of that fate, Stowe seems to say, we need to see alcoholism as a profoundly inward, private phenomenon, and to approach it from the inner perspective of the alcoholic's own experiences and consciousness.

Before turning to the development of these patterns in Stowe's fiction, I wish to address an issue highly pertinent to that fiction—the nineteenth-century moral-medical debate over intemperance. Understanding that debate not only will illuminate specific Stowe texts, but will help clarify the relationship between her work and the larger temperance context in which it was produced.

The controversies surrounding alcoholism as a "disease" continue today. Certainly among those engaged in the treatment and counseling of alcoholics, the disease model prevails, having gained considerable prestige from its acceptance in the 1950s by both the World Health Organization and the American Medical Association.[2] But the medical model is far from universally dominant. Despite the proliferation of medical terminology in talking about alcoholism in our society, many alcoholics still feel a stigma they would not have with most other diseases. Moreover, in public opinion the medical model still lags behind the moral one; although many people putatively accept the disease interpretation and mode of speaking about alcoholism, the "moral weakness" concept remains strong, coexisting in a vague, undefined relationship with the medical model (Ames, 24–25). Recent years have also witnessed articulate, explicit challenges to disease theories of alcoholism, most notably in two books: philosopher Herbert Fingarette's *Heavy Drinking: The Myth of Alcoholism as a Disease* (1988), and psychologist Stanton Peele's *Diseasing of America: Addiction Treatment Out of Control* (1989). These authors, writing from the perspectives of different disciplines, vigorously argue against what they see as the biological determinism and moral irresponsibility of the disease concept. Others, such as the psychologist and physician George E. Vaillant, in *The Natural History of Alcoholism* (1983), and literary critic Thomas B. Gilmore, in his lengthy review of Fingarette, just as forcefully argue for the values of the disease model and against those who would dispense with it. The debate remains unresolved, and often seems unresolvable, at least in the light of present scientific knowledge.[3]

Current as the concerns outlined above seem, reflecting modern discussions of addiction theory, nature versus nurture, guilt, psychological "health," and a panoply of related contemporary issues, it is a common error to see the disease concept and the debates surrounding it as recent developments. The disease concept of alcoholism received new impetus from the influence of Alcoholics Anonymous (founded in 1935) and from the work of various researchers, most notably E. M. Jellinek, in the decades following World War II. But references to chronic drunkenness as a disease actually extend as far back as the classical author Seneca, with the modern theory of addiction itself emerging in the late eighteenth century.[4] In his definitive study of the genesis of modern addiction theory, Harry G. Levine points out that it is in the work of Dr. Benjamin Rush— eminent colonial physician and signer of the Declaration of Independence— that "we can find the first clearly developed modern conception of alcohol addiction" (Levine, "Discovery," 151). When he published the first of the many editions of his pamphlet, *An Inquiry into the Effects of Ardent Spirits upon the Human Mind and Body* (1784), Rush directly contradicted the prevailing view of his times, expressed earlier in the Puritan theologian Jonathan Edwards's *Freedom of the Will*, that desire and will cannot be divorced. Using the example of the habitual drunkard, Edwards "rejected the idea that the drunkard can be compelled by appetite or desire to do something against his will" (Levine, "Discovery," 150). Rush's challenge to this belief, along with his identification of habitual drunkenness as a "disease," dramatically changed the way that many people perceived alcoholism, and profoundly influenced the nineteenth-century temperance movement, as is evident in the number of physicians and temperance supporters emphasizing the medical aspects of addiction.[5]

In the early nineteenth-century world in which Harriet Beecher Stowe grew up, concepts of alcoholism as disease *and* as depravity coexisted, clashed, and sometimes even intersected. The English physician Thomas Trotter, for example, one of the earliest proponents of the disease concept, nonetheless wrote of drink in moralistic terms, as did Rush, even as he urged a more medical understanding of the progressive course of addiction.[6] Conversely, some of the staunchest moralists occasionally tempered their attacks on the sin of drunkenness with medical language. The charismatic temperance lecturer John B. Gough, arguably the nineteenth century's best-known reformed drunkard, explicitly described intemperance as both disease and, with some exceptions, sin. The antiliquor writings of the popular antebellum preacher Mason Locke Weems labeled intemperance a "disease" even as Weems castigated drink in the most lurid terms.[7] And the eminent Lyman Beecher, father of Harriet Beecher Stowe and author of the huge publishing success *Six Sermons on Intemperance*

(1826), departed from his usual references to drunkenness as the most heinous of sins to describe the alcoholism of a friend's son in surprisingly medical terms. In his autobiography, Beecher observes that a young acquaintance, having failed in his attempts to conquer his own intemperance, "became bound hand and foot" by alcohol. Stressing the physicality of the young man's condition, Beecher further noted that "the thirst was in his constitution." In words most unlike the diatribes leveled at drink and drinkers in his sermons, but curiously anticipating his daughter Harriet's late-in-life fictional accounts of alcoholism, Beecher stated, after the young man's death, "I indulge the hope that God saw it was a constitutional infirmity, *like any other disease*" (my italics).[8] For the most part, however, Beecher unambiguously attacks intemperance in the strongest possible terms of moral condemnation.

The deeper one goes into nineteenth-century temperance attitudes, and into the attitudes of society in general, the more complex the entire issue of drunkenness as disease or sin becomes. As if in testimony to this fact, America's most famous temperance author, T. S. Arthur, openly admitted his own confusion about alcoholism's moral/medical status. In his *Strong Drink*, Arthur writes that he does not, finally, know whether "drunkenness is a disease, for which after it has been established, the individual ceases to be responsible and should be subject to restraint and treatment as for lunacy or fever; a *crime* to be punished; or a *sin* to be repented and healed by the Physician of souls. . . ."[9]

The metaphor "Physician of souls" may remind us of another fact that adds to the complexity of the disease concept—its inescapable metaphorical dimension. To speak of alcoholism as a disease is to speak, in part, metaphorically, as a recent commentator on the issue has pointed out (Gilmore, "The Critic Criticized," 27). Although groups like the World Health Organization and the American Medical Association readily include alcoholism on their lists of officially recognized illnesses, a metaphorical element persists in contemporary descriptions of alcoholism as a disease, given that the condition depends so much not only on biology but on sociocultural and psychological factors, and on the interplay of all of these in an individual human being. This metaphorical element was all the more strong in the early, eighteenth- and nineteenth-century definitions of alcoholism as a disease. Even then, the argument that alcoholism should be thought or spoken of as an illness could provoke considerable hostility, particularly in the United States, where Thomas Trotter's moralistic tone did not prevent his work from being condemned by those who opposed the medicalization of what they saw as a distinctly moral issue and, indeed, as a sin.[10]

A further complication is the fact that the disease model itself has changed since physicians like Benjamin Rush and Thomas Trotter introduced it some two centuries ago. As Genevieve Ames reminds us, "the disease model of Rush . . . was defined not in terms of disease pathology as we know it today," but rather "as a 'disease of the will', and as an addiction brought on by a gradual breaking down of moral willpower" (Ames, 30). Nor is it always clear in earlier writings whether "disease" means physical susceptibility to alcohol, as the term is often used today, or a subsequent addiction to alcohol, along with addiction's attendant physical debilities. For Stowe as well, these issues would always remain blurred, although, by the 1870s, she inclined to the view that alcoholism is at least partly dependent on a preexisting psychological and physical susceptibility to drink, for which susceptibility, in and of itself, the alcoholic is blameless.

Despite the incursion of medical language into the discourses of morality, prominent nineteenth-century temperance leaders like Beecher and Gough were far more emphatic in addressing habitual drunkenness as a moral rather than physical phenomenon. And, despite the persistence of exceptions, the tendency from the 1850s on was to label alcoholism as a moral failing that *led* to various diseases, rather than to call the sensitivity or predisposition to alcohol itself a disease. The antidisease faction became more vociferous as the century went on, with arguments in favor of the medical model being countered by attacks such as J. E. Todd's pamphlet, *Drunkenness a Vice, Not a Disease*, and by the general tone of those who, like the Reverend Jonathan Townley Crane, father of Stephen Crane, blisteringly condemned the drunkard as the apotheosis of depravity. This increasing negativity toward the drunkard reflects sociologist Joseph Gusfield's now-classic model of the shift from "assimilative" to "coercive" reform in the nineteenth-century temperance movement. Describing this attitudinal shift in her historical analysis of the medical-moral controversy, Genevieve Ames observes that "As hard drinking became increasingly prevalent and problematic on both the American frontier and in urban slums, traditional thinking about alcohol use and misuse began to change," resulting in the "eventual treatment of alcoholics as criminal, immoral, depraved, or insane" (Ames, 32). Thus, while historians like Mark Edward Lender and James Kirby Martin have shown that the Women's Christian Temperance Union, founded in 1874, and some other temperance groups exhibited "genuine sympathy for the drunkard," the general image of the heavy drinker as social misfit became already widespread during the 1850s. "After the Civil War, this image crystallized in the skid row stereotype. And, given the fears for the sanctity of the middle-class home, the demands of industrial efficiency, and the premium on good citizenship in a rapidly changing society, the individual drunkard's aberrant behavior and apparent lack of regard for neorepublican virtues was intolerable, at least in temperance eyes.[11]

These negative views of the drunkard, while conflicting with more sympathetic attitudes within the temperance movement, dominated temperance literature, especially in the latter half of the nineteenth century. True, antiliquor fiction often acknowledged the factors that could lead to intemperance, such as heredity, social pressures to drink, and personal or professional anxiety. Simultaneously, however, individual drunkards were often portrayed as morally reprehensible and personally disgusting, for example, as "irreligious wife-beaters, thugs, murderers and loafers, whose profligate ways finally impoverished entire families."[12] Despite the numerous exceptions to this pattern that one would expect from so large and increasingly diverse a population as that of the United States in the 1800s, the hostile, unforgiving view of the alcoholic became increasingly dominant in both American literature and society during Stowe's lifetime. It is against the backdrop of this pattern that I now wish to place Stowe's depiction of alcoholism, tracing its development from her earliest temperance works to the two late novels mentioned before.

Little in Stowe's early temperance work distinguishes it from the cataract of sentimental temperance fiction published in antebellum America. Certainly Stowe never engaged in the kind of subversive sensationalism that David S. Reynolds describes as the "dark temperance" mode, although her stories are often tinged with a vitality and an irony absent from temperance's more cloyingly lachrymose productions, such as those of Lydia Sigourney or T. S. Arthur.[13] In Stowe's early work, such as the stories published in the *New York Evangelist* in the 1830s, we find individual variations on several themes familiar to temperance readers: poverty and distress caused by drink; drunkenness as the source of personal and domestic unhappiness quite apart from its disastrous financial impact; attacks on moderate drinking as leading, by means of a domino effect, to chronic drunkenness; the description of addiction in terms of stages of progressively greater dependence on alcohol; and an insistence on total abstinence as the only path to sobriety. In addition, a few glimmerings of the later Stowe shine through, as in her sympathetic account of the rationale for the drinking of those who seek solace or escape from suffering, in her gently ironic jabs at temperance sanctimoniousness, and in her emphasis on redeeming the drunkard, rather than on doling out the horrible punishments that typified most temperance works.[14] In her early work, however, Stowe does not seem interested in alcoholism as a disease. Only much later, under the presumed influence of the alcoholism of her son, Frederick, and the morphine addiction of her daughter, Georgiana, does Stowe return to the disease models of alcoholism circulating in her youth, and present them with passionate conviction in the novels featuring the alcoholic character Bolton.[15]

Representative of Stowe's early temperance fiction is the 1839 story "The Drunkard Reclaimed" (subsequently retitled "Let Every Man Mind His Own Business" when Stowe published it in her elegant collection, *The Mayflower*). The tale vividly depicts a refined family's decline as the result of social drinking, but ends on a note of familial reconciliation and personal redemption for the alcoholic. In fact, the story's original title, when it appeared in *The New York Evangelist*, testifies to Stowe's penchant for lifting the fallen rather than casting them into a black hole of moral condemnation. Just as Stowe urged Rebecca Harding Davis to do in her own fiction, so too Stowe here refuses to show the drunkard as beyond redemption. Not that Stowe never punishes her drunks; the most notorious of them, the alcoholic slave driver Simon Legree, one of nineteenth-century American fiction's vilest characters, is made to suffer the agonies of delirium tremens and drink-related, terror-inducing guilt before his grisly death. But for the most part, Stowe shows that even the sorriest drunkard, sunk in an abyss of shame, can be plucked out by some combination of religion, abstinence, and, usually , a woman's caring guidance.[16] This last point is particularly strong in "The Drunkard Reclaimed," where the once flighty Augusta Elmore, now married to alcoholic Edward Howard, refuses to desert him even when urged to do so by respectable members of society, and helps him eventually to achieve sobriety and a modicum of material comfort. Similarly, another short story, "The Coral Ring," focuses on a woman's gentle influence in persuading a freely drinking male acquaintance (not a romantic interest) to become temperate before it is too late.

Stowe did not, however, invariably associate drink with male vice, or sobriety with female virtue. "Uncle Enoch," originally published (like "The Drunkard Reclaimed") in *The New York Evangelist*, is unusual in being one of the few fictional works of its time to acknowledge the almost unspeakable topic of female intemperance.[17] Similarly, female as well as male drinkers appear in Stowe's most famous work, but there is no implication in *Uncle Tom's Cabin* that a female drinker is somehow more reprehensible than a male one; drunkenness is an evil to be eschewed by all, and no "special stigma," to use drink historian Mark Edward Lender's term, attaches to such female drinkers as Cassy because of their gender.[18]

It is, in fact, with *Uncle Tom's Cabin* that we begin to see Stowe becoming more interested in and sympathetic to the inner processes of the alcoholic's mind. Not that this interest and sympathy extend to every drunkard. In the case of Simon Legree, heavy drinking serves mainly to accentuate his generally hateful, sadistic character. Indeed, Legree's drinking is worse than that of an out-and-out addict, since he "was not an habitual drunkard." Legree drinks not because he has to but, *horribile dictu*, because he wants to: "His coarse, strong nature craved, and could endure, a continual stimulation, that would have utterly wrecked and crazed a finer one" (2: 158). In contrast to Legree, Stowe clearly sympathizes with the genial St. Clare, whose excessive tippling is a foible corrected through the wise advice of Uncle Tom, and she takes pains to explain the extenuating circumstances behind the drinking of Cassy and of the "old rusk-woman" whom Uncle Tom seeks to turn to temperance. In both cases drinking, while unequivocally evil, results not from the coarse cravings of a Legree, but from the understandable desperation of those needing some anodyne from physical and psychic suffering. The old woman's suffering stems from her daughter's death, while Cassy's comes from Legree's exploitation of her both as woman and as slave, and from her separation from her daughter (1: 285, 2: 157–58).

In Stowe's next novel, *Dred* (1856), Simon Legree reappears decked out in upper-class garb as the dissolute, obsessively racist, and boorish drunkard Tom Gordon. As with Legree, Gordon's drinking—set up in implicit contrast to the rebellious slave Dred's abstinence from alcohol—only deepens his villainy. But Gordon is a less complicated, less varied figure than Legree since his entire personality consists of bullying and posturing. Gordon's character lacks the multidimensionality and vividness of Legree's, and his drinking functions as a boring generalized attribute without the richness of detail we find in the so enjoyably despicable Legree.

Curiously, in *Dred* it is the unpromising figure of the hapless poor white, Cripps, that provides a brief but intriguing exploration of the drinker's consciousness and motivation. All of temperance literature's stereotypes regarding lower-class squalor and drunkenness appear in Cripps—the laziness, the craven toadying before one's "betters," the filthy living conditions, the abuse of wife and children, the monetary irresponsibility, the personal repulsiveness. But in one fascinating passage, Stowe anticipates William James's comments, in *The Varieties of Religious Experience*, on the complexity and depth of motive that, whether conscious or not, often lie behind even the most mundane drinking. "Not out of mere perversity do men run after it," writes James of alcohol. "To the poor and the unlettered it stands in the place of symphony concerts and of literature; and it is part of the deeper mystery and tragedy of life that whiffs and gleams of something that we immediately recognize as excellent should be vouchsafed to so many of us only in the fleeting earlier phases of what in its totality is so degrading a poisoning."[19] In a strikingly similar passage on the unfortunate Cripps, sitting drunk in his squalid hut, Stowe writes, "despite the exhortations of Tiff [a kind of Uncle Tom *redivivus*, who constantly urges Cripps to stop drinking] he had applied to the whiskey-jug immediately on his departure. Why not? He was uncomfortable—gloomy; and every one, under such circumstances, naturally inclines towards *some* source of consolation. He who is intellectual reads and studies; he who is industrious flies to business; he who is none of these—what has he but his whiskey?" (3:133–34).

The above passages testify to the importance of drink-related issues for Stowe. But it was late in her career that Stowe most specifically and pointedly dealt with the alcoholic as an individual rather than as a stereotype or mere instrument for moral instruction. This Stowe accomplished with the character of Bolton, to whom I now turn, first in *My Wife and I* (1871), and then in its sequel, *We and Our Neighbors* (1873).

The often stilted, cloyingly sentimental prose of the Bolton novels should not prevent the modern reader from recognizing their author's challenge to the discourses of "coercive" reform and of the moralistic model of alcoholism.[20] Explaining his own susceptibility to drink, which requires him to ask the narrator of *My Wife and I*, Harry Henderson, to act as a kind of temperance watchdog over him, Bolton describes his alcoholism as a virtually inevitable fate, and thus asserts the essential innocence, at least on one level, of the alcoholic. Key to Bolton's self-analysis is loss of control—a phrase ubiquitous in current alcohol research and treatment. At first a servant, drink soon "becomes the most tyrannical of masters," says Bolton. Turning to another metaphor, Bolton compares himself to a shipmaster who, at the edge of a whirlpool, learns to his horror "that the ship *no longer obeyed the rudder*"—as his dependence on alcohol outweighs his reason and willpower (12: 328). This involuntary nature of Bolton's condition, and, by implication, of all or at least many alcoholics, receives fuller development in a subsequent chapter whose very title—"The Fates"—allows Stowe both to stress the irrelevance of volition in analyzing addiction, and to set up an analogy between the drunkard's affliction and the great, destiny-driven misfortunes portrayed in ancient Greek literature and myth. After going on at length about the futility of his attempts to avoid intoxication when drinking, Bolton tells Henderson of the nearly irresistible attraction that alcohol exerts on his senses in spite of his shame, regret, and determination not to drink again. He goes on to tell Henderson that "you know we read in the Greek tragedies of men and women whom the gods have smitten with unnatural and guilty purposes, in which they were irresistibly impelled toward what they abominated and shuddered at! Is it not strange that the Greek fable should have a real counterpart in the midst of our modern life?" (12: 345). That counterpart is, of course, the alcoholism from which Bolton suffers and by which he feels doomed.

One important result of comparing alcoholism to the curses laid on victims of the gods in Greek tragedy is to raise the subject of intemperance out of its usual context of sordid physical details, lurid violence, and paternalistic contempt on the part of sober authors and readers. While Stowe never hesitates to show drunkenness in its most offensive aspects, in *My Wife and I* she gives the inner turmoil of the individual drinker—or at least of Bolton—an unusual measure of personal dignity. The alcoholic's sufferings that we saw in "The Drunkard Reclaimed" and in *Uncle Tom's Cabin* rise in the Bolton novels to the level of tragic art, rather than remaining in the shabby realm of the pathetic misfit to which Stowe's temperance-supporting contemporaries often consigned the alcoholic. But an equally, if not more important effect of the comparison to Greek tragedy is the imputation of innocence to the alcoholic for his susceptibility to drink. The drunkard *has* this susceptibility; he cannot change it. As far as alcoholism is concerned, Stowe seemingly believes that biology is destiny. But, although the alcoholic cannot change his condition, he can and must recognize it, acknowledge its power, and fight it with the best weapon he has—total abstinence, as Bolton himself determines to do.[21]

In Bolton's case, although drunkenness causes evil—the profligacy and irresponsibility he describes at length to Henderson in *My Wife and I*—it does not proceed from an evil motivation (as, for example, do Simon Legree's cravings for sensual stimulation) but from a kind of inherent flaw or temperamental fault line. "I shall be a vessel with a crack in it, always," says Bolton, to which Henderson replies, "Well, a vase of fine porcelain with a crack in it is better than earthenware without" (12: 346). At this late stage in Stowe's career, the alcoholic's susceptibility is nothing of which to be ashamed in any moral sense. Although regrettable and even terrible in its possible consequences, the condition is more a constitutional imperfection than a sign of the moral turpitude and gross self-indulgence that, as we have seen, it was for Jonathan Edwards or, in Stowe's own time, Jonathan Townley Crane.

We and Our Neighbors extends this idea of alcoholism as at least a partially inherent trait, rather than a deliberately chosen path of sin. Here Stowe makes more explicit her medical approach to alcoholism, although—somewhat confusingly—traces of a morally disapproving tone remain. In this novel, religious faith is, as elsewhere in Stowe, crucial to a virtuous and successful life. Without that faith, for example, Bolton declares that he would almost certainly commit suicide (13: 204). But religion for Stowe is no longer sufficient in and of itself to reclaim the drunkard. Indeed, she has her devout narrator, Harry Henderson, reject the solely religious cure for intemperance that was a mainstay of such popular antiliquor texts as Harriette Newell Baker's *Cora and the Doctor* (1855). Affirming the interrelations of the physical and the moral, Henderson says, "our souls have got to be saved in our bodies and by the laws of our bodies; and a doctor who understands them will do more than a minister who doesn't. Why just look at poor Bolton. The trouble that he dreads, the fear that blasts his life, that makes him afraid to marry, *is a disease of the body*" (my italics). "Fasting, prayer, sacraments, couldn't keep off an acute attack of dipsomania, but a doctor might" (13: 137). This idea reappears in the novel when Bolton himself qualifies the optimistic belief of the Anglican minister, Mr. St. John, in the Church's power to redeem the dissolute: "I know something of the difficulties, physical and moral, which lie in the way," warns Bolton (13: 201). Similarly, the narrator, Henderson, reminds the even more enthusiastic Mr. James, who seeks to reform drunkards through religion, that "the craving for drink gets to be a physical disease" (13: 367). To be sure, Stowe never condemns either Mr. St. John or Mr. James, but she pointedly balances their effusive faith with the medically informed, more physically oriented views of Henderson and Bolton.[22]

The fullest medical statement on alcoholism in this or any other Stowe novel comes, however, not from either of the male principals, but from Caroline, the young woman Bolton loves and eventually marries. Refusing to accept Bolton's request that she keep a "safe distance" from him because of his fear that at any moment he may succumb to drink (13: 205), Caroline writes to Bolton that "the sad fatality which clouds your life makes this feeling [her devotion to him] only the more intense; as we feel for those who are a part of our own hearts when in suffering and danger" (13: 206). Precisely because she has studied medicine, Caroline feels herself to be "at a standpoint where my judgment on these questions and subjects is different from that of ordinary women"—i.e., those women for whom alcoholism and alcoholics are objects only of fear and loathing. Just as Henderson stresses the physicality of alcoholism, so too Caroline asserts that "An understanding of the laws of physical being, of the conditions of brain and nerve forces, may possibly at some future day bring a remedy for such sufferings as yours." She goes on to distinguish once again between her own attitudes and those of more conventional women: "I shall not be to you what many women are to the men whom they love, an added weight to fall upon you if you fall, to crush you under the burden of my disappointments and anxieties and distresses. Knowing that your heart is resolute and your nature noble, a failure, supposing such a possibility, would be to me only like a fever or a paralysis—a subject for new care and watchfulness and devotion, not one for tears or reproaches or exhortations" (13:206). Caroline's next statement even more explicitly supports the medical view of alcoholism: "There are lesions of the will that are no more to be considered subject to moral condemnation than a strain of the spinal column or a sudden fall from paralysis" (13: 206).

Could the most ardent advocate of A.A. more forcefully describe alcoholism as a disease? Probably not, but Stowe's statement is, nonetheless, problematic, haunted by the difficulty of labeling alcoholism as a subject belonging to any single, exclusive category—mind, body, soul, psyche, character. The phrase "lesions of the will" perfectly expresses this problematic quality, revealing as it does the incursion of "willpower" and moral or personal value judgments into the purely medical discourse that Stowe's text ostensibly promotes. The connotations of the word "lesions" by itself are emphatically physical and medical, pointing toward the disease notion of alcoholism. But the phrase "of the will" points away from the body and from medicine toward a more intangible area which, for lack of a better term, we may call "character," and which impinges on questions of moral evaluation. "Lesions of the will" also makes it clear that the illness of alcoholism, for Caroline and for Stowe, is in some sense not "really" an illness. Just as Benjamin Rush's late-eighteenth-century disease theory of inebriety was, finally, not as firmly pathological as the disease theory is today (as Genevieve Ames observed in a passage cited earlier), so too Stowe cannot completely shed moral overtones in her discussion of Bolton. After all, "lesions of the will" are not lesions in the medical sense. The things signified by the word "lesions" here may very well exist, but they are not literally "lesions." Rather, the word is a vivid and valiant attempt to medicalize the condition, but it is not a denotative signifier of an objective, medically verifiable reality, as lesions of the arm or scalp or leg would be. Obviously a metaphor, the term "lesions" takes us back to the ineluctable, problematic, *metaphorical* nature of the disease concept of alcoholism, both in Stowe's day and our own.

However medical, metaphorical, or moral one's views of it may be, alcoholism involves a wide range of cultural perceptions and meanings. As the foregoing discussion demonstrates, these perceptions and meanings play a major role in Stowe's fiction, revealing nuances and changes over time that should help to dispel the notion of Stowe as a one-dimensional proselytizer for teetotalism. That proselytizing tendency is, admittedly, a genuine part of Stowe's work both as author and as leading cultural spokesperson, but it is only a part, coexisting and sometimes conflicting with other, often paradoxical elements in a complex structure built up of Stowe's own ideals, experiences, impressions, and convictions. Study of that structure and of its constituent parts shows that Stowe not only reflected but also challenged the dominant perspectives of her own culture and of late-nineteenth-century temperance. To understand this pattern of reflection and challenge is, then, to put into sharper outline the artistic and ideological profile of one of the United States' most potent, influential, and controversial cultural icons. And it is also to see more clearly where we have been as a culture and, thus, where we are now.

Notes

1. For Baldwin, see his essay, "Everybody's Protest Novel," in *Notes of a Native Son* (New York: Bantam, 1964), 9–17. Joan D. Hedrick's study, *Harriet Beecher Stowe: A Life* (New York & Oxford: Oxford UP, 1994), which blends intellectual and literary analysis with biography, represents the increasing sophistication of Stowe studies, as do a number of the texts found in Hedrick's bibliography. Where convenient, further references to Hedrick will appear in the text.

2. Genevieve M. Ames, "American Beliefs About Alcoholism: Historical Perspectives on the Medical-Moral Controversy," in Linda A. Bennett and Genevieve M. Ames, eds., *The American Experience with Alcohol: Contrasting Cultural Perspectives* (New York: Plenum, 1985), 25. Further references to this source will appear in the text.

3. Herbert Fingarette, *Heavy Drinking: The Myth of Alcoholism as a Disease* (Berkeley: U of California P, 1988); Stanton Peele, *The Diseasing of America: Addiction Treatment Out of Control* (Lexington, MA: Heath, 1989); George E. Vaillant, *The Natural History of Alcoholism* (Cambridge, MA: Harvard UP, 1983); Thomas B. Gilmore, Jr., "The Critic Criticized," *Dionysos: The Literature and Intoxication Triquarterly* 1 (1989): 19–30.

4. On Alcoholics Anonymous views of alcoholism as a disease, see Ernest Kurtz, *Not God: A History of Alcoholics Anonymous* (Center City, MN: Hazelden Educational Materials, 1979), and Nan Robertson, *Getting Better: Inside Alcoholics Anonymous* (New York: Morrow, 1988). See also E. M. Jellinek, *The Disease Concept of Alcoholism* (New Brunswick: Hillhouse P, 1960). On ancient views of alcoholism, including that of Seneca, see Frank A. Seixas, "What! Still using that old term Alcohol-

ism? And still calling it a Disease?" *British Journal on Alcohol and Alcoholism* 16 (1981): 78–87.

5. Harry G. Levine, "The Discovery of Addiction: Changing Conceptions of Habitual Drunkenness in America," *Journal of Studies on Alcohol* 39 (1978): 143–74; see also Levine, "The Alcohol Problem in America: From Temperance to Alcoholism," *British Journal of Addiction* 79 (1984): 109–19. For a representative expression of a nineteenth-century doctor's medical view of alcoholism, see Samuel B. Woodward (superintendent of Worcester Hospital), *Essays on Asylums for Inebriates* (Worcester, MA, 1838), especially p. 2: "Like insanity, intemperance is too much of a physical disease to be cured by moral means only."

6. See Thomas Trotter, *An Essay, Medical, Philosophical, and Chemical, on Drunkenness* (Philadelphia: Anthony Finley, 1813); on Trotter's "moral overtones" see also Brian Harrison, *Drink and the Victorians* (Pittsburgh: U of Pittsburgh P, 1971), 21–22. Harrison also points out that Erasmus Darwin "conceived a medical rather than moral objection to intoxicants," but later English reformers rarely mentioned the more medically inclined Darwin and Trotter: see Harrison, 92.

7. Mason Locke Weems, *Three Discourses: Hymen's Recruiting Serjeant, The Drunkard's Looking-Glass, God's Revenge Against Adultery* (New York: Random, 1929, originally published 1813), 55.

8. On Beecher's views of intemperance as a sin, see Lyman Beecher, *Six Sermons on the Nature, Occasions, Signs, Evils, and Remedy of Intemperance* (New York: American Tract Society, 1827), especially 5–7; on the incident with a youthful acquaintance, see Barbara M. Cross, ed., *The Autobiography of Lyman Beecher* (Cambridge: Harvard UP, 1961), 2:23.

9. T. S. Arthur, quoted in Joan L. Silverman, " 'I'll Never Touch Another Drop': Images of Alcoholism and Temperance in American Popular Culture, 1874–1919" (Ph.D. diss., New York University, 1979), 77.

10. On the hostile response to Trotter's medical interpretation of alcoholism, see Berton Roueché, *The Neutral Spirit: A Portrait of Alcohol* (Boston: Little, 1960), 106.

11. Unlike Stowe, who at least saw some extenuating circumstances for heavy drinking in the suffering of characters such as Cassy in *Uncle Tom's Cabin*, Jonathan Townley Crane castigated escapist drinkers for their "cowardice" and "meanness of spirit": see Crane, *Arts of Intoxication: The Aim, and the Results* (New York: Carlton & Lanahan, 1870), 219. For similar instances of Crane's animosity to any and all who drink, see his "Drugs as an Indulgence," *Methodist Quarterly Review* 40 (1858): 551–66, and *Popular Amusements* (Cincinnati: Hitchcock & Walden, 1869). See also J. E. Todd, *Drunkenness a Vice, Not a Disease* (Hartford: Case, Lockwood, & Brainard, 1882). Gusfield's influential analysis of temperance history is found in his *Symbolic Crusade: Status Politics and the American Temperance Movement* (Urbana: U of Illinois P, 1963, 1986). For the comments on the WCTU and post–Civil War attitudes, see Mark Edward Lender and James Kirby Martin, *Drinking in*

America: A History (New York: Free, 1982), 116–17. Where convenient, further citations of these sources will appear in the text.

12. Mark Edward Lender and Karen R. Karnchanapee, " 'Temperance Tales': Anti-liquor Fiction and American Attitudes Toward Alcoholics in the Late 19th and Early 20th Centuries," *Journal of Studies on Alcohol* 38 (1977): 1351.

13. David S. Reynolds, *Beneath the American Renaissance: The Subversive Imagination in the Age of Emerson and Melville* (New York: Knopf, 1988), especially 55–73.

14. As Lender and Karnchanapee point out, "The image of alcoholics as social outcasts and physically dissipated derelicts was firmly entrenched in the American mind by the end of the antebellum Temperance Movement" (1347). It is, thus, not surprising that many temperance works "portrayed the worst possible view of the alcoholic, an individual as confirmed in his poverty and dissolution as he was in his drinking." Such works also tended to punish their drunkards, showing them being "hit by trains or trampled by horses in the end" (1351). On the negative portrayal of the drinker, see also Silverman, 77–79.

15. On the alcohol- and drug-related problems of Stowe's children see the appropriate index entries for Frederick Stowe and Georgiana Stowe Allen in Hedrick.

16. In 1869, Stowe wrote to Rebecca Harding Davis urging Davis to conclude her serial, "The Tembroke Legacy," on a happy rather than tragic note. "Frighten us dreadfully, but dont quite kill us," wrote Stowe (quoted in Hedrick, 336). On Stowe's generally enthusiastic view of Davis, whom she never met, but who shared Stowe's concern with the medical dimensions of alcoholism, see also Sharon M. Harris, *Rebecca Harding Davis and American Realism* (Philadelphia: U of Pennsylvania P, 1991), 147.

17. As Hedrick observes, "Uncle Enoch" addresses the problem of women drinkers "at a time when drunkenness was assumed to be a male problem" (134). Stowe's awareness of female drinking, though rare, was not unique, as evidenced by examples like the American author Ann Stephens's *The Old Homestead* (1855), with its alcoholic mother, or, in England, George Eliot's haunting portrait of a female alcoholic in "Janet's Repentance" (1858) and various drunken female characters in Dickens (e.g., Mrs. Gamp in *Martin Chuzzlewit*) and Gaskell (Esther in *Mary Barton*), among others.

18. See Mark Edward Lender, "A Special Stigma: Woman and Alcoholism in the Late 19th and Early 20th Centuries," in David L. Strug et al., *Alcohol Interventions: Historical and Sociological Approaches* (New York: Haworth P, 1986), 41–57. For Stowe's fiction, I have, except where noted otherwise, used *The Writings of Harriet Beecher Stowe* (Boston: Houghton, 1896), in 16 vols. Page references to the appropriate volume from this edition appear in the text. For "The Drunkard Reclaimed," I use the retitled version, "Let Every Man Mind His Business," in Stowe, *The Mayflower* (New York: Harper & Bros., 1843), 112–33. For "The Coral Ring," first published in 1843, see *The Writings of Harriet Beecher Stowe*, 14: 164–75.

19. William James, *The Varieties of Religious Experience*, ed. Martin E. Marty (New York: Viking Penguin, 1982, originally published 1902), 387.

20. Alice C. Crozier emphasizes a similar point when she writes that, "In seeking to understand Mrs. Stowe's achievement as a novelist and a polemicist, we need sufficient historical imagination to restrain the modern reader's impatience with the extravagance of some of the language of Victorian sentimentality"; see Crozier, *The Novels of Harriet Beecher Stowe* (New York: Oxford UP, 1969), 3. With regard to the Bolton novels, Crozier briefly anticipates my argument when she observes that Stowe's "treatment of Bolton's alcoholism in *My Wife and I* is a far cry from the shrill speeches on temperance one is apt to find in her earlier writing. . . ." (186).

21. These ideas are strikingly similar to some of the major concepts of Alcoholics Anonymous that have received pithy recent expression from Dr. Steven Hyman, director of the Mind, Brain, Behavior Institute at Harvard University. "The great A. A. insight," declares Dr. Hyman, "was not just that alcoholism is a disease but that having this disease is not an excuse for anything—not for missing work, messing up your family, killing people in automobiles. . . . In terms of cause, alcoholism does have genetic causes, cultural causes, circumstantial causes. But there's nothing deterministic about its *consequences.* That's the strange paradox A.A. understood, and it seems to be more and more difficult for people to accept"; quoted in Andrew Delbanco and Thomas Delbanco, "Annals of Addiction: A.A. at the Crossroads," *The New Yorker*, March 20, 1995, 61. The views of alcoholism expressed through Bolton also anticipate the mentality behind A.A.'s famous Serenity Prayer:

> God grant me the serenity
> To accept the things I cannot change;
> Courage to change the things I can;
> And wisdom to know the difference.

See Nan Robertson, *Getting Better: Inside Alcoholics Anonymous* (New York: Morrow, 1988), 119.

22. A late temperance story by Stowe, "Betty's Bright Idea" (1876), curiously ignores this medical orientation, although it does reflect the concern with the drunkard's perspectives and dignity that we find in the Bolton novels. The tale quickly brings up the drunkard's inner life as we follow down-and-out John Morley's interior monologue. Through this device, Stowe begins her temperance tale with the unlikely ploy of implicitly mocking, through Morley's thoughts, temperance priggishness and condescension. We learn that Morley has not touched a drop of liquor for a whole year, and is then fired for going off on a "spree." "And now just because I fell once I'm kicked out!" laments Morley. "No use to try. When a fellow once trips, everybody gives him a kick. Talk about love of Christ! Who believes it? Don't see much love of Christ where I go. Your Christians hit a fellow that's down as hard as anybody" (14: 238). The subtext here is directed, of course, not at the intemperate, nor at religion as such, but at the respectable and sober from one of their own flock, the celebrated author herself.

Stowe also challenges the drunkard-bashing found in many other temperance tales: "We have heard much about the sufferings of the wives and children of men who are overtaken with drink; but what is not so well understood is the sufferings of the men themselves in their sober moments, when they feel that they are becoming a curse to all that are dearest to them" (14: 245). With these words, Stowe encapsulates the drift of this particular tale, and echoes her interest in the addict's inner life and motivations for drinking that we saw in such characters as Cassy in *Uncle Tom's Cabin* and Bolton in *My Wife and I* and *We and Our Neighbors.*

The tale's resolution, however, is disappointingly facile. Contemplating suicide, Morley hears a hymn from a nearby prayer meeting, joins the meeting, hears a sermon on Christ as savior, and rushes home a changed man. In Stowe's words, "He passed the drinking-saloon without a thought or wish of drinking. The expulsive force of a new emotion had for the time driven out all temptation. Raised above weakness, he thought only of this Jesus, this Saviour from sin, who he now believed had followed him and found him, and he longed to go home and tell his wife what great things the Lord had done for him" (14: 218). Published *after* the Bolton novels, "Betty's Bright Idea" remains silent about alcoholism as a disease, seeming instead to typify the notion of conquering addiction *solely* through religion that Stowe explicitly rejects in discussing Bolton. Even her conviction that alcoholism was a disease could not destroy Stowe's lasting faith in religion's miraculous power.

Deracialized Discourse

Temperance and Racial Ambiguity in Harper's "The Two Offers" and *Sowing and Reaping*

☙ Debra J. Rosenthal

Frances E. W. Harper's short story "The Two Offers" (1859) and novel *Sowing and Reaping: A Temperance Story* (1876–77) are works written by a black woman, serialized in black journals for black readers, yet they avoid any mention of race. In Harper's novels *Minnie's Sacrifice* (1869), *Trial and Triumph* (1888–89) (both serialized in the African Methodist Episcopal Church journal *Christian Recorder*), and *Iola Leroy* (1892), African American characters figure predominantly. Yet characters in "The Two Offers" and *Sowing and Reaping* are not marked as either black or white. In an era when African American writers pledged their talents to the abolition cause and other aspects of black uplift, the deracialized discourse of "The Two Offers" and *Sowing and Reaping* stands in curious contrast to its contemporaries. This renunciation of racial difference questions the role of race in reading the novel and critical assumptions about color that we as readers bring to the text. Most significant to this essay, Harper's deracialized discourse facilitates the reform ambitions of antialcohol literature.

Given the notable lack of blackness or whiteness in "The Two Offers" and *Sowing and Reaping*, race seems to be unimportant. The vast majority of antebellum or Reconstruction novels, written by white authors, presume characters' whiteness.[1] Readers open the works of Thoreau, Alcott, Poe, Hawthorne, Howells, James, and others, confident that the heroes and heroines are white, unless of course the novel treats the tragic mulatta stereotype. These novels seem "raceless" since the assumption of whiteness is so pervasive that race is never acknowledged. Black novelists, however, do not assume this default whiteness; instead, they generally create characters recognized as black.

The novels of such writers as William Wells Brown, Harriet Jacobs, Harriet Wilson, and Pauline Hopkins are peopled with black protagonists, and the subject of race is a central narrative concern. Harper's deracialized discourse thus challenges our critical readerly assumptions of race—that characters are white unless otherwise indicated. By including in her other novels racial markers to signal whiteness or blackness, Harper creates interpretive dilemmas of embodiment when she portrays characters as racially indeterminate.

As late-twentieth-century readers consumed with issues of race, we note this ambiguous suspended discourse. This apparent game of fill-in-the-gap, when combined with an American racism that presumes respectable middle-class characters to be white, makes us hesitate to read the novel as black. In her work on racial discourse and the law, Patricia J. Williams investigates "how the blind application of principles of neutrality, through the device of omission . . . make[s] the reader participate in old habits of cultural bias."[2] In other words, the equalizing ambition of race neutrality undermines its democratic potential by reinforcing the reader's bias of assuming a baseline whiteness. Williams further interprets race neutrality as a "suppression, an institutionalization of psychic taboos." Following Williams's terms, Harper's deracialized discourse could be said to suppress difference, thus veiling the presence of black identity in American literature and creating what Williams calls an "invisible black, a phantom black."[3]

Emma Dunham Kelley also wrote a novel with racially unmarked characters who at first glance seem white—the narrative describes the female characters' light hair and fair skin. *Megda* (1891) was published in Boston with a frontispiece photo of the author, clearly an African American woman, but the characters could easily be Caucasian. *Megda* stands apart from two other works by black women published a year later—Harper's *Iola Leroy* and Anna Julia Cooper's *A Voice from the South*—because *Megda* is not a novel of social protest. These other two works advocate racial equality and uplift, but Kelley's novel barely mentions race. Although Megda and her circle could be white, the novel simultaneously tempts the reader to interpret the characters as black: Megda's brother has dark skin, and the novel's locale is modeled on the black bourgeoisie town of Oak Bluffs, Massachusetts.[4]

This tension between Harper's career, which was devoted to black distinction, and the racelessness of "The Two Offers" and *Sowing and Reaping* questions the relationship between writer and reader. If author-audience ties abide by affiliations of race, then color may determine who reads and misreads the texts. Possibly Harper modulated her stories to suit her audience. For example, in her best-known novel, *Iola Leroy*, Harper targets a wider audience of both races. In her "Note" to that novel she writes that her express goal is to inspire blacks and to "awaken" in whites "a stronger sense of justice and a more Christlike humanity towards blacks."[5] Aimed at blacks who had yet to see positive literary role models and at whites who enjoyed sentimental novels,[6] *Iola Leroy* illustrates Deborah McDowell's distinctions between public and private readership because the novel addresses concerns both inside and outside the black community. To garner support from her white women readers, Harper wrote in a way that stylistically and aesthetically appealed to white "social and literary expectations."[7]

Perhaps Harper's readers understood the elision of blackness in "The Two Offers" and *Sowing and Reaping* differently and recognized that she was not silencing or slighting her heritage. While Harper aimed *Iola Leroy* at a mixed-race audience, she wrote "The Two Offers" and her three other novels specifically for black readers. These three novels, *Minnie's Sacrifice* (1869), *Sowing and Reaping: A Temperance Story* (1876–77), and *Trial and Triumph* (1888–89) were all serialized in the African Methodist Episcopal Church's journal, the *Christian Recorder*.[8] Publication of these novels in the Afro-Protestant press evidences a substantial African American reading population: 86 percent of black Bostonians were literate in 1850, and 92 percent by 1860.[9] "The Two Offers," considered the first short story published by an African American, likewise appeared in a journal that appealed specifically to black Americans, the *Anglo-African*. The *Anglo-African* instructed and inspired black readers, and committed itself to printing "the products of the pens of colored men and women."[10]

Since the type of publication influences certain assumptions readers can make, readers of the Afro-Protestant press probably did not find the deracialized discourse curious, but instead assumed Harper's characters to be black. By giving the rhetorical figuration of racial ambiguity the interpretive meaning of "black," readers would have found the normalizing of blackness to be empowering and the departure from the "black-as-victim-of-racism-and-discrimination"[11] characterization to be confirming. Assuming a default black identity also releases the writer from the burden of race: Harper was free not to focus on contentious issues of race but could instead center her attention on the institution of marriage and on her moral reform project of temperance.[12] The racial uncertainty of "The Two Offers," *Sowing and Reaping*, and *Megda* could offer an additional liberating possibility since they "speak about and to African Americans themselves,"[13] and "reflect some of the ambivalence that an upwardly mobile group of mixed-race people might experience when representing themselves to the outside world—or, for that matter, to each other."[14] Such self-reflection as the norm or default race removes the black experience from the realm of the invisible and returns black Americans to the center, where the triumphs and foibles of personhood are more important than surface skin color.

Harper's deracialized discourse appropriates and politicizes the raceless conventions of white-authored novels. Because Harper is race-conscious and progressive in her other writings, her emptying this temperance fiction of racial markers serves specific purposes and aligns her thinking with some of the most radical assimilation discourse of her day. While conservative antislavery proponents, such as colonizationists and separatist abolitionists, called for a separation of blacks and whites, more radical figures such as Frederick Douglass called for racial integration. As a black woman appropriating and claiming for blacks a discourse traditionally understood to be white, Harper implicitly advocates an assimilationist agenda by absorbing one discourse into another.[15]

The racelessness of these works and their implied normalizing of black identity posits a progressive credo that contrasts with the conservative dogma of the temperance movement. The dual narrative tensions between liberally resisting racial stereotypes while encouraging a conservative resistance to drink is paralleled in temperance literature's generic tension between its aim to unbind drunkards from the bottle and its method of achieving this aim through the binds of self-limiting reform. These opposite narrative pulls are partially resolved by Harper's belief that if African Americans' "talents are to be recognized we must write less of issues that are particular and more of feelings that are general."[16] To that end, Harper devoted energy to writing about such racially transcendent afflictions as intoxication, in addition to such race-specific problems as slavery and the quest for freedom.

Harper's temperance writings that normalize blackness smooth the narrative tensions between coextensive progressive and conservative discourses by showing both to be a search for middle-class respectability. Temperance fiction portrays individual decorum suppressed by besottedness; those who remain sober or regain sobriety achieve a level of dignity. The racial ambiguity in "The Two Offers" and *Sowing and Reaping*, which suggests that characters who could be black lead lives indistinguishable from those of white Americans, indicates that middle-class respectability is a right in itself. The deracialized discourse signals that blacks have just as much entitlement and ability as whites to circulate in brilliant society and be concerned with moral reform.

Harper's Temperance Poetry

Years before the appearance of *Sowing and Reaping*, Harper expressed her interest in temperance in poetry. Her temperance poems were published in volumes of her verse, not in a black publication such as the *Christian Recorder.* Many of the other poems in the volumes were abolitionist verses, thus continuing Harper's concern with political action and social reform. Harper's aims aligned with those of other black leaders who hoped that moral suasion would lead to temperance, abolition, and the absence of prejudice.[17] Yet many temperance poems suggest the race of the poetic personae and therefore seem directed to a targeted audience. For example, in "The Drunkard's Child," the alcoholic's dying boy has "golden curls" and a "marble brow."[18] The male persona in "Signing the Pledge" vows that his son, "With brow so fair and mild," will not be called a drunkard's child, and never will the boy's "young face / Whiten with grief and dread" at his father's inebriation.[19] Two of Harper's temperance poems implore women to marry a temperate man; I will return to this strategy of twinning romance and social action. These two poems are racially marked, one signifying white and the other black: in "The Contrast," the "fair" bride becomes "pale" when she realizes she married an alcoholic.[20] But the narrating voice of "Advice to Girls" contains adjectives that Harper uses to describe African Americans, urging young women to judge a man carefully and not fall in love with his "raven hair or flashing eyes."

While these poems rhetorically signal race-specific personae and appeal to such readers, other poems lean on a deracialized discourse, thus posing interpretive uncertainties. For example, poems like "Nothing and Something," "The Fatal Pledge," and "Save the Boys" make no mention of race. Through moral persuasion the poems try to win readers to the temperance cause. A typical stanza reads, ". . . by the wine-cup's ruddy glow / I traced a path to shame and woe. . . . The cup allures and then destroys. / Oh! from its thraldom save the boys."[21] In these poems, as in her novel *Sowing and Reaping*, Harper omits black or white signifiers.

Harper's Temperance Fiction

As temperance fiction, "The Two Offers" and *Sowing and Reaping* are part of Harper's lifelong commitment to the antialcohol movement. "The Two Offers" presents the dilemma of Laura Lagrange, an heiress who receives two requests for her hand in marriage. Her poor cousin, Janette Alston, advises

Laura to refuse both on the grounds that it is better to remain an old maid than to marry a man simply because he makes a good offer. Laura heedlessly marries a drunkard whose lack of affection drives her to an early grave. Janette prevails into old age as a single woman. Heavily didactic, the plot of *Sowing and Reaping* is similar to contemporaneous temperance novels: characters must decide between temptation and sobriety, and those who distance themselves from alcohol and take the temperance pledge are rewarded. The novel focuses on two cousins, Belle Gordon and Jeanette Roland, who live in an unnamed northern city. Belle is courted by the wealthy Charles Romaine, but refuses him because she disdains his drinking habit. Instead, she marries the poorer, but temperate, Paul Clifford and lives happily ever after with him, working together for the temperance cause. Jeanette marries Charles Romaine, who leads her into a life of misery through his inebriation. He finally passes out and dies in the street.

As temperance texts concerned with domesticity, "The Two Offers" and *Sowing and Reaping* aim to elevate the moral and ethical precepts of readers by instructing women on the importance of marrying a temperate man, by positively influencing husbands and children, and by encouraging drunkards to sign the temperance pledge. The story's and novel's unflagging moralizing is common to Harper's other works concerned with racial uplift, but the deracialized discourse of "The Two Offers" and *Sowing and Reaping* stands in contrast to *Iola Leroy*, which is critical of white temperance workers who solicit the black vote, and which portrays grog shops as a trick by whites to keep blacks poor and ignorant. These themes echo Harper's work as the head of the colored division of the Women's Christian Temperance Union. Other northern black leaders also championed the temperance cause as a key to social improvement and a means of channeling blacks' energy and money in more productive directions.[22]

"The Two Offers" and *Sowing and Reaping* diverge from most white-authored temperance novels in that they do not resort to the dark-temperance mode that marks the writings of moral fictionists who gleefully detail the horrific depravity of drunkenness. Although the temperance genre began in the 1820s with didactic tracts, it became more and more sensational and subversive, with readers eager to read about the degeneracy and wickedness they supposedly protested. There are two scenes that teeter on the sensational in *Sowing and Reaping*: in one, a poor woman whom Belle aids recounts how her husband, desperate for money to buy alcohol, threatens her with scissors and cuts off her hair to sell. But this scene is reported to the readers by the woman;

we do not experience the terror as it happens. In the second scene, at the end of the novel, we see Charles Romaine, despairing for a drink, running wildly to saloons and quivering with excitement and anguish as he slakes his thirst, only to slip on the ice and die in the cold street. Yet this scene is brief and is notable more for the psychological insight into Charles's pathetic state than for any illicit thrill it might evoke in the reader. Far from titillating, Harper's style in *Sowing and Reaping* remains didactic and dedicated to her cause of social and political uplift.

Politically, Harper was marginalized by white women's temperance and suffrage organizations. For seven years she served as chair of the "Colored Chapter" of the Philadelphia and Pennsylvania Women's Christian Temperance Union.[23] Harper disagreed with Elizabeth Cady Stanton and Susan B. Anthony, who opposed giving black women the vote.[24] In *Sowing and Reaping*, Harper urges women to campaign for their voting rights in order to further the temperance cause. When one woman character asserts that she has as many rights as she wants, that she is content to let her father and brothers vote for her, and that she fears the drunken crowd of men at the polling booth, the character Mrs. Gladstone retorts that women, taxed without representation, need power. And, most important to the novel, with suffrage rights women can vote for prohibition or to close saloons. As Mrs. Gladstone says, men "refuse to let us vote and yet fail to protect our homes from the ravages of rum."[25] The power of women's temperance crusades is evident in saloon owner John Anderson's lament that "this crusading has made quite a hole in my business," and that it has "affected the revenue of the state" (167). Again, the deracialized discourse makes it wholly plausible that Harper is advocating the vote for black women.

Just as she hoped to change society's acceptance of drinking, Harper hoped to change radically society's perceptions of black women by replacing images of them as passive and sexually exploited with images of strong and intelligent figures. To counteract the negative descriptions of blacks in Thomas Nelson Page's novels and in Joel Chandler Harris's Uncle Remus stories, black novelists often accorded their mulatta characters such attributes as virtue, intelligence, and idealized white beauty.[26] Because of the long history of debased images of black women, Deborah McDowell argues that "black women novelists have assumed throughout their tradition a revisionist mission aimed at substituting reality for stereotype."[27] But often writers trying to break the mold of negatively stereotyped black characters have been criticized for creating new stereotypes that present equally flat, overly idealized characters.[28] For example, Harper was faulted for her assimilationist views, for portraying the black middle class as mulattos, and for creating light-skinned black characters in order to appeal to white readers.

The character of the light-skinned mulatta appealed both to white audiences who saw her as a fallen white woman, and to black readers who could identify with the prejudice leveled against her. The mulatta is a "narrative device of mediation" who explores and expresses the relationships between the races, as well as a figure that acts, in Hazel Carby's words, "as a literary displacement of the actual increasing separation of the races."[29] Harper uses light-skinned blacks and racially unmarked characters to appeal to black and white readers as well as to urge black betterment by depicting African Americans leading middle-class lives indistinguishable from those of whites. The deracialized discourse of "The Two Offers" and *Sowing and Reaping* participates in this project by depicting to a black readership racially indeterminate characters engaged in social and moral elevation. Because of the novel's authorship and appearance in the Afro-Protestant press, we do not readily assume a default whiteness; therefore the intelligent, prosperous, honorable characters defy easy stereotyping.

Harper's romantic marriage plots further politicize her novels even as they appeal to her readers' warm sentiments. Harper's mix of politics and romance supports Jane Tompkins's argument about the inherently political nature of sentimental novels. Tompkins charges that the sentimental novel is "complex and significant in ways *other than* those that characterize the established masterpieces" and that it is "a political enterprise, halfway between sermon and social theory, that both codifies and attempts to mold the values of its time."[30] Because nineteenth-century black women's texts focused on marriage, they were less valued than black men's, and were thus disparagingly deemed "sentimental." Men's texts, such as Frederick Douglass's *Narrative* and Richard Wright's *Black Boy*, were perceived as focusing on more "important" subjects such as the escape to freedom, and were thus more highly regarded.[31] Although a marriage plot may stand as the antithesis to a freedom plot so cherished by male writers, the civil right to marry, denied to slaves, was as important to newly emancipated slaves as was the right to vote. To participate fully in American culture and society, blacks insisted on the right to vote (although for men only) and the right to marry, which constituted "twin indexes for measuring how black people collectively viewed their civil liberties."[32]

The vehicle of the temperance novel permitted Harper to attack the injustice of women's dependence on an intemperate husband. The saloon pulled men away from their families to establish a male domain that excluded women and children.[33] In the eighteenth century, drinking was a community event used to mark celebrations and to repay for help with occasions such as the harvest and house raising.[34] In the nineteenth century, drink became masculinized as it moved from the home to the tavern.[35] Temperance literature therefore allowed women writers to foray into the male world to criticize it.

With this in mind, the marriage and temperance plots of "The Two Offers" and *Sowing and Reaping* are mutually constitutive: both value women's autonomy to choose a temperate husband because being beholden to a drunkard replicates the condition of bondage to a cruel master. Since nineteenth-century women were dependent on men, many temperance stories, including "The Two Offers" and *Sowing and Reaping*, contrast the devastation and loneliness of the drunkard's family with the happiness and security of the temperate man's family.[36] Some young women members of the WCTU even pledged to marry only abstainers: "Lips that have touched liquor shall never touch mine."[37]

Temperance Fiction and Deracialized Discourse

The deracialized discourse of "The Two Offers" and *Sowing and Reaping* is intricately connected to the temperance concerns of these works, and serves to make radical claims for the position of the black American in the nineteenth-century literary imagination. In "The Two Offers," the unmarried Janette finds satisfaction in life, achieves a degree of success in her writing, and devotes herself to abolition. Through these worthy accomplishments, Janette learns "one of life's most precious lessons, that true happiness consists not so much in the fruition of our wishes as in the regulation of desires and the full development and right culture of our whole natures."[38] This temperance theme ramifies to other aspects of life to conclude the story with an image of an old unmarried woman content with her life. Were this woman black, "The Two Offers" powerfully suggests that black women do not need to rely on marriage for happiness, and that single black women, applying the principles of moderation espoused by the temperance movement, can cultivate meaningful lives.

A deracialized discourse combined with temperance themes places black men in an exceptional position of strength in *Sowing and Reaping*. In most nineteenth-century texts, the narrative figure of the father who wields patriarchal control is represented by a white man who denies such power to black men.[39] In *Sowing and Reaping*, Belle ministers to Mary Gough and her husband Joe, a drunken father weakened physically, financially, and spiritually by alcohol. Yet Joe Gough wields narrative control because the aim of the temperance text is to bring the drunkard to sobriety, thereby reinstating his authority. Through Belle's efforts, Joe takes the temperance pledge, secures a job, and regains patriarchal control. As opposed to slave narratives that portray black men being beaten down, *Sowing and Reaping*'s racially ambiguous discourse presents to readers a society rallying to restore the respect and power of a man who can be interpreted as black. As a text authored by a black woman, *Sowing and Reaping* also suggests that black women view black men as peers, and that wives benefit by helping their husbands to achieve sobriety.

In many ways, then, "The Two Offers" and *Sowing and Reaping* are about identity and alcohol consumption. The deracialized discourse presents a cipher for interpreting the racial identity of Harper's characters. Through moral suasion the short story and novel proffer a utopian vision, for alcoholism equally affects blacks and whites and therefore levels the difference between the races. In an 1891 issue of the *A.M.E. Church Review*, Harper asserted that as "bad as was American slavery the slavery of intemperance is worse. Slavery was the enemy of one section, the oppressor of one race, but intemperance is the curse of every land and the deadly foe of every kindred, tribe and race."[40] In an essay on the WCTU and black women, Harper wrote that after Emancipation, "it was found that an enemy, old and strong and deceptive, was warring against the best interests of society; not simply an enemy to one race, but an enemy to all races."[41] Because the temperance movement recognizes and addresses the downfalls and vulnerabilities of all alcoholics, the deracialized discourse of temperance in the novel points to a shared identity between black and white and a common goal of achieving middle-class respectability, thereby radically suggesting communality between the races.

Notes

1. William J. Scheick also noted the lack of concern about racial issues in "The Two Offers," but he assumes the heroines are white. See his "Strategic Ellipsis in Harper's 'The Two Offers,'" *Southern Literary Journal* 23.2 (Spring 1991): 14–18.

2. Patricia J. Williams, *The Alchemy of Race and Rights* (Cambridge, MA: Harvard UP, 1991), 48.

3. Ibid., 119.

4. Molly Hite, "Introduction," Emma Dunham Kelley, *Megda* (New York: Oxford UP, 1988), xxvii–xxx.

5. Frances E. W. Harper, *Iola Leroy, or Shadows Uplifted* (Boston: Beacon, 1987), 282.

6. Marilyn Elkins, "Reading Beyond the Conventions: A Look at Frances E. W. Har-

per's *Iola Leroy, or Shadows Uplifted*," *American Literary Realism, 1870–1910* 22.2 (Winter 1990): 45.

7. Deborah McDowell, " 'The Changing Same': Generational Connections and Black Women Novelists," *New Literary History* 18.2 (Winter 1987): 287.

8. The Protestant church vigorously opposed the use of alcohol and was instrumental in promoting temperance among American blacks. At its 1896 general conference, the A.M.E. Church adopted a set of resolutions strongly discouraging the use of alcoholic beverages. See Denise Herd, "Ambiguity in Black Drinking Norms: An Ethnohistorical Interpretation," in *The American Experience with Alcohol: Contrasting Cultural Perspectives*, ed. Linda A. Bennett and Genevieve M. Ames (New York: Plenum P, 1985), 157–58.

9. Frances Smith Foster, "Introduction," Frances E. W. Harper, *Minnie's Sacrifice, Sowing and Reaping, Trial and Triumph: Three Rediscovered Novels by Frances E. W. Harper*, ed. Frances Smith Foster (Boston: Beacon, 1994), xxi.

10. Quoted in Frances Smith Foster, ed., *A Brighter Coming Day: A Frances Ellen Watkins Harper Reader* (New York: Feminist P, 1990), 105.

11. Foster, "Introduction," *Minnie's Sacrifice*, xxviii.

12. Elizabeth Ammons, "*Legacy* Profile: Frances Ellen Watkins Harper," *Legacy* 2.1 (Fall 1985): 63.

13. Foster, "Introduction," *Minnie's Sacrifice*, xxviii.

14. Hite, "Introduction," *Megda*, xxxi.

15. I thank David S. Reynolds for reminding me of the importance of this historical context.

16. J. Saunders Redding, *To Make a Poet Black* (New York: McGrath, 1968), 39; quoted in *Twentieth Century Literary Criticism*, vol. 14, Dennis Poupard and James E. Person, Jr., eds. (Detroit: Gale, 1984), 257.

17. Donald Yacovone, "The Transformation of the Black Temperance Movement, 1827–1854: An Interpretation," *Journal of the Early Republic* 8 (Fall 1988): 284.

18. Frances E. W. Harper, "The Drunkard's Child," in Foster, *A Brighter Coming Day*, 64.

19. Frances E. W. Harper, "Signing the Pledge," in Foster, *A Brighter Coming Day*, 256.

20. Frances E. W. Harper, "The Contrast," in Foster, *A Brighter Coming Day*, 73.

21. Frances E. W. Harper, "Save the Boys," in Foster, *A Brighter Coming Day*, 250–51.

22. Jane H. Pease and William H. Pease, *They Who Would Be Free: Blacks' Search for Freedom, 1830–1864* (New York: Atheneum, 1974), 124, 126.

23. Foster, "Introduction," *A Brighter Coming Day*, 21.

24. Hazel Carby, *Reconstructing Womanhood: The Emergence of the Afro-American Woman Novelist* (NY: Oxford UP, 1987), 67.

25. Frances E. W. Harper, *Sowing and Reaping: A Temperance Story*, in *Minnie's Sacrifice, Sowing and Reaping, Trial and Triumph: Three Rediscovered Novels by Frances E. W. Harper*, ed. Frances Smith Foster (Boston: Beacon, 1994), 162.

26. Vashti Lewis, "The Near-White Female in Frances Ellen Watkins Harper's *Iola Leroy*," *Phylon: A Review of Race and Culture* 45.4 (Winter 1984): 314–22.

27. McDowell, " 'The Changing Same,' " 284.

28. Ibid.

29. Carby, *Reconstructing*, 89, 90.

30. Jane Tompkins, *Sensational Designs: The Cultural Work of American Fiction, 1790–1860* (New York: Oxford UP, 1985), 126.

31. Claudia Tate, "Allegories of Black Female Desire; or, Rereading Nineteenth-Century Sentimental Narratives of Black Female Authority," in *Changing Our Own Words: Essays on Criticism, Theory, and Writing by Black Women*, ed. Cheryl Wall (New Brunswick, Rutgers UP, 1989).

32. Ibid., 103.

33. Barbara Leslie Epstein, *The Politics of Domesticity: Women, Evangelism, and Temperance in Nineteenth-Century America* (Middletown, CT: Wesleyan UP, 1986), 106.

34. Ian R. Tyrell, *Sobering Up: From Temperance to Prohibition in Antebellum America, 1800–1860* (Westport, CT: Greenwood P, 1979), 20.

35. Epstein, *Domesticity*, 108.

36. Ibid., 105.

37. Joseph R. Gusfield, *Symbolic Crusade: Status Politics and the American Temperance Movement* (Urbana: U of Illinois P, 1963), 85.

38. Frances Ellen Watkins Harper, "The Two Offers" [1859], in Foster, *A Brighter Coming Day*, 114.

39. Hazel V. Carby, " 'On the Threshold of Woman's Era': Lynching, Empire, and Sexuality in Black Feminist Theory," in Henry Louis Gates, Jr., ed., *"Race," Writing, and Difference* (Chicago: U of Chicago P, 1986), 315.

40. Frances Harper, "Temperance," *A.M.E. Church Review* 7 (1891): 373. Cited in Melba Joyce Boyd, *Discarded Legacy: Politics and Poetics in the Life of Frances E. W. Harper, 1825–1911* (Detroit: Wayne State UP, 1994), 75.

41. Frances E. W. Harper, "The Women's Christian Temperance Union and the Colored Woman," in Foster, *A Brighter Coming Day*, 281.

"Alcoholism" and The Modern Temper

✍ John W. Crowley

IN DEFINING "THE MODERN TEMPER" OF HIS PREMATURELY JADED contemporaries, Joseph Wood Krutch outlined in 1929 a dark vision of the dehumanized new world in which "man must henceforth live if he lives at all." Painfully aware of its predicament, this Lost Generation had "awakened to the fact that both the ends which its fathers proposed to themselves and the emotions from which they drew their strength seem irrelevant and remote." For Krutch, the epitome of "The Modern Temper" was T. S. Eliot in his "bleak, tortuous complexities": "Here disgust speaks with a robust voice and denunciation is confident, but ecstasy, flickering and uncertain, leaps fitfully up only to sink back among the cinders." Thoreau's "quiet desperation" defined the intellectual's status quo; "and the more highly developed the reflective powers of the individual," the more likely was quiet desperation to become "an active rebellion which expresses itself in self-regarding vices."[1]

The chief modernist vice was habitual drunkenness. Donald W. Goodwin has convincingly argued that the modernists—the white males especially— were a decidedly drunken lot: "well-known writers in America during the first half of the twentieth century were extraordinarily susceptible to the disease called alcoholism." Within this group, alcoholism was nothing short of "epidemic," in fact. "What is hard," says Goodwin, "is to think of *non*alcoholics among American writers of the twentieth century."[2] Robin Room likewise finds "a clear association of problematic drunkenness not only with American writers, but with a particular generational cohort that came of age in 1909– 1921."[3]

The attitudes of the Lost Generation, those children of the century who believed they had come too soon into a world too old, were formed as much by growing up in the heyday of Prohibition as by living through the Great War.

Both experiences bred deep skepticism about the wisdom and integrity of the elders and provoked rebellion against authority that exceeded the ordinary friction between generations. Simply because it became illicit, drinking possessed a singular importance; drinking in defiance of Prohibition was a sign of solidarity with the rising generation's resistance to what it called "Puritanism" and to what it deemed to be the oppression of bourgeois American life.

As A. J. Liebling recalled, his contemporaries felt a particular "reverence for strong drink" because, for them, liquor was both "the symbol of a sacred cause" and a "self-righteous pleasure": "Drinking, we proved to ourselves our freedom as individuals and flouted Congress. . . . It was the only period during which a fellow could be smug and slopped concurrently."[4] Prohibition thus inspired a perverse reaction from those, in revolt from their native villages, who stormed Greenwich Village, capital of the old American Bohemia. "Its effect upon the intellectual life was severe: from being a mild accompaniment to dining and conversation, alcohol became almost a primary and constant necessity."[5]

One suggestive sign of a generational shift in American attitudes toward drinking was the proliferation of terms for drunkenness. By 1927, Edmund Wilson had collected over a hundred of them, noting that the "vocabulary of social drinking . . . seems to have become especially rich: one gets the impression that more nuances are nowadays discriminated than was the case before Prohibition. Thus, *fried*, *stewed*, and *boiled* all convey distinctly different ideas; and *cock-eyed*, *plastered*, *owled*, *embalmed*, and *ossified* evoke quite different images." It was significant, Wilson thought, that as new terms were coming into vogue, some of the old ones were falling out of use. Fewer persons, it seemed, were going on "*sprees*, *toots*, *tears*, *jags*, *bats*, *brannigans* or *benders*," perhaps because such words suggested "not merely extreme drunkenness, but also an exceptional occurrence, a breaking away by the drinker from the conditions of his normal life." Wilson speculated that the disappearance of these terms reflected "the fact that this kind of fierce protracted drinking has now become universal, an accepted feature of social life instead of a disreputable escapade."[6]

Writing for an audience of liberal intellectuals in *The New Republic*, Wilson was overgeneralizing. Fierce and protracted drinking—or even ordinary drinking, for that matter—was far from "universal" under Prohibition. As might have been expected, despite the wholesale failure of enforcement, the consumption of alcohol declined overall during the 1920s. At the same time, however, it increased among young and educated city dwellers, in whose sophisticated circles heavy drinking was not merely tolerated, but actively encouraged. As Room points out, this group came to maturity when "temperance had become a majority sentiment in the country at large and a sentiment associated by and large with conservative or reactionary political forces." In such circumstances, drunkenness could be construed as "an act of political dissent."

Room also observes that drinking among some members of the Lost Generation was an act of cultural reaffiliation. Those who migrated to Paris tended to adopt the drinking habits of a country that had "the highest recorded per capita alcohol consumption in the world"; they also followed the French tradition in which intoxication was closely tied to political radicalism and the artistic avant-garde.[7]

The commercial success of a few novels during the 1920s—notably F. Scott Fitzgerald's *This Side of Paradise* (1920) and Ernest Hemingway's *The Sun Also Rises* (1926)—magnified the Lost Generation's influence on American culture. Alfred Kazin notes that one key element of "the great changeover from the old rural and small-town America" during this period was "the triumph in the marketplace of 'advanced,' wholly 'modern' writers and books, ideas, and attitudes"—which made heavy drinking stylish and created an enduring association between modernism and alcoholism. Booze came "to seem a natural accompaniment of the literary life—of its loneliness, its creative aspirations and its frenzies, its 'specialness,' its hazards in a society where values are constantly put in money terms."[8]

Jack London was perhaps the first American writer to drink in the modern spirit; and in *John Barleycorn* (1913), he helped to create the cultural climate for "advanced" ideas. *John Barleycorn* suggests that The Modern Temper itself may have been one by-product of the "epidemic" of alcoholism among writers and intellectuals early in the twentieth century. For even as London celebrates an ideology of despair, in part by emphasizing the "manliness" required to espouse it, he acknowledges an epistemological dilemma. Does alcohol merely unveil what is otherwise hidden from common view? Or, rather, does alcohol itself produce the "pitiless, spectral syllogisms"? " 'Temperamentally I am wholesome-hearted and merry,' " London observes of himself. " 'Yet when I walk with John Barleycorn I suffer all the damnation of intellectual pessimism.' " It is the curse of the White Logic—"the argent messenger of truth beyond truth, the antithesis of life, cruel and bleak as interstellar space, pulseless and frozen as absolute zero, dazzling with the frost of irrefragable logic and unforgettable fact"—that blights the dreams of the dreamer and compels him to cry out, "as in 'The City of Dreadful Night': 'Our life's a cheat, our death a black abyss.'" Then, in vain hope of relief from the "sickness of pessimism, caused by drink," the victim "must drink further in quest of the anodyne that John Barleycorn promises but never delivers."[9]

If alcohol in its physical, psychological, and spiritual impact on so many writers was not solely responsible for The Modern Temper, then it was certainly inseparable from the modernist ideology of despair—what Saul Bellow once called "The Thinking Man's Waste Land." Bellow complained in 1965 that American literature had been dominated too long and too uncritically by a tradition in which the "alienation" of the artist is "accompanied by the more or less conscious acceptance of a theory of modern civilization." According to this theory, "modern mass society is frightful, brutal, hostile to whatever is pure in the human spirit, a waste land and a horror. To its ugliness, its bureaucratic regiments, its thefts, its lies, its wars, and its cruelties, the artist can never be reconciled."[10]

The horrors of modern life may account, perhaps, for the Waste Land mentality of so much modernist literature. But this ideology of despair was propagated largely under the influence of alcohol: by writers for whom writing and drinking were conjoined. Many Americans of the Lost Generation who bellied up to the bars of Paris or frequented the speakeasies back home came to believe that ardent spirits and artistic inspiration went hand in glove. In communion with the White Logic, these writers fashioned a literature steeped in what Donald Newlove calls "the authentic rhetoric of the true drunk, its shadow and ironies, universal overcast, the last red dingdong of doom breaking ecstatically over a dying landscape."[11]

The modernist understanding of alcoholism derived from the medicalized model of "inebriation" that was constructed by psychiatrists and physicians during the nineteenth century. In fact, two competing concepts of habitual drunkenness coexisted throughout the nineteenth century. According to Harry Gene Levine, the older paradigm, dating from colonial times, held that because "there was nothing inherent in either the individual or the substance which prevented someone from drinking moderately," a person had "final control" over the intake of alcohol: "Drunkenness was a choice, albeit a sinful one, which some individuals made." This moral paradigm of "intemperance" as a sin was gradually overshadowed by the medical idea of "inebriation" as an addiction: "a sort of disease of the will, an inability to prevent oneself from drinking." The "disease" model, often traced to Benjamin Rush's influential Inquiry into the

Effects of Ardent Spirits upon the Human Body and Mind (1784), posited "that habitual drunkards are alcohol addicts, persons who have lost control over their drinking and who must abstain entirely from alcohol."[12]

The emergent medical paradigm, which was deeply influential within the temperance movement, fostered a sympathetic attitude toward drunkards and gave rise to reformist attempts to save them from their powerlessness over alcohol, now thought by some to be inevitably addicting. But habitual drunkenness was never entirely freed from moral stigma. In the nineteenth-century disease model, insofar as intemperance was linked to attenuated willpower, addiction was not located exclusively in the substance; it was inseparable from defective "character," for the proper building of which Victorians held each other morally accountable. Of the confluence of moral and medical values in the idea of "inebriation," Virginia Berridge and Griffith Edwards remark: "Moral values were inserted into this apparently 'natural' and 'autonomous' disease entity. Addiction, clearly not simply a physical disease entity, was a 'disease of the will.' It was disease *and* vice." An addict's moral weakness, then, was an important causal element: "the disease was defined in terms of 'moral bankruptcy,' 'a form of moral infirmity,' terms deriving from similar formulations in insanity."[13]

"Inebriation" (or "inebriety") covered addiction both to alcohol and to other drugs as well. "Alcoholism," the strict connotations of which were more narrowly clinical in Victorian than in modern usage, referred to the long-term physical consequences of alcohol addiction. "Alcoholism" in this sense was more or less synonymous with "dipsomania," another medical term. By the early twentieth century, however, "alcoholism" was being used more loosely to refer to habitual drunkenness; and in this sense it was more or less synonymous with "intemperance," a term with moral and religious overtones.

The idea of dipsomania as a congenital, "chemical" form of insanity was widely disseminated throughout the later nineteenth century, mainly through the mandatory drug education programs that were initiated in public schools during the 1880s under the aegis of the Women's Christian Temperance Union and other antidrink organizations. A definition from an 1883 textbook designed for such classroom use may be taken as typical of the prevailing view. "Certain writers on diseases of the mind allude especially to a form of insanity called *dipsomania*, in which state a man has a maddening thirst for alcoholic drinks." Dipsomania describes the extreme case of an "appetite for alcoholic liquors" that, according to "some of the best medical authorities," may be "inherited, just as people inherit such diseases as scrofula, gout, or consumption."[14] Within the Social Darwinian framework of such textbooks, the drunkard (or dipso-maniac) is regarded as clinically insane: the defective offspring of degenerate stock. By definition, such a creature is radically different from a "normal" person.

These ideas still had currency early in the twentieth century.[15] In a popular book published just two years after *John Barleycorn*, for example, a journalist identified two different types of the drunkard: "one is morally defective from the start—a moral imbecile of a sort; that was the cause of his taking to drink. The other drunkard had to set up a pathological process which would bring him to the same state of moral imbecility. The one was born to his drunken inheritance, the other prepared himself for it. The one was diseased at the start; the other took his self-appointed way, through vice, to the identical degenera-tive condition of disease."[16] The first type is recognizable as the Victorian "dipsomaniac"; the second as the "alcoholic" in the broader modern sense of the habitual drinker who devolves into a dipsomaniac. Although both ul-timately attain the same "condition of disease," the alcoholic seems more normal; and because he is more normal, he is also held more responsible for his "self-appointed way," his choice of an avoidable vice.

In the Victorian paradigm, "inebriation" was disease *and* vice, dipsomania *and* intemperance. In the modern paradigm, "alcoholism" became less a vice than a disease—and less degrading a disease than dipsomania had been thought to be. In *John Barleycorn*, the conflation of Victorian and modern paradigms and their accompanying terminologies results in some confusion in Jack Lon-don's depiction of the "alcoholic." This term is used inconsistently: sometimes in the clinical Victorian sense as a synonym for *dipsomaniac* (a drunkard through bad heredity), and sometimes in the modern sense (a drunkard through bad habits). London is "no hereditary alcoholic," he says, because he was not born with any "organic, chemical predisposition toward alcohol." He considers himself, therefore, to be "a normal, average man" who drinks "in the normal, average way, as drinking goes." He also regards his drinking as funda-mentally different from an addiction to opiates or tobacco: "Drinking, as I deem it, is practically entirely a habit of mind."[17] *John Barleycorn* traces the incremental progression of this "habit of mind" into a mental obsession—and, in effect, reveals the subtle transformation of a "normal" person into an "alcoholic."

Like London, most of the modernists held views of "alcoholism" that were partly Victorian, partly modern, and thus somewhat contradictory. The con-tradictions have carried over into biography and criticism. Consider, for example, some recent work on Fitzgerald's *Tender Is the Night* (1934), in which Dick Diver's drunken downfall is played out against a backdrop of Spenglerian cultural decline. "It is apparent," Tom Dardis writes, "that Fitzgerald, by using alcohol as both cause *and* effect in the creation of Diver's malaise, was drawing a parallel between his fictional couple and Zelda and himself." Although he does not emphasize Diver's drinking until late in the novel, he nevertheless "permits us to observe that nearly all of Dick's troubles—professional and marital—have alcohol behind them."[18] Against such assertions, Diver might have argued, as Fitzgerald himself once testily remarked: "The assumption that all my troubles are due to drink is a little too easy."[19] This point is well taken for Julie M. Irwin:

> If, as seems incontestable, F. Scott Fitzgerald was an alcoholic and not merely a drunk, what exactly does acceptance of this fact mean for his life, his work, and his literary reputation? We know that alcoholism made Fitzgerald's days hellish and clearly brought about his early death. Yet one mustn't push this too far. Certainly Fitzgerald's alcoholism cannot—ought not—be pressed into service to shoulder all the blame for his downfall. . . . Until some of the basic questions about alcoholism are answered, one cannot know for sure whether, in Fitzgerald's case, the disease was solely to blame or whether it was a combination of the disease and his own weakness of character that brought him down.[20]

This passage exposes the underlying confusion that also characterized Fitzgerald's and other modernists' understanding of habitual drunkenness. In accord with the modern paradigm that emerged in the 1930s and became predominant in the second half of the twentieth century, Irwin assumes that alcoholism is a "disease." But she is uneasy with the disease concept to the extent that its determinism would lift all moral responsibility from the alcoholic's shoulders. In her proscription about what "ought not" be done by critics with the disease model, and in her reference to "blame" and "weakness of character," Irwin betrays a residual adherence to the Victorian paradigm of intemperance that accounts for her otherwise puzzling distinction between Fitzgerald's being "an alcoholic" and his being "merely a drunk."

Or "drunkard"? This old-fashioned term is relevant because Fitzgerald, despite what he learned about the "disease" of alcoholism from Zelda's psychiatrists, never completely cast off the Victorian influences of his youth. "Drunkard" and "alcoholic" were not interchangeable terms for him because he perceived a subtle difference between them. Fitzgerald was repelled by "intemperance" at the same time that he was strangely attracted to "alcoholism"; whereas the former was stigmatized as a vice, the latter was distinguished (in both senses) as a sign of the modern.

"Alcoholic" and "alcoholism" were to become more and more common terms in ordinary American usage, mainly through the success of what historians have called the "Alcoholism Movement" in recasting American attitudes toward habitual drunkenness. Between the 1930s and the 1960s, as Bruce H. Johnson observes, a new consensus took shape as "the traditional moralistic interpretations of this form of deviant behavior were abandoned in favor of a 'scientific' or medical point of view according to which the chronic drunkard is the victim of a physiological or psychological aberration."[21]

This transformation of public opinion was accomplished, with remarkable efficiency, by a relatively small band of dedicated campaigners associated with a trio of allied institutions with overlapping memberships and interlocking purposes: Alcoholics Anonymous, the National Committee for Education on Alcoholism (later renamed the National Council on Alcoholism), and the Yale Center for Studies of Alcohol (later renamed the Yale Center of Alcohol Studies).

During its first decade (1935–1945), Alcoholics Anonymous branched out from its two original groups in New York and Akron, Ohio, to several other cities, and membership rose exponentially from its founding pair (William Griffith Wilson, a.k.a. "Bill W.," and Robert Holbrook Smith, a.k.a. "Dr. Bob") to include a few dozen and then about fifteen thousand persons, nearly all of them white, middle-class men.[22] Thanks in large part to extensive and favorable press coverage, the A.A. fellowship mushroomed to over one hundred thousand members by 1951.

Much of this coverage was generated and orchestrated by Marty Mann, founder of the NCEA, who combined a genius for public relations with an ambition to proselytize for the "disease" concept of alcoholism she had encountered in Alcoholics Anonymous. (Having first joined in 1939, she became the first female member to remain sober.) Although Mann officially dissociated herself and the NCEA from A.A., her mission was to develop the grassroots organization needed to spread the fellowship's message.

The academic wing of the Alcoholism Movement, which revolved around the research center created at Yale by Howard W. Haggard and Elvin Morton Jellinek, maintained a dispassionately scientific distance from the more fervent elements of the coalition. But the goal was much the same: to detach the study and perception of habitual drunkenness from the moral frame of reference associated with temperance and Prohibition.

The planks of the Alcoholism Movement's platform, already nailed down by the late 1930s, were: that alcoholism is an illness rather than a failure of character and, therefore, a medical rather than a moral issue; that treatment of alcoholism is a public health imperative; that, fortunately, complete rehabilitation is possible if the alcoholic is placed in competent hands. In one 1938 magazine article, "an eminent physician" put the weight of medical authority behind the new common sense:

> "Alcoholism," he insists, "is not a vice but a disease. The alcoholic is not a moral weakling. He is tragically ill with a mental malady. If taken in time he can often be cured. The spread of the disease can be stemmed and turned back, but only with the aid of the doctors and the psychologists who have made it their field of research and experiment. To try to do so by sumptuary laws [i.e. Prohibition] is like trying to cure and prevent tuberculosis with a cough-drop."[23]

The visibility and respectability gained by the allied organizations of the Alcoholism Movement reflected one of its major goals: not only to promote a medicalized understanding of alcoholism, but also to create an improved image for the alcoholic—one commensurate with the perception of a post-Prohibition increase in problem drinking within the American middle classes. By the 1940s, as ever more such families were affected by habitual drunkenness, the public became receptive to the idea, as Johnson says, that if "well educated, industrious members of the upwardly-mobile middle class could succumb to [the] ravages of habitual drunkenness," then perhaps "problem drinking was not merely a matter of weak willpower and moral degeneracy." Not surprisingly, the temperance stereotype of the drunkard as a skid-row derelict gradually gave way to a far more sympathetic view as the NCEA disseminated "the image of the alcoholic as a hard-working business executive who was the unfortunate victim of a disease" that strikes indiscriminately at every social level.[24]

As articulated by Jellinek, the acknowledged spokesman for the Yale Center, the new paradigm of alcoholism posited a sharp distinction between "normal" drinkers and "alcoholics," whose "addiction" was evinced by an intense craving for drink and a complete loss of control over drinking. Alcohol, that is, was seen to be addictive only for a certain group: those who developed an increased tolerance, who experienced withdrawal symptoms if they tried to quit drinking, and who exhibited bodily deterioration as a result of heavy and habitual consumption. The disease of alcoholism was thought to be progressive (in the sense that it moved from psychological to physiological dependence) and irreversible (in the sense that the alcoholic could never safely return to normal drinking). The only effective treatment, according to the Alcoholism Movement, was lifelong abstinence.

Except for its absolute distinction between alcoholics and normal drinkers—a distinction that won the praise and support of the liquor industry for locating addiction in the person rather than the substance—the modern disease model offered little that was new. Its major ideas were derived from the old concept of "inebriety" and a wealth of scientific investigations dating from the late nineteenth century. Jellinek himself first came into prominence through his work of digesting and summarizing all the old published research on drinking and drunkenness.

The new paradigm was, in essence, a triumph of publicity and conceptual packaging. "What was scientific about the disease concept of alcoholism besides its articulation by scientists is . . . not apparent," one historian drily observes. "Neither of its key terms—*alcoholism* and *disease*—was clearly or consistently defined. . . . Nor were any of its key propositions supported by controlled empirical research."[25] Jellinek himself later retreated from his own theories.[26] And by the 1950s, several of the scientists associated with the Alcoholism Movement were troubled by a continuing lack of validation: "In spite of all the propaganda that had been distributed, the scientific evidence supporting the disease was extremely tenuous."[27]

Once the Alcoholism Movement had reconstructed the framework within which Americans understood excessive drinking, once habitual drunkenness had been medicalized as well as psychologized, then "alcoholic" writers began to become self-conscious of their "alcoholism," and fiction about drinking changed accordingly. The pivotal text was *The Lost Weekend* (1944), on which Charles Jackson brought to bear his own experience as an alcoholic as well as his understanding of the "disease" paradigm, including its freight of psychoanalytic theory.

The modernists had reacted against the Victorian idea of "inebriation" by producing a literature that idealized intoxication as iconoclasm and lionized the drunk as an anti-"Puritan" rebel. A major element in such texts was the representation of excessive drinking as an inevitable response of the sensitive consciousness to the nightmarish human condition. *The Lost Weekend* began to close the book on the modernist *drunk narrative* by exposing the literariness of its alcoholic despair.

In his sober moments, Jackson's protagonist realizes that his existence does not live up to the high romantic tragedy of the sort he admires in *Tender Is the*

Night, in which the alcoholic culture hero learns the bitter wisdom of the ages from John Barleycorn. The drunken life is "merely ludicrous—ludicrous but not worth laughing at, something merely to put up with and bear with because there was nothing else to do about it."[28] In its demystification of the White Logic, *The Lost Weekend* inaugurated a new mode of American fiction in which habitual drunkenness was figured less as a sign of The Modern Temper than as the symptom of a disease.

Since the 1940s, what might be called the *recovery narrative* has largely superseded the modernist drunk narrative. American novelists have continued to produce powerful stories of alcoholic degeneration. More common, however, have been fictions about relief from alcohol (and other drugs) that reflect the influence of the Alcoholism Movement in general and the success of A.A. in particular. Numerous Hollywood films, some derived from popular plays or best-selling books, have also dealt explicitly with alcoholism. In several of these, too, A.A. is explicitly endorsed.[29]

Recovery narratives have always played an important part in A.A. meetings, as well as in all three editions of the Big Book. Members routinely tell of their personal adventures before and after joining the fellowship and retrace their progress from drunkenness to sobriety.[30] These stories, which constitute a type of spiritual autobiography, have been adapted to fiction and have also created a discourse for the rapidly expanding "recovery" movement of the late twentieth century.

A.A. itself was another creation of the Lost Generation of middle-class Americans who came of age during the early 1920s and who made excessive drinking a hallmark of their youthful rebellion. When this cohort reached middle age at mid-century, it was faced with the resultant drinking problems. (A common pattern in male drinkers is for alcoholism to develop gradually for twenty years or so and then to become acute when they reach their forties.) "The founding of Alcoholics Anonymous in 1935, and its emergence as a national movement around 1940," says Robin Room, "must be seen as the reaction of the initial 'wet generations' to the predicament in which they found themselves." Both the approach and the rhetoric of A.A., moreover, "were carefully attuned to the mind-set of members of the initial 'wet generation' and, in particular, to the men of the generation." The antidrink discourse of A.A. provided an alternative to the now "discredited invective of the temperance movement."[31]

The blunt and deflationary pragmatism of A.A. also provided an alternative to the seductive grandiosity of The Modern Temper. Donald Newlove recalls how in his drinking days he sought "the just, pure expression of a kind of holy blackness I admired as the richest resource for dark language." Life's gruesome side, which he had often experienced on the job as an ambulance driver, had initiated him, he believed, into the darkest secrets of the White Logic. The deadliest ordeal was having to wrestle with a corpse wedged upside down between a bathtub and toilet:

> [A]s I got down and pried I told myself that if I lived through this, that then I had gone through my Guadalcanal, my Iwo Jima, my Saipan, my Tarawa, my King Lear tree-splitting storm, my Godot, my *No Exit*, my holocaust, my pie-slice of the universal horror and tragedy and that I was now an accredited Twentieth-Century Writer and fully empowered to seek and state the definitive negative statement for my times and to hold a mirror up to the power of blackness, the night within the night, my Dachau, Berlin, Hiroshima, a spiritual desolation that granted me the clear right to drink. I deserved to drink to keep my good cheer and avoid suicide.

Newlove later came to realize that he had been aggrandizing his capacity for suffering: "I still, of course, didn't know I was a drunk or that my bottom was far, far off, and that I was now only groping about in my graveyard period, a merely literary agony."[32]

In contrast to the truly horrific suffering enduring at Guadalcanal or Dachau or Hiroshima, the agony of the alcoholic "Twentieth-Century Writer"—agony that was largely self-inflicted through drinking and that served in turn to justify drinking—*was* "merely literary" more often than these writers wished to recognize. When F. Scott Fitzgerald gravely opined, "There are no second acts in American lives,"[33] he neglected to mention that he and many other modernists, stuck in their "graveyard period," had gotten drunk during the first act and passed out during intermission.

Notes

This chapter derives from material originally published in chapters 1, 2, 4, and 7 of *The White Logic: Alcoholism and Gender in American Modernist Fiction* (Amherst: University of Massachusetts P, 1994).

1. Joseph Wood Krutch, *The Modern Temper: A Study and a Confession* (1929; rpt. New York: Harcourt, Brace & World, 1956), 16–17, 24–25.
2. Donald W. Goodwin, *Alcohol and the Writer* (Kansas City, MO: Andrews and McMeel, 1988), 4.
3. Robin Room, "A 'Reverence for Strong Drink': The Lost Generation and the

Elevation of Alcohol in American Culture," *Journal of Studies on Alcohol* 45 (September 1984): 540.

4. Liebling quoted in Room, "A 'Reverence for Strong Drink,' " 543.

5. Frederick J. Hoffman, *The Twenties: American Writing in the Postwar Decade*, rev. ed. (New York: Free, 1962), 36.

6. Edmund Wilson, "The Lexicon of Prohibition," in *The American Earthquake: A Documentary of the Twenties and Thirties* (Garden City, NY: Doubleday Anchor, 1958), 91.

7. Room, "A 'Reverence for Strong Drink,' " 542–43.

8. Alfred Kazin, " 'The Giant Killer': Drink and the American Writer," *Commentary* 61 (March 1976), 46, 44.

9. Jack London, *John Barleycorn* (New York: Century, 1913), 8, 308, 303.

10. Saul Bellow, "The Thinking Man's Waste Land," *Saturday Review* 48 (3 April 1965), 20.

11. Donald Newlove, *Those Drinking Days: Myself and Other Writers* (New York: Horizon Press, 1981), 61.

12. Harry Gene Levine, "The Discovery of Addiction: Changing Conceptions of Habitual Drunkenness in America," *Journal of Studies on Alcohol* 39 (January 1978): 149, 158.

13. Virginia Berridge and Griffith Edwards, *Opium and the People: Opiate Use in Nineteenth-Century England* (New Haven: Yale UP, 1987), 155.

14. Orestes M. Brands, *Lessons on the Human Body; An Elementary Treatise Upon Physiology, Hygiene, and the Effects of Stimulants and Narcotics on the Human System* (Boston: Leach, Shewell, & Sanborn, 1883), 202.

15. Mark Edward Lender and Karen R. Karnchanapee point out that for at least fifty years, between the 1880s and 1930s, "the drunkard of the schoolroom was the drunkard of the Temperance Tales. 'The drunkard, with his foul breath, his noisy tongue, his foolish and dangerous acts, his bloated face, and reeling gait,' a typical text related, 'is in many communities an everyday warning to young and old. . . .' " Long after repeal of the Eighteenth Amendment, "alcohol education still contained a heavy temperance strain." " 'Temperance Tales': Antiliquor Fiction and American Attitudes Toward Alcoholics in the Late 19th and Early 20th Centuries," *Journal of Studies on Alcohol* 38 (July 1977): 1366.

16. Vance Thompson, *Drink and Be Sober* (New York: Moffat, Yard, 1915), 108–9.

17. London, *John Barleycorn*, 6, 11, 339.

18. Tom Dardis, *The Thirsty Muse: Alcohol and the American Writer* (New York: Ticknor and Fields, 1989), 124.

19. *As Ever, Scott Fitz—: Letters Between F. Scott Fitzgerald and His Literary Agent, Harold Ober, 1919–1940*, ed. Matthew J. Bruccoli and Jennifer M. Atkinson (Philadelphia: Lippincott, 1972), 209–10.

20. Julie M. Irwin, "F. Scott Fitzgerald's Little Drinking Problem," *The American Scholar* 56 (Summer 1987): 427.

21. Bruce Holley Johnson, "The Alcoholism Movement in America: A Study in Cultural Innovation" (Ph.D. diss., University of Illinois, 1973), 148. Johnson asserts that "by the mid-1960's those who had not yet brought their opinions into line with this new point of view were forced to contend with the fact that their ideas were inconsistent with practically all of the statements on this subject emanating from the centers of national culture" (148). Johnson bases this conclusion on his review of literature produced by various institutions responsible for the dissemination of public discourse: religious organizations, medical associations, state and federal governments, the judicial system, corporations, magazines, encyclopedias and dictionaries.

22. Jack S. Blocker remarks: "Viewed in historical perspective, Alcoholics Anonymous represents a flowering among middle-class and upper-class men of the self-help tradition that flourished primarily within the ranks of working-class men from the early nineteenth century to the early twentieth century." *American Temperance Movements: Cycles of Reform* (Boston: Twayne, 1989), 142–43. Blocker goes on to point out a connection between the self-help impulse among workers and periods of pronounced economic instability and/or technological change. Alcoholics Anonymous was founded, of course, in the midst of the Great Depression, when economic anxieties and real hardships were more widely shared than ever before in America by middle-class and even upper-class men.

23. Genevieve Parkhurst, "Drinking and Alcoholism," *Harper's Monthly Magazine* 177 (July 1938): 159.

24. Johnson, "The Alcoholism Movement in America," 183, 427. Ernest Kurtz points out that when *Alcoholics Anonymous* (the so-called Big Book) was being assembled during the late 1930s, the homogeneity of current A.A. membership made it difficult to furnish any variety in the part of the book devoted to personal narratives. "The problem was met by editing to accent different phases of the drinkers' common experience." *Not-God: A History of Alcoholics Anonymous* (Center City, MN: Hazelden, 1979), 73.

25. Blocker, *American Temperance Movements*, 146. One early critique of the "disease" paradigm was mounted during the 1960s by the radical psychiatrist Thomas S. Szasz. See "Alcoholism: A Socio-Ethical Perspective," *Western Medicine Medical Journal* 7 (December 1966): 15–21. The attack has since been taken up by a variety of alcohol researchers, and it has now reached the level of popularization. See, for instance: Herbert Fingarette, *Heavy Drinking: The Myth of Alcoholism as a Disease* (Berkeley: U of California P, 1988); Stanton Peele, *Diseasing of America: Addiction Treatment Out of Control* (1989; rpt. Boston: Houghton, 1991).

26. See the evasive preface to Jellinek's book, which finally appeared in 1960, years after he had established his reputation as the premier scientific exponent of the disease paradigm. Jellinek's convoluted prose may be read as symptomatic of the ambivalence he developed about the ideas that had made him famous: "It goes against my grain to use the expression disease concept—the proper wording would be disease conception. But the publisher's objection that conception sounds awkward must

be admitted. . . . Strictly speaking, alcoholism is a concept; so is disease. But that alcoholism is a disease is a viewpoint and thus a conception. Nevertheless I have bowed to the prevalent usage of concept, especially for the title of this book. Indeed, alcoholism itself is only a part issue—but this book is limited to the disease concept issue." *The Disease Concept of Alcoholism* (New Haven, CT: College and University Press, 1960), ix. For signs of Jellinek's dis-ease with the disease concept(ion), see also 11–12, 158–59, 165–66.

27. Johnson, "The Alcoholism Movement in America," 328.

28. Charles Jackson, *The Lost Weekend* (New York: Farrar and Rinehart 1944), 216.

29. See Robin Room, "Alcoholism and Alcoholics Anonymous in U.S. Films, 1945– 1962: The Party Ends for the 'Wet Generations,'" *Journal of Studies on Alcohol* 50 (July 1989): 368–83.

30. Published originally in 1939, *Alcoholics Anonymous* was reissued in 1955 and 1976. Although the main body of the text has remained virtually unchanged from the first to the third edition, the "Personal Stories" section has been revised to reflect the changing demographics of the membership. See Kurtz, *Not-God*, 132.

31. Room, "Alcoholism and Alcoholics Anonymous," 380.

32. Newlove, *Those Drinking Days*, 71, 48.

33. Fitzgerald, *The Last Tycoon: An Unfinished Novel* (1941; rpt. New York: Scribner's, 1969), 163.

"Bill's Story"

Form and Meaning in A.A. Recovery Narratives

⚐ Edmund O'Reilly

Stories may be the best means we have for comprehending alcoholism, since only stories can begin to contain alcoholism's bewildering, intractable, contradictory, protean nature. In Alcoholics Anonymous, stories are the essential medium of currency, the means by which consolation and admonition, theory and counsel are exchanged. Oral autobiographical narratives in particular—with the main body of evidence, the speaking subject, on full view—are told and retold as the key part of the routine of A.A. meetings. The life story of A.A.'s charismatic founder, the Vermont stockbroker William Griffith Wilson (1895–1971), is an important precedent for A.A. speakers, providing a formal paradigm for narrative performance as well as a conceptual model of how recovery from alcoholism might occur.

Bill Wilson's life has been told many times in stories of varying scope, insight, and complexity; by biographers with different perspectives and degrees of sympathy; and often by Wilson himself, both orally and in writing. There are book-length accounts, such as Robert Thomsen's popular *Bill W.* (1975) and A.A.'s collectively prepared "official" life, '*Pass It On*' (1984). Ernest Kurtz brings the discipline of a trained historian to bear in *Not-God* (1979), his superb interpretation of Wilson's life and work and the growth of A.A. More recently, in *Getting Better: Inside Alcoholics Anonymous* (1988), journalist Nan Robertson has retold the story acknowledging Wilson's personal shortcomings—his egocentricity, his "womanizing," and his moodiness. Robertson projects a credible "contemporary" Wilson for readers taught by popular psychology and mass media that wealthy, powerful, and celebrated figures must be inwardly troubled and less than exemplary.[1]

Wilson told his own story at A.A. meetings and frequently shared it with outside groups as well in the course of his unabating pursuit of acceptance for the fellowship; printed versions of his talks appear in *Alcoholics Anonymous Comes of Age* (1957) and the pamphlet *Three Talks to Medical Societies* (n.d.), and in A.A.'s central text, *Alcoholics Anonymous: The Story of How Many Thousands of Men and Women Have Recovered from Alcoholism* (1976).[2]

These versions of Wilson's autobiography, and the manner in which he customarily delivered it, have percolated throughout the secondary literature on alcoholism and treatment, sometimes with misleading consequences. Hostile or ill-informed critics of A.A. have been willing at times to attribute Wilson's idiosyncracies to the membership at large. His personal dramatic white-light conversion, for example, continues to trouble even some of the A.A. membership, who regard it as inconsistent with their own conceptions of dignified spiritual bearing, if not frankly embarrassing. Robertson mentions Wilson's "old-fashioned" prose style, his use of "outdated slang," and "a boosterist tone of onward and upward with George Follansbee Babbitt" (72–73). Critics of A.A. seem disposed to believe that this manner is current, widespread, and obligatory.

Clues to specific influences on Wilson's development as a writer and thinker are sparse. His prose style is a mid-1930s transformation of a popular inspirational strain in American writing, dating from the eighteenth century or earlier, bearing the marks of Franklin's influence (perhaps traceable to Bunyan), codified in the mid-nineteenth century by, among others, T. S. Arthur (*Ten Nights in a Bar-Room*, 1854; *Six Nights with the Washingtonians*, 1871), and carried on in our own time by legions of authors of self-help and popular psychology tracts, numbering among them such figures as Norman Vincent Peale, Fulton J. Sheen, Joshua Loth Leibman, M. Scott Peck, Leo Buscaglia, and Dr. Joyce Brothers.[3] The style is aggressively plain, with frequent irruptions of a kind of oafish "poetic" excess to signal a surplus of emotion.

Wilson's manner of speaking and writing bears an interesting correspondence to that of the advertising executive Bruce Barton; indeed, a suggestive affinity is evoked by a glance at the two men's roughly contemporaneous careers. Both were schooled in American ideals of entrepreneurial success, and pursued those ideals uncritically and without cynicism; and both seem to have felt an insufficiency at the heart of the dream. In *The Man Nobody Knows* (first published in 1925, the same year that saw the publication of *The Great Gatsby*), Barton reinterpreted the life of Christ for the instruction and profit—both spiritual *and* fiscal—of modern businessmen. "Every one of His conversations, every contact between His mind and others, is worthy of the attentive study of

any sales manager," Barton said of "the most popular dinner guest in Jerusa-
lem." Wilson, too, would link therapy, persuasion, and the bottom line, and
bear witness in his writing to a confluence of the pragmatic and the inspirational in the language of modern advertising. The key difference between the
two may be that Wilson ultimately discovered a product he really believed in.[4]

"Jesus hated prosy dullness" (Barton, 94). Justified by this proposition,
Barton provided a recipe for effective communication in business that includes conciseness, simplicity, sincerity, and repetition—values that also inform A.A. stories. Whether or not Wilson was acquainted with Barton's work
is uncertain, but we may be sure that he knew Franklin, the novels of Horatio
Alger, and had at least passing familiarity, from his small-town Vermont Protestant upbringing, with the available range of popular Christian inspirational
literature.

Wilson's life story has attained a certain canonical character in A.A., and acts
as an important reference point, both historically and structurally. There is an
agreeable congruence between the story of Wilson's recovery from alcoholism
and the story of A.A.'s origin. The founding of the program was no afterthought, conceived by Wilson subsequent to becoming sober, but rather was
integral to his attainment of sobriety: the precise moment of A.A.'s conception
is said to have occurred when Wilson, feeling that his own sobriety depended
on communicating with another alcoholic, located Dr. Robert Smith in Akron,
Ohio, and pressed upon him the message of submission and spiritual regeneration. At this juncture—according to the celebration of these events in the
literature—Wilson's own sobriety was reinforced, Dr. Bob's was inaugurated,
and Alcoholics Anonymous was set in forward motion. A complex typology
will henceforth obtain.

The historical moment of the formation of the fellowship—the bonding of
the two founders in Akron—becomes analogous to the moment of commitment to the group in the life of the individual alcoholic, whether that individual is Wilson or a contemporary. As the world prior to the formation of A.A.
was without recourse for suffering alcoholics, so is the individual before commitment to A.A. desolate, hopeless; and as the world since A.A.'s inception is a
place where the alcoholic may now find a happy alternative to institutionalization and early death, so is the individual subsequent to commitment to A.A.
liberated from degradation, mental chaos, and despair. The story of the
group's origin is a historicized and globalized version of the story of personal
recovery; a subject telling his or her own story according to the pattern set out
by Wilson is making a complex affirmation of identification with the founding

member, with others who align themselves in the same pattern, and with the group as an emergent entity in the social world. Pivotal biographical and historical decisions coincide, and inform and deepen one another.

It is appropriate, then, that we should look at the first telling of Wilson's life, "Bill's Story," from *Alcoholics Anonymous* (1976), originally published in 1939. We might hope to find here a certain ingenuousness and freedom from political and propagandistic motives that could have contaminated later tellings. This task should provide useful historical and conceptual data as well as interpretive leverage.

The "Big Book," as *Alcoholics Anonymous* is universally known among the A.A. membership, was first published only four years after the founding of the program. Wilson wrote the expository first section of the book, to which "Bill's Story" acts as prelude and representative anecdote, and carefully edited the rest—a collection of twenty-nine first-person stories of recovery by other A.A. members—for consistency of content and tone ('Pass It On,' 200). Since 1939 the Big Book has been modified twice—personal stories were added or deleted—"to represent the current membership of Alcoholics Anonymous more accurately, and thereby to reach more alcoholics," but "Bill's Story" and opening arguments have remained unchanged (*Alcoholics Anonymous*, xii).

Alcoholism is, among other things, a disease of authority; that is, centers of power and patterns of hierarchy are misperceived or displaced; existing social and political structures are repudiated or ignored; the texture of human life—situated, interwoven, dependent—is denied; phantom authority is arrogated to the self, and a potent illusion of control is contrived to maintain the false edifice.

Bill Wilson's craving for praise despite his avowal of the need for "the destruction of self-centeredness" (*Alcoholics Anonymous*, 14) and his struggles between anonymity and celebrity, humility and self-aggrandizement, are well documented, often reported by Wilson himself. It is not difficult to understand why "Bill's Story" has pride of place in the Big Book. By virtue of its position as well as its name, the primacy of "Bill's Story" and of Bill himself within the fledgling fellowship is asserted; "Bill's Story" becomes, as if by fiat, *the* paradigmatic story for A.A.—at the same time that the singularity of its author is emphasized. Bill writes his personal evolution as a chronicle of the reapportionment of authority, and it is not inappropriate by A.A. standards for the renovated self to affirm its own worth as refurbished moral and behavioral principles strengthen in recovery. But at the same time the story bears traces—perhaps necessarily—of defiant gestures of repudiated "self-centeredness," an inescapable residue of persisting conflict. An apparent contradiction develops in the paradox of "prideful humility." This problem in one form or another is often examined in the course of A.A. discussions, and is often confronted by A.A. speakers as they experience a tension between the ambiguities of self-display and the commitment to service.

The notion of alcoholic pride is central to Gregory Bateson's important contribution to the understanding of alcoholism. In "The Cybernetics of 'Self': A Theory of Alcoholism" (1972), Bateson develops a conceptual vocabulary to describe the mechanism of alcoholic progression.[5]

According to Bateson, the basic fault in the alcoholic personality system is an erroneous, encultured self-concept that is experienced as a hierarchical, compartmental structure in which interests are pitted against one another—almost like class interests in a nineteenth-century factory. Some components of this incorrectly delimited self-system are experienced as controllable by other components, and particular sets of position are prized. A complex internal dynamic develops from shifting patterns of dominance and subordination among reified "parts" of the system. Some demarcated sectors of the self are felt to be at war with others (as in "part of me knows this is wrong"; "I can beat this thing"; or even, "I didn't know what I was doing"). We are in the somewhat shopworn domain of the schizoid sensibility, of course—for which the blame for incalculable damage done to Western cognitive processes is customarily laid to Descartes and, subsequently, the ideals of Enlightenment science. *Body* and *mind* are incorrectly perceived as discrete and in some sense adversarial, just as *self* and *environment* may be felt to exist in opposition to one another rather than as complementary aspects of an integrated totality.

Alcoholic pride develops from within the adversities of the segmented self to become a defining and potentially lethal influence in the life of an active alcoholic. Alcoholic pride is based not on past achievement, but on the mastery of one component of the self by another—a controlling, rational element against an impulsive, insurgent affect, for example. Hence, it is a point of pride, a challenge, to be able to drink well, to hold one's liquor; or, when that fails, to seem to be able to *stop* drinking in the face of powerful physical cravings (for short periods, at least: "going on the wagon," "cleaning up [one's] act"). But then, having achieved the short-term goal of a provisional renunciation, the situation reverses itself and the relocated challenge is provided by the risks of returning to drink—usually to "controlled" drinking. Playground metaphors—*seesaw* and *merry-go-round*—abound in the language of A.A., suggestive at once of "meaningless" compulsive repetition and of inadequately repudiated child-hood egocentrism.

Implicated in the alcoholic's pride is a "real or fictitious other," a performer created out of materials from the alcoholic's own private psychic playpen, or a real person, pathologically mediated, with whom the alcoholic can coexist only competitively or symmetrically. The *other* challenges the alcoholic to seemingly ever more destructive behavior.

> As things get worse the alcoholic is likely to become a solitary drinker and to exhibit the whole spectrum of response to challenge. His wife and friends begin to suggest that his drinking is a *weakness* and he may respond, with symmetry, both by resenting them and by asserting his strength to resist the bottle. But, as is characteristic of the symmetrical responses, a brief period of successful struggle weakens his motivation and he falls off the wagon. Symmetrical effort requires continual opposition from the opponent.
>
> Gradually the focus of the battle changes, and the alcoholic finds himself committed to a new and more deadly type of symmetrical conflict. He must now prove that the bottle cannot kill him. (Bateson, 326)

Bateson believes that symmetrical escalation is inescapable until the alcoholic is utterly degraded. (A.A. speakers often use escalators, elevators, and moving trains as metaphors for the progress of their drinking careers.) The condition of radical defeat—if it does not kill—breaks the cycle and forces an epistemological restructuring that is more "correct." This is termed "hitting bottom" in A.A., and compels recognition that "the 'self' as ordinarily understood is only a small part of a much larger trial and error system which does the thinking, acting, and deciding. This system includes all the informational pathways which are relevant at any given moment to any given decision. The 'self' is a false reification of an improperly delimited part of this much larger field of interlocking processes" (Bateson, 331).

"Bill's Story" begins during the First World War, a time made emblematic here by virtue of social dislocation and stark polarities. "War fever ran high in the New England town to which we new, young officers from Plattsburg were assigned," Wilson writes, "and we were flattered when the first citizens took us to their homes, making us feel heroic" (*Alcoholics Anonymous*, 1). World-wide military conflict mirrors Bill's doomed, escalating efforts at inward self-determination; "fever" immediately suggests loss of control. There may be a measure of justification in war itself, but "war fever" denotes discord overlaid with delirium, hallucination, rashness, and the unpredictability of high heat. "Flattery" makes note of the capriciousness, the mutability of social definition, and the narrator's susceptibility to it; he is made to feel heroic, but the feeling is without depth; his situation is altogether spurious.

"Here was love, applause, war," says Wilson. "I was part of life at last" (1). But definition is supplied from without; the sense of participation in "life" is felt to be a social fabrication, false as flattery—although even a false sense of participation provides recompense for intimated antecedent loneliness. Loneliness and estrangement are only suggested here, and the recognition of any possible underlying social dysfunction is barely a whisper of implication. The role of social pathologies in the genesis of individual alienation will never become a powerful theme in A.A.: the restoration and maintenance of sobriety and the development of autonomous moral responsibility are reckoned sufficiently formidable tasks from which, within the framework of the group, engagement with social and political critique could only prove a distraction. This is not to suggest that A.A. members are incapable of, or enjoined from, social activism—only that platforms for it must be found outside the boundaries of the program. Nothing in A.A. precludes activism of any sort, provided it is not chemically buttressed, but this is beyond the reclamatory therapeutic A.A. purview and irrelevant to it. There is, of course, a quietist strain in A.A. philosophy that might be construed as socially prescriptive; but probably more to the point is the utopian content of "mere" sobriety: survival of passage through active alcoholism renders humble acquiescence to everyday life contrastingly so superior to dissonance of any sort that willful disruption is, for many, wholly unthinkable. Still, almost all A.A. stories contain at least germinally the suggestion of radical social dysfunction.[6]

Throughout the first part of "Bill's Story," a terminology of reciprocal motion is employed—both vertical (rising and falling) and horizontal (arriving and departing)—corresponding to repetitions of the cycle of sobriety and relapse. In the opening paragraphs Bill goes away to the war in Europe and returns to enter the world of Wall Street. The rise and fall of stocks and money values becomes a leitmotif, replicated in the fluctuations of commercial enterprises, in business successes and failures. As the story progresses, the alternation between sobriety and drunkenness reflects these first oppositions, but then absorbs their force and takes on a life of its own. A qualitative change in Bill's drinking coincides with the stock market disaster of 1929; as before, institutional history and personal history coalesce, this time in the single image of the Crash: "I was finished and so were many friends. The papers reported men jumping to death from the towers of High Finance. That disgusted me. I would not jump. I went back to the bar. My friends had dropped several million since ten o'clock—so what? Tomorrow was another day. As I drank the old fierce determination to win came back" (4).[7]

The movements of alternation and opposition persist. Bill and his wife leave New York and return twice (3, 4); Bill repeatedly makes and loses money, finds and loses jobs (4, 5). He begins to follow the course described by Bateson: prideful periods of "fierce determination" are inevitably succeeded by demoralizing drinking bouts; symmetrical patterning is established, and a predictable intensification, which is deterioration in social and therapeutic terms, occurs:

> Liquor ceased to be a luxury; it became a necessity. "Bathtub" gin, two bottles a day, and often three, got to be routine. Sometimes a small deal would net a few hundred dollars, and I would pay my bills at the bars and delicatessens. This went on endlessly, and I began to waken very early in the morning shaking violently. A tumbler full of gin followed by half a dozen bottles of beer would be required if I were to eat any breakfast. Nevertheless, I still thought I could control the situation, and there were periods of sobriety which renewed my wife's hope. (5)

The alcoholic tremor itself becomes emblematic of the forward and backward movement that dominates Wilson's life. He refers to his diminished capacity to "surmount obstacles," and refers to his worsening condition as a "plunge into the dark." Despair is likened to a "morass" and to "quicksand" (8). Bill apprehends his newly sober friend Ebby in terms of retroaction: "escape" and a "recapturing [of] the spirit of other days" (9); Ebby looks to him like someone "raised from the dead" (11). Even after he attains sobriety, Bill is bedeviled by oscillating apprehensions: "waves of self-pity and resentment . . . sometimes nearly drove me back to drink" (15). But the emergent A.A. program, "the path that really goes somewhere" (15), cuts at the perpendicular across the futility of tidal repetition.

"The path that really goes somewhere" denotes the breaking of the patterns of symmetrical escalation, and also implies a new construction to be placed upon the idea of success. Success, for Wilson, had been a version of the common received American ideal: "My talent for leadership, I imagined, would place me at the head of vast enterprises which I would manage with utmost assurance" (1). "Business and financial leaders were my heroes" (2).[8]

The success Wilson craves is, of course, meretricious; things are not what they seem. "Unhappy scenes" are enacted behind the façade of Bill's "sumptuous apartment"; the boom of the twenties, "seething and swelling"—like something about to explode, or like a nest of larvae—is built on "paper millions" (3); both are symptomatic of an erroneous system of values based in misperceptions. Success, for Wilson, is a lethal illusion. The initial false materialist utopia of "vast enterprises" is counterbalanced, by the time we reach the end of "Bill's Story," with a realized utopia of a starkly different character: "We have it with us right here and now. Each day my friend's simple talk in our kitchen multiplies itself in a widening circle of peace on earth and good will to men" (16).

The friend referred to, Ebby, is a former drinking buddy who had achieved sobriety in the Oxford Group, a Christian revival fellowship with Lutheran pietist roots;[9] the "simple talk" is Ebby's presentation of the Oxford Group's "simple religious idea and . . . practical program of action"; and the practical program of action, which had yet to be filtered and codified as the Twelve Steps of Alcoholics Anonymous, was a rudimentary and somewhat folksy six-point procedure:

1. We admitted that we were licked, that we were powerless over alcohol.
2. We made a moral inventory of our defects or sins.
3. We confessed or shared our shortcomings with another person in confidence.
4. We made restitution to all those we had harmed by our drinking.
5. We tried to help other alcoholics, with no thought of reward in money or prestige.
6. We prayed to whatever God we thought there was for power to practice these precepts. (*Alcoholics Anonymous Comes of Age*, 160)

Bill searches out elemental images to convey Ebby's overwhelming impact. In his conversion, Ebby's "roots grasped a new soil" (*Alcoholics Anonymous*, 12), and not the quicksand or morass of before; his arrival is "an oasis in this dreary desert of futility"; Ebby is "on fire" (9), his effect "electric" (14). Ebby enables Bill to stand "in the sunlight at last" (12), to make contact with the "Father of Light who presides over us all" (14). "Scales of pride and prejudice fell from my eyes," Bill writes. "A new world came into view" (12). "How blind I had been" (13). Unifying, clarifying images of light replace dissonant figures. Bill's language stabilizes, takes on a compelling self-assurance. "There was a sense of victory, followed by such a peace and serenity as I had never known. There was utter confidence" (14).[10]

The final third of "Bill's Story" is taken up with a presentation of the Twelve Steps in a nonprogrammatic, anecdotal manner. For example, Steps Eight and Nine, in their present, codified form, read:

8. Made a list of all persons we had harmed, and became willing to make amends to them all.

9. Made direct amends to such people wherever possible, except when to do so would injure them or others.

In "Bill's Story" these steps are narrativized: "My schoolmate visited me, and I fully acquainted him with my problems and deficiencies. We made a list of people I had hurt or toward whom I felt resentment. I expressed my entire willingness to approach these individuals, admitting my wrong. Never was I to be critical of them. I was to right all such matters to the utmost of my ability" (13).

At last on that "path that really goes somewhere," Bill celebrates the "fellowship [that] has grown up among us of which it is a wonderful thing to feel a part." Families are reunited, "feuds and bitterness of all sorts" have been wiped out, and "business and professional men have regained their standing" (15). Out of the abjection occasioned by ever-accelerating alcoholic degeneration, a new concept of success emerges based on the fellowship of complementarity rather than symmetrical competition, sympathetic human interaction rather than self-serving instrumentality, voluntary gift giving rather than compulsory market exchange, unity rather than fragmentation based on misperception. In prospect is the restoration of an Edenic natural harmony, uncongenial to greed and the hunger for power.

"Bill's Story" falls into three parts, anticipating and enacting the narrative formula that Wilson will provide in Chapter 5 of the Big Book ("How It Works"), and establishing the dominant pattern for stories of addiction and recovery to come: "Our stories disclose in a general way what we used to be like, what happened, and what we are like now" (58). This is not the first occurrence of trichotomy.

The phrase "love, applause, war," in the opening paragraph of "Bill's Story," is the first of a succession of Wilsonian triads that often seem to control his rhetoric and his thought. He writes of "remorse, horror, and hopelessness" (6), of "happiness, peace, and usefulness" (8), of struggles that are "strenuous, comic, and tragic" (16); he studies economics, business, and law (2); on a camping trip he carries "three huge volumes of a financial reference service"

(3). He describes three similar failed attempts to control his drinking before learning the impotence of willpower against the craving for alcohol—an important premise in A.A. doctrine. There are deltoid icons, as well: Wall Street is a "maelstrom" (2), and financial speculation is like a "boomerang" (2).[11] At a moment of illumination, Wilson feels the melting of an "icy intellectual mountain" in whose shadow he has lived (12). His victorious sobriety is like a wind from a "mountain top" (14). Images of trajectory form a subset of the imagery of triangulation. Bill's health declines "like a ski-jump" (7); he is "catapulted" (8) into a "fourth dimension" of existence—which, presumably, subsumes and transcends the first three.

Trichotomy does not stop with "Bill's Story" but seems to saturate the program. The A.A. "Preamble," read at the start of every meeting, characterizes the fellowship as composed of men and women who share "experience, strength and hope" with each other for the sake of sobriety. "Experience, strength and hope" may be understood as a recipe for story production in speaking before groups, each element matching a phrase from the more explicit Big Book story formula, "what we used to be like, what happened, and what we are like now." A bit of A.A. folk wisdom has it that each speaking occasion consists of three parts—the message you planned to give, the message you gave, and the message you wish you'd given. Some members like to recite a three-part figure, playing on the language of Step Two, that claims to summarize a probable line of spiritual development in A.A.: "I came; I came to; I came to believe" (a triplex variant of the duplex "bring the body and the mind will follow"). A similar model of progress is elaborated by Wilson in a chapter of *Alcoholics Anonymous Comes of Age*, called "The Three Legacies of Alcoholics Anonymous: Recovery, Unity, Service." The words *recovery*, *unity*, and *service* are identified with the three legs of an equilateral triangle inscribed in a circle, a standard A.A. emblem, often with two triangular *A*'s in the center.

Several common A.A. slogans are made up of three words: "Easy does it"; "First things first"; "Keep it simple"; "Keep coming back"; "Listen and learn." New members are told they would do well to avoid "people, places, and things" associated with their drinking habits. The main points of the Twelve Steps of A.A. are sometimes reduced to three and rendered formulaically as "I can't; He can; let Him," the third-person pronouns denoting, of course, the Higher Power. The Serenity Prayer, now generally associated with A.A. and cognate enterprises, has frequently made its way into the printed literature of the program and is reproduced on one side of a widely distributed wallet-sized card produced by A.A. World Services. The prayer is often recited in unison by a group, sometimes as an alternative to the Lord's Prayer, to close their meeting. The Serenity Prayer, too, is tripartite: "God grant me the serenity to accept the things I cannot change, courage to change the things I can, and wisdom to know the difference." Acceptance, wisdom, and courage are cognate with experience, strength, and hope, and name qualities or attitudes of mind that may be rightly aspired to with respect to the past, the future, and the present; the suggestion of a rudimentary but unitary approach to a method of deliberation over warring ideas is also present.[12]

Alcoholism is characterized throughout A.A. as "a threefold disease—physical, mental, and spiritual." "The clear message," Ernest Kurtz writes, "is that there is a unity in human life, ill or healthy. The parts of the human experience are so interconnected that to suffer disturbance in one is to suffer dislocation in all; and in recovery, all must be attended to if any is to be healed" (Kurtz, 202). (In characterizing the A.A. speaking process, one A.A. member remarked, "This is just pure religion, medicine, and psychology.") By Kurtz's account, the comprehension of this triform creates the basis in a receptive subject—the alcoholic in defeat—for the idea of the "wholeness of accepted limitation." This wholeness is conceptually near-of-kin to what we have identified as epistemological reintegration under the principle of complementarity.[13]

In "The Number Three in American Culture," Alan Dundes (1980) has documented the pervasiveness of trichotomy as an important principle in the Occidental cognitive landscape, operative in every expressive and regulative mode, from the rhymes and games of children to the most rigorous rules of "scientific" procedure. The play of this native category in "Bill's Story" and throughout A.A. is normative, then, somehow deeply familiar, in no way odd or exceptional; a similar array of triforms could probably be produced using everyday-speech-based evidence from any ideologically informed institution or association. In A.A., however, trichotomy seems to play a special, integrated, structural role.

To put it succinctly (and in only three words): trichotomy subverts symmetry. In a list of generalizations about the uses of the number three as a native category, Dundes observes that "a third term may be the result of splitting a polarity," or that a third term may be formed by the "merging or combining of two terms so that one has *A, B,* and *AB.*"[14] It is then only a short step to the production of a third term that depends upon the two members of a polarity but is not contained by them, or even necessarily and specifically implied by them. The third term may be qualitatively distinct, a synthesis that is something other than a mean or a sum, but is perhaps a transcendence. Analogies from genetics or chemistry might be suggested, but they would fail, as always, to convey the intricacies of symbolic process, especially in its characteristic ability to elude or defy categorical rigidity. Transcendence, in the imagination, is not answerable to falsifiability strictures, or even to brute facts.

I suggest that the imposition of a dynamic trinary structuring process on the relentless binary alternation of alcoholic hopelessness creates the possibility for new patterns of cognitive practice to develop through accustomed linguistic channels, primarily the narrative modes. The mere introduction of trichotomy as a concept to be comprehended in a binary framework challenges the very utility of that framework and forces an expansive renovation of the cognitive system. Similarly, the process of reformulating the materials of experience according to the three-part story format encourages retroactive overhaul of the meanings of the experience. Duality may continue to inhere in the recollected materials of experience; but trichotomy, introduced as a function of the narrative discourse, becomes the mainspring of reinterpretive options.

In the pragmatics of alcoholic progression, "hitting bottom" compels the recognition of a need for a term beyond the two terms governing the malevolent machinery of symmetry and escalation. Optimally, the term "sober" will transcend and replace the opposition "drunk/not drunk," and an entire new range of possibilities will become available for the creation of an amended life. Wilson's defeat is total in "Bill's Story"; the binary schema in which he has operated confidently at first and then with diminishing faith is finally undone even before the propitious advent of Ebby: "I had met my match. I had been overwhelmed. Alcohol was my master" (8). At this point, Wilson has "taken" the First Step, and is on the way to "working" the all-important Second and Third, a triangulation that points, like an arrowhead, toward the further particulars of A.A. practice. Trichotomy has been superimposed upon the dualistic world, opening it up, liberating the subject from the bondage that dualistic contrastive relevance has become.[15]

Further, trichotomy in its transcendence of dualism now comes to represent a new unity; a sense of personal integrity accompanies the new cognitive amplitude. Dundes recalls the "special case" of trichotomy, the triune, or "three-in-one." Christian theology furnishes our best and most familiar example in the Trinity, of course, but other instances might be mentioned: the *Moirai* of the Greeks—Atropos, Clotho, and Lachesis, the "Fates"—or Freud's early model of the mind. It may be that trichotomy is a cultural and not a natural category, but there is a fact of physical structure underlying the symbolic force of the triune: the immutability of the triangle. Given sides of a determined length, the triangle alone among polygons can assume only one shape. Its unity is its strength, which is unassailable, granted the integrity of the limbs. The rigid three-part structure of the A.A. narrative forces a restriction of scope and limitation of focus upon the narrator; benevolent but austere confinement to a particular form and direction is imposed. The structure encourages an evocation of A.A.'s utopian ideology without concession to any alternative narratorial designs.

A.A. story structure is strikingly like the narratologists' definition of the "minimal story": "A narrative recounting only two states and one event such that (1) one state precedes the other state in time (and causes it); (2) the second state constitutes the inverse (or the modification, including the 'zero' modification) of the first."[16] Adherence to this structure in A.A. is virtually irresistible, not only because of the weight of A.A. convention, but, underlying that, because of the structure's conformity to a "natural" conception of narrative and communicative felicity. As Dundes abundantly demonstrates, the play of threes pervades our everyday suppositions about causality and our received ideas of social dynamics and individual and corporate success.

In "Bill's Story," the initial state is the dualistic world of binary thinking and symmetrical drinking behavior, with all of its concomitant disasters and pains culminating in total abjection; the modifying event is a succession of educating experiences resulting in a "spiritual awakening" that allows Bill to understand that he may choose his own conception of a Higher Power to which to relinquish his impotent and now defeated will; the second state is the "widening circle of peace on earth and good will to men" inhabited by Bill as a consequence of submission to the Higher Power (*Alcoholics Anonymous*, 16). That circle expresses the unifying power of complementarity, offering a conceptual alternative to the jagged symmetricality of the initial state, in consequence of the restructuring of basic cognitive categories. An intensity of crystalline light symbolically erases the shadows of false discriminations enjoined in binary perception; trichotomic process points the way to the remedial attitudes, symbolic strategies, and cognitive positions that we have subsumed under the idea of complementarity. The emblem of the triangle inscribed in a circle becomes an instruction concerning how to think: trichotomy or dialectic is to be employed within a horizon of inclusiveness, community, integration, and acceptance.

The shape of an ideal A.A. narrative is easy enough to chart on the basis of what we have determined so far. The representation of the first state, "what we used to be like," must illustrate the qualities and repercussions of alcoholic drinking, and suggest the untenable situation devolved around the speaker as a consequence of symmetrical thinking. Important themes must include the sense of isolation and the amelioration of loneliness initially provided by drink; the recognition of false conviviality; the material and spiritual privations of addictive drinking; the development of despair and the fear of madness based in the inability to reverse what has become an obviously suicidal progression. The middle-term event, "what happened," must emphatically if not dramatically represent the mental changes that led the speaker to discover A.A., the growth of a willingness to comply with the ideology of A.A., and the advent of authentic, unbroken sobriety. The second state, "what we are like now," should evince in some measure its own inverse relation to the first state. Now composure has replaced mental disorder; material losses have perhaps been replaced, but these grains are understood to be far less valuable than the spiritual enrichment that has occurred; real conviviality is discovered in fellowship and service through the enactment of A.A. principles.

Schematically, the story looks something like this (the conditions above and below the central event, "spiritual awakening," mirror each other):

I   Salutation ("Hi, my name is X
     and I'm an alcoholic.")[17]

II   First state   isolation/self-preoccupation
     (what we used to be like):   false conviviality
                                     reasons for drinking
                                     privations
                                     despair, fear of madness

III Event (what happened):   discovery of A.A.—skepticism, slips
                                     "spiritual awakening"
                                     acceptance of A.A.—authentic sobriety

IV   Second state   serenity, rule of reason
     (what we are like now):   material and spiritual restoration
                                     reasons for not drinking
                                     real conviviality
                                     service/community orientation

V   Coda

The content of "first-state" representations, "what we used to be like," may be, to some degree, quantified, itemized, and pressed into a scheme of narrative functions after the manner of Vladimir Propp. First-state narrative often matches the classical models of alcoholic progression that have been proposed from Benjamin Rush to E. M. Jellinek. Rush showed alcoholic deterioration on a descending scale, like marks of decreasing temperature on the "Moral and Physical Thermometer" he devised for graphic impact; an 1846 Nathaniel Currier lithograph depicts *The Drunkard's Progress from the First Glass to the Grave* in nine steps; Arthur's 1854 novel *Ten Nights in a Bar-Room* measures alcoholic decline at the community level in the intervals between the narrator's successive visits to the intemperate Cedarville; Jellinek counts out forty-three characteristic symptoms divided according to degree of severity among a Prodromal, a Crucial, and a Chronic phase. The triplet follows on the heels of a prealcoholic period.[18]

Predicated upon the speaking subject, the forty-three symptoms of Jellinek's phase model act as a tentative inventory of functions for the construction of A.A. stories. The predictive value of the list for narrative analysis is limited in that there is no obligation on the speaker to include any function or cluster of functions; the list is like a menu from which the speaker may "select"—in harmonious patterns, capriciously, or not at all. Many stories told by "high-bottom" drinkers—that is, those who were able to achieve sobriety before experiencing extreme degradation—are structured as if functions had been selected only from the Prodromal Phase; others range throughout the list, apparently at random, and certainly without regard to an idealized model of progression. Most A.A. stories are top-heavy with occurrences of these functions. Still, the functions differ from Propp's kind of morphological schedule in two important ways: they are not bound to occur in any order and they do not, of themselves, produce a story.

Middle-term representations, the "event" or statement of "what happened," are rarely as abrupt, intense, and precisely framed as the moment in "Bill's Story" when Ebby's question, *"Why don't you choose your own conception of God?"* instantly liberates Bill from the "vestiges" of "prejudice," enabling him to build a private spirituality not bounded by rejected theological orthodoxy and to submit to an authentic Higher Power. "That statement hit me hard. It melted the icy intellectual mountain in whose shadow I had lived and shivered many years. I stood in the sunlight at last. *It was only a matter of being willing to believe in a Power greater than myself. Nothing more was required of me to make my beginning.* I saw that growth could start from that point. Upon a foundation of complete willingness I might build what I saw in my friend. Would I have it? Of course I would!" (*Alcoholics Anonymous*, 12). (Wilson's "spiritual awakening" is presented with considerable restraint in its Big Book version. In *Alcoholics Anonymous Comes of Age*, Bill tells of a moment of revelation that matches some of the more dramatic conversions recorded in William James's *The Varieties of Religious Experience*. James, in fact, has identified the appearance of vivid white light—"photisms"—as the distinguishing mark of a virtual subgenre of mystical experience.)[19]

The modifying event, the "what happened" stage in A.A. narratives, may be related in tones that range from an awestruck gravity appropriate to the extravagance of a supernatural visitation, perhaps accompanied by upwelling tears of gratitude, to a drier kind of analytic bemusement or a detached irony. (While it is true that mystical illuminations occur from time to time in spoken A.A. narratives, they seem to be, in the urban Northeast at least, in a clear minority.) Most commonly, I think, "what happened" is represented not by a moment of abrupt change at a single point in the past, some cataclysmic disruption of the cognitive universe, but rather by an account of gradual accommodation to A.A. folkways and a set of adjustments—some major, many microscopic—to everyday life without drink. The narrative location of a moment of surrender is probably in most cases a retrospective contrivance, an interpretive interpolation in what seems to be a long and faltering journey toward present stability.

The description of "what we are like now" is often a condensed, allusive coda to the first two parts of the story. The concentration of most A.A. stories is on the depiction of "what we used to be like." And while there is a disapproving category in A.A. aesthetics for the prideful recitation of unevaluated drinking exploits—the reviled "drunkalogue"—it is possible to satisfy an A.A. audience with only the smallest spoken homage to the boundless rewards of sobriety. Overly effusive self-proclamations of inner harmony, tranquility, and emotional growth—especially in a national cultural climate of mistrust and cynicism—veer too close to the display of pride or complacency for the liking of A.A. audiences; and a too-rigorously structured story, drawing attention to its own clever parallelisms and repetitions, could imply a dualistic thought pattern that shadows too closely the transcended restrictions of binary opposition. It may be simply that the past drinking life, for all its liabilities, is more interesting—taking that term to suggest the capacity to generate funny or lurid anecdotes—than the sober present. For St. Augustine, history ended and exegesis began at the moment of his conversion; and so it is with the alcoholic who has entered A.A. A period of purposeful commentary is inaugurated that coincides with the beginning of a time of mental restructuring based on the principle of complementarity; the production of new tellable incidents is brought to a close—although the raw materials of good tale-making remain in stock.

The real weight of "second-state" representation comes not from the words of the narrative, but from the presence of the speaker. The effect of this presence is most powerfully experienced at meetings, of course, during the delivery of the stories; but even given a story separated from its speaker in time, space, and discursive community, the *idea* of the living narrator continues to inform the text. Knowledge of the nature of the source of the discourse is vital to the judicious evaluation of any personal narrative; this is especially important to remember when the very existence of a narrative is the primary demonstration of that narrative's truth, and the animate presence of the speaker its embodiment.

Much of the second state, the "what we are like now" segment, of the A.A. narrative, then, is implied or signaled by information that is, strictly speaking, outside of the narrative: the presence of the speaker, the speaker's governing intention to enter into a compact with the group by means of the act of speaking, and the dramatic negotiations that this intention might imply, such as confronting the past and overcoming temperamental resistance.

The coda in A.A. stories is precisely a "functional device for returning the verbal perspective to the present moment."[20] Often, the speaker addresses the audience directly, linking the final moments of the historical account with the immediate present of the speaking situation. Wilson moves into the progressive present tense to round out "Bill's Story" with its widening circle of peace and goodwill. The coda is, in fact, a significant gesture of unity, bonding the past to the present, audience to narrative substance, speaker to audience, unalterable historical data to continuing interpretive process, subjectivity to objectivity.

The coda carries out a complex unifying operation and points to an ancillary principle of totalization. The idea of unity in A.A. bears the sense not just of solidarity or mutuality, but of the necessary integration of program principles into all aspects of the subject's life. Embedded stories of slips and failures are invariably interpreted as a failure to adhere to an A.A. "suggestion," to follow an A.A. rule, to understand a simple principle. Ultimately, each A.A. precept stands in synecdochic relationship to the whole, and, similarly, seemingly casual utterances may be expressive of the entire body of suppositions, principles, implications, lore, and shared history.

The simple coda, then, is more than a structural afterthought and, like other components of the narrative pattern, may enact a signifying purpose supplementary to its ostensible content. The A.A. verbal universe aspires toward the anagogic, and analysis will be inadequate to the degree that it loses sight of that aspiration. Perhaps the figure of the triune is, after all, the most appropriate to impose upon A.A. stories, and the stories best imagined as units of verbal action that are themselves only atoms in the larger entity. A list of phase symptoms, the change of heart, and the presence of the speaker—these notations for representing the form and meaning of A.A. stories are incommensurate with the potency of the lived storytelling event. The correspondences, harmonies, and inversions in a multidimensional grid, together with the gravity and immediacy of the issues—the *fact* of something at stake—generate a highly charged performance. In an interview with me, "Scott," a New York attorney with more than fifteen years of sobriety in A.A., summarized the galvanic effect of a good speaker upon an A.A. audience:

> I can see in myself, and I think I experience it with others, that the telling of a story enriches the sense of the joint effort to be well. . . . The person who tells the story sort of commits himself to the effort; he's taking a risk in telling a story, and nobody really ought to believe otherwise; it's not that you're there bathed with love and therefore you're perfectly safe. . . . The person who's telling a story is taking a chance, and it's not just that it'll be misunderstood, it's the very risk of being intimate in a big room full of people. And so he's committed to doing something difficult . . . because he's been told it'll . . . help him to get well. And that commitment . . . engages the commitment of the other people in the room. I just know it does, and . . . aside from its content, the very act is a way of joining, as it was with me when I gave my first qualification.
>
> It's a rite of passage . . . it's a commitment to this mode of therapy, or this way of life, or this . . . getting better, and . . . it's a big step. And everybody who listens accepts it as a big step; it's not considered a trivial thing. Because after all there are these thirty or forty people willing to sit there for half an hour and listen to something that isn't on television, isn't a movie, it isn't exciting, it isn't a ball game, and their act of listening is a form of sharing as well, because they're sharing his life and they're committing themselves to this whole methodology, in a way that very few people are prepared to commit themselves—that is by shutting up and letting someone else do the talking. And . . . everybody's casting their lot with the process when they attend a meeting where there's a speaker. And that's all a vote for sobriety and getting well, and I think it's a terribly unifying, mentally unifying experience. I know I've never left a meeting when I didn't come away feeling

more purposeful, and my molecules, which lay at random up till then, are now organized until I need another meeting. It just gives me a sense of purpose and a sense of belonging to something, and a sense of direction; that is to say, I'm there to be well and that's the most important thing in my life.

Notes

This chapter is an altered version of "Paradigm and Form," published in my book, *Sobering Tales: Narratives of Alcoholism and Recovery* (Amherst: University of Massachusetts Press, 1997).

1. See Robert Thomsen, *Bill W.* (New York: Harper, 1975); Alcoholics Anonymous World Services, *'Pass It On': The Story of Bill Wilson and How the A.A. Message Reached the World* (New York: A.A., 1984); Ernest Kurtz, *Not-God: A History of Alcoholics Anonymous* (Center City, MN: Hazelden, 1979); and Nan Robertson, *Getting Better: Inside Alcoholics Anonymous* (New York: Morrow, 1988).

2. Alcoholics Anonymous World Services, *Alcoholics Anonymous Comes of Age: A Brief History of A.A.* (New York: A.A., 1957); *Three Talks to Medical Societies by Bill W., Co-Founder of Alcoholics Anonymous* (New York: A.A., n.d.); and *Alcoholics Anonymous: The Story of How Many Thousands of Men and Women Have Recovered from Alcoholism*, 3d ed. (New York: A.A., 1976).

3. See T. S. Arthur, *Ten Nights in a Bar-Room*, ed. C. Hugh Holman (1854; rpt. New York: Odyssey, 1966), and *Six Nights with the Washingtonians* (Philadelphia: Peterson, 1871); James D. Hart, *The Popular Book: A History of America's Literary Taste* (Berkeley and Los Angeles: U of California P, 1961); Richard Hofstadter, *Anti-Intellectualism in American Life* (New York: Vintage, 1963); Russel Nye, *The Unembarrassed Muse: The Popular Arts in America* (New York: Dial, 1970); and Jane Tompkins, *Sensational Designs: The Cultural Work of American Fiction 1790–1860* (New York: Oxford UP, 1985).

4. Bruce Barton, *The Man Nobody Knows* (Indianapolis: Bobbs, 1952), 12, 72. See T. J. Jackson Lears, "From Salvation to Self-Realization: Advertising and the Therapeutic Roots of the Consumer Culture, 1880–1930," in *The Culture of Consumption*, ed. Richard Wightman Fox and T. J. Jackson Lears (New York: Pantheon, 1983), and Warren I. Susman, *Culture as History* (New York: Pantheon, 1984), for discussions of Barton. Lears's complex and essential argument in "From Salvation to Self-Realization" is continuous with his account of antimodernism in *No Place of Grace: Antimodernism and the Transformation of American Culture, 1880–1920* (New York: Pantheon, 1981). Alcoholism was recognized and problematized in the context of emergent industrial modernity, and must to some extent be reckoned a disorder specific to the modernist transformations of mechanization, rationalization, dehumanization, overdevelopment, surveillance, and bureaucratic distension. It might be argued that the therapeutic gesture of Alcoholics Anonymous is to offer

an authentic experience based in ideals of primitive communalism—care, face-to-face interaction, meaningful reiteration—to replace the spurious comforts of drink-induced self-erasure.

For interesting if tangential reflections on American literary style and sensibility, see Hugh Kenner, *A Homemade World: The American Modernist Writers* (New York: Morrow, 1975). According to *Dr. Bob and the Good Oldtimers* (Alcoholics Anonymous, 1980), literature influential upon early A.A. included the Book of James, Henry Drummond's *The Greatest Thing in the World*, and a Methodist periodical, *The Upper Room*. Later in his life, Dr. Bob's favorite reading included *The Varieties of Religious Experience*, Augustine's *Confessions*, Lloyd C. Douglas's *The Robe*, and Ouspensky's *Tertium Organum*.

5. Gregory Bateson, "The Cybernetics of 'Self': A Theory of Alcoholism," in *Steps to an Ecology of Mind* (New York: Ballantine, 1972), 309–37.

6. Wilson's felt isolation in childhood and adolescence is explored in Thomsen (1975) and in *'Pass It On'* (Alcoholics Anonymous, 1984). One of A.A.'s quasi-official "slogans" is "live and let live," a commendable enough position when there are no real problems in the neighborhood. But "live and let live" may cease to be tenable equipment for living when one is confronted with a virulent bigot or an armed psychotic.

7. This passage may be compared interestingly with Fitzgerald's recollections in *The Crack-up* (New York: New Directions, 1945).

8. We must take him at his word; but it is curious to note that the only historical figures named—in fact, the only proper names that occur—in "Bill's Story" are Napoleon and the golf superstar Walter Hagen. Cawelti's interpretive history of the concept of success in America is interesting and helpful: John G. Cawelti, *Apostles of the Self-Made Man* (Chicago: U of Chicago P, 1965).

9. Alan Eister is thorough on the Oxford Group in his *Drawing-Room Conversion: A Sociological Account of the Oxford Group Movement* (Durham, NC: Duke UP, 1950), and Kurtz discusses its influence upon A.A. in *Not-God*. See also Alcoholics Anonymous, *Alcoholics Anonymous Comes of Age*; *Dr. Bob and the Good Oldtimers: A Biography, with Recollections of Early A.A. in the Midwest* (New York: A.A., 1980); and *'Pass It On'*. The Oxford Group phenomenon seems bizarre today; some of its internal contradictions surfaced dramatically when leader Frank Buchman made flattering remarks about Hitler to the press. See also Edmund Wilson, "Saving the Right People and Their Butlers," in *The American Earthquake: A Documentary of the Twenties and Thirties* (New York: Farrar, 1958), 518–26. Wilson's lacerating 1934 profile of the Buchmanites is, happily, not generally applicable to contemporary A.A.:

> The whole occasion makes an impression infinitely sad and insipid. I have seen these people before: these people whom their work does not satisfy . . . who are coming to realize that their functions in society are not serious and to seek anxiously for something to hang on to. . . . If they were a little more uncomfortably neurotic, they would be going to psychoanalysts; if they were sillier, they

would be nudists; if they were cleverer, Gurdjieff would get them. . . . They have invested [Christ] with the fatuous cheerfulness of the people in the American advertizements and of the salesmen who try to sell you what they advertize. One of the characteristic features of the Oxford Group is the continual chuckling and bubbling, the grinning and twinkling and beaming which goes on among its members, and which makes an outsider feel quite morose. (525–26)

10. Light here, clarifying and harmonizing, is an image of complementarity and as such must necessarily be discriminated from the kind of whiteness that plagued Jack London in *John Barleycorn*, or the whiteness of the whale in *Moby-Dick*. Whiteness, unlike the crystalline transparency of pure light, is opaque, signaling a kind of blockage; it is a malignant transform of light—light gone wrong, light that has rotted.

This shifty signifier puts in a brief appearance in Lewis Hyde's *The Gift*. In his discussion of Ezra Pound, Hyde says, in passing: "Twitted once by Eliot to reveal his religious beliefs, Pound (after sending us to Confucius and Ovid) wrote: 'I believe that a light from Eleusis persisted throughout the middle ages and set beauty in the song of Provence and of Italy.' This 'undivided light' occasions beauty in art, and vice versa—that is, beauty in art sets, or awakens, the knowledge of this light in the mind of man." And, a moment later: "The liquid light, the *nous*, the fecundity of nature, the feeling of the soul in ascent—only the imagination can articulate our apprehension of these things, and the imagination speaks to us in images." Lewis Hyde, *The Gift: Imagination and the Erotic Life of Property* (New York: Vintage, 1983), 218–20.

11. In both Thomsen (1975) and *Alcoholics Anonymous Comes of Age* (1957), an anecdote from Wilson's childhood involving a boomerang is used to demonstrate that his pride and tenacity were well established even in his tenderest years.

12. An A.A. joke refers to the "short form" of the Serenity Prayer: "Fuck it." This is more than just a cynical gloss on the principles of acceptance and passivity enjoined in much A.A. literature; it also underscores the unitary character of the three-part prayer.

13. Edward Sapir—in a different context—describes religion as "the haunting realization of ultimate powerlessness in an inscrutable world, and the unquestioning and thoroughly irrational conviction of the possibility of gaining mystic security by somehow identifying oneself with what can never be known." Sapir's language carries us into the heart of what Bateson identifies as complementarity. This is "religion" not in the sense of an ideological orthodoxy, but rather a deeply felt, unmediated recognition of limits.

> Religion is omnipresent fear and a vast humility paradoxically turned into bedrock security, for once the fear is imaginatively taken to one's heart and the humility confessed . . . the triumph of human consciousness is assured. There can be neither fear nor humiliation for deeply religious natures, for they have intuitively experienced both of these emotions in advance of the declared hostility of an overwhelming world, coldly indifferent to human desire.

... It is the pursuit, conscious or unconscious, of ultimate serenity following total and necessary defeat that constitutes the core of religion. Edward Sapir, *Culture, Language and Personality*, ed. David G. Mandelbaum (Berkeley: U of California P, 1956), 122–23.

14. Alan Dundes, "The Number Three in American Culture," in *Interpreting Folklore* (Bloomington: Indiana UP, 1980), 136.

15. In acknowledging a greater power and deferring to it, the alcoholic situates himself as a system within a nested structure of larger pertinent systems—within, and not outside or against that structure. The pathology is identified and located not as a discrete and antithetical other with which the alcoholic is engaged in interminable contest (the Bottle, John Barleycorn, the Bright Lights, the Boss, the Wife, the Government), but as an inherent and pervasive aspect of the entire perceptual, cognitive, affective system. Ideally, smaller and larger systems become reoriented, achieving congruence and harmonious relationship with one another; complementarity becomes an ordering principle in the subject's mental life. In its social dimension, the principle of complementarity engenders a sense of implication and involvement in the human community and fosters an aspiration to participate usefully. The humility attained in the experience of absolute surrender gives rise to a service orientation which is codified in A.A. as Step Twelve, Tradition Five, and the Preamble, all of which affirm a commitment to help other alcoholics.

The Twelve Steps of A.A. are as follows:

> 1. We admitted we were powerless over alcohol—that our lives had become unmanageable. 2. Came to believe that a Power greater than ourselves could restore us to sanity. 3. Made a decision to turn our will and our lives over to the care of God *as we understood Him*. 4. Made a searching and fearless moral inventory of ourselves. 5. Admitted to God, to ourselves, and to another human being the exact nature of our wrongs. 6. Were entirely ready to have God remove all these defects of character. 7. Humbly asked Him to remove our shortcomings. 8. Made a list of all persons we had harmed, and became willing to make amends to them all. 9. Made direct amends to such people wherever possible, except when to do so would injure them or others. 10. Continued to take personal inventory and when we were wrong promptly admitted it. 11. Sought through prayer and meditation to improve our conscious contact with God *as we understood Him*, praying only for knowledge of His will for us and the power to carry that out. 12. Having had a spiritual awakening as the result of these steps, we tried to carry this message to alcoholics, and to practice these principles in all our affairs.

The Preamble, in full, reads:

> Alcoholics Anonymous is a fellowship of men and women who share their experience, strength, and hope with each other that they may solve their common problem and help others to recover from alcoholism.

The only requirement for membership is a desire to stop drinking. There are no dues or fees for A.A. membership; we are self-supporting through our own contributions. A.A. is not allied with any sect, denomination, politics, organization, or institution; does not wish to engage in any controversy; neither endorses nor opposes any causes. Our primary purpose is to stay sober and help other alcoholics to achieve sobriety.

16. Gerald Prince, *A Dictionary of Narratology* (Lincoln: U of Nebraska P, 1987), 53.

17. The declaration "I'm an alcoholic," at the start of a narrative, establishes with certainty the conditions under which the narrative to follow may be contemplated, just as the clues that arouse particular expectations in literary genres are contained in titles, opening lines, and initial situations, not to mention packaging and marketing appurtenances. To say to an A.A. group "I'm an alcoholic" is to affirm a commitment to the avowed purposes of the group, to claim credibility as a witness and participant, and to petition for the authority to admonish, exemplify, beseech, advise, and so on. As a speech act, the statement possesses a rich density.

18. See Vladimir Propp, *Morphology of the Folktale* (Austin: U of Texas P, 1968); Elvin Morton Jellinek, "Phases of Alcohol Addiction," in *Society, Culture, and Drinking Patterns*, ed. David J. Pittman and Charles R. Snyder (Carbondale and Edwardsville: Southern Illinois UP, 1962), 356–68; and Mark Edward Lender and Karen R. Karnchanapee, " 'Temperance Tales': Anti-Liquor Fiction and American Attitudes Toward Alcoholics in the Late 19th and Early 20th Centuries," *Journal of Studies on Alcohol* 38 (1977): 1347–70.

This is a summary of Jellinek's phase model:

Symptoms or functions of the Prodromal Phase: palimpsests (blackouts); surreptitious drinking; preoccupation with alcohol; avid drinking; guilt feelings about drinking behavior; avoidance of reference to alcohol; increasing frequency of palimpsests.

Symptoms or functions of the Crucial Phase: loss of control; rationalization of drinking behavior; social pressures; grandiose behavior; marked aggressive behavior; persistent remorse; periods of total abstinence; changing the pattern of drinking; dropping friends; quitting jobs; behavior becomes alcohol centered; loss of outside interests; reinterpretation of interpersonal relations; marked self-pity; geographic escapes; change in family habits; unreasonable resentments; protection of supply; neglect of proper nutrition; first hospitalization; decrease of sexual drive; alcoholic jealousy; regular matutinal drinking.

Symptoms or functions of the Chronic Phase: prolonged intoxication; marked ethical deterioration; impairment of thinking; alcoholic psychoses; drinks with persons far below social level; recourse to "technical products" (Sterno, after-shave lotion, vanilla extract); loss of alcohol tolerance; indefinable fears; tremors; psychomotor inhibition; drinking takes on obsessive character; vague religious desires develop; entire rationalization system fails. At this point, there may be susceptibility to rehabilitation, especially in A.A., but, failing the appropriate intervention, probable outcomes are insanity and death.

19. William James, *The Varieties of Religious Experience* (1902; rpt. New York: Penguin, 1982).

20. William Labov and Joshua Waletzky, "Narrative Analysis: Oral Versions of Personal Experience," in *Essays on the Verbal and Visual Arts*, ed. June Helm. Proceedings of the 1966 Annual Spring Meeting of the American Ethnological Society (Seattle: U of Washington P, 1967), 39.

Drink and Disorder in the Classroom

⚒ Joan D. Hedrick

Y<small>OU MAY HAVE TURNED TO THIS ESSAY FOR THE SOME OF THE SAME</small> reasons students signed up for my class, "Drink and Disorder in America": curiosity, amusement, a wan hope that instead of the usual academic fare you would be served up a headier brew. On the first day of class when I walked into McCook Auditorium at Trinity College, Hartford, ranged in the ascending, amphitheater-style seats were 125 students, 75 of whom were men. My strategy had worked. The problem I had set myself was how, as director of women's studies, to reach beyond the converted and those on the "anxious bench" to the generality of student who would not ordinarily consider signing up for a course on women and gender. A handful of curious, adventuresome men regularly sign up for "Introduction to Women's Studies," but rarely do men make up more than 10 percent of the population in such classes. "Drink and Disorder," on the other hand, attracted half of the football team and a goodly proportion of fraternity brothers. Some students felt betrayed when they received the syllabus and saw that this was indeed a course with the usual papers and exams; several left. But most were lured into academic waters of a deeper sort than they would ordinarily have ventured into. This experiment had unexpected consequences in my own consciousness as well.

I think of "Drink and Disorder" as a mainstream "men's studies" course.[1] The connection between masculinity and drinking has often been observed. As Norman Clark has written, for many Americans "getting drunk . . . is an almost ceremonial validation of masculinity or individuality or social class identity."[2] "Drink and Disorder" attempts to situate drinking culturally and historically and explores the links between identity and alcohol consumption, paying particular attention to the ways in which drinking patterns vary across gender and ethnic groups. Besides reaching a general audience, this course integrates men's history and women's history via the temperance movement. It also asks students to think critically and historically about drinking as an *institution*—much as Adrienne Rich's 1977 classic, *Of Woman Born: Motherhood as Experience and Institution* did for motherhood. The ability to step back and examine as cultural constructs behaviors and institutions that we have taken for granted as "natural" is essential to women's studies and, I would add, to a liberal arts education. And just as women's studies pedagogy classically unites the personal and the political, I encourage students in "Drink and Disorder" to examine their own culture of drinking with a critical eye.

The first exercise in the course, a "Group History" (see Appendix A), was adapted from my "Introduction to Women's Studies."[3] As a glance at it will reveal, it provides a structure in which students can experience the consciousness-raising group of the 1970s. It functions both as an icebreaker in a large class and as an early signal that a dialectic between personal experience and historical analysis is part of the course. Meeting outside of class in small groups, students come prepared to discuss three moments: their most recent experience with alcohol, their most historically significant experience with alcohol, and the earliest time in their childhood that they became aware of alcohol. (In "Introduction to Women's Studies" this exercise is carried out with "sex/gender" substituted for "alcohol"; men in that course have a hard time with the assignment because they find that, unlike women, they are rarely reminded of their sex/gender. None reported problems with the drinking history exercise.) They then report back to the class, each group having its turn to come to the front of the auditorium and introduce themselves via their drinking histories.

This exercise has the virtue of allowing us to learn names and faces of students, some of which are indelibly impressed upon one's memory by their vivid stories. Students clearly enjoy the chance to hear from their peers, and having small chunks of their contemporary experience introduced into the framework of the course, where we handle evidence analytically and culturally, is appetizing. They are often surprised and stimulated by the questions and discussion that arise in response to their presentations. Patterns emerge from the individual stories and they are surprised to see that what they thought was their own experience is in fact part of a cultural phenomenon, a group experience. Racial and ethnic differences also sharply emerge: it is usually clear that alcohol plays a smaller social role in African American cultures than in many white ethnic cultures.[4] (On a campus in which drinking is an important ritual in the acculturation of process, this has large social implications for who gets included and on whose terms.) Details of the campus drinking culture and patterns of socialization and acculturation are often unself-consciously elaborated. I see patterns of generational difference that are illuminating.

The course takes a broad, interdisciplinary, and chronological approach consistent with its introductory-level format (see syllabus, Appendix B) and cross-listings with history, American studies, and women's studies. It includes popular culture material via speakers, films, and advertising. My broad goals are to make students curious about patterns in their own culture, better observers of contemporary life, reflective about their own choices, and open to differences. Like a typical women's studies course and in the tradition of good liberal arts pedagogy, the course seeks to unsettle and challenge assumptions. Many of these assumptions and debates will be familiar to historians, whose stock-in-trade is patterns of continuity and change.

Many students bring to the study of history an unexamined and contradictory set of assumptions about progress and the superiority of their own culture. In this popularized version of Whig history, they assume that history is an upward trajectory in which things get bigger, better, and badder. The contemporary hysteria around drugs has led them to believe that use of drugs, including alcohol, is at an all-time high. They are surprised to learn in William Rorabaugh's excellent monograph, *The Alcoholic Republic*, that in 1830 the per capita consumption of absolute alcohol was 3.9 gallons—almost twice the level consumed in 1975.[5] This unexpected finding makes them engage the critical term of historical inquiry—change. Rorabaugh, however, is completely unattuned to gender. My criticism of his unexamined assumptions opens up a new term of critical inquiry and encourages students to question what they are reading. It also begins to push a standard history course toward a more revisionist agenda.

I assign chapters from monographs that pose contrasting interpretations of the nineteenth-century temperance movement, Gusfield's *Symbolic Crusade*[6] and Clark's *Deliver Us from Evil*. Gusfield pursues the now-classic argument about benevolence as social control by a privileged elite, whereas Clark's *Deliver Us from Evil* sees temperance as a bourgeois attempt at self-improvement. The better students readily see that Gusfield and Clark are in fact discussing different historical phases of the temperance movement—Gusfield the early phase when temperance was dominated by the clergy, and Clark the post-1840 phase when self-help groups like the Washingtonians set the tone—and that therefore both could be right. The key to reconciling these conflicting views is thus history itself—the change from one period to another. Here the goal is historiographic: to dislodge the high school notion of history as fact and replace it with a more sophisticated understanding of history as contested story, underlying which are such questions as point of view and the nature of evidence. We talk about the difference between primary and secondary sources and the different values they hold for students of the past. The two primary sources we examine with Gusfield and Clark are Lyman Beecher's *Six Sermons on Intemperance* (1826) and Edgar Allan Poe's "The Black Cat" (1843). Both present rich texts for the analysis of symbolic language and cultural patterns. Poe's narrator presents a homely tale, a record of "mere household events" in which, under the influence first of drink and then of what he calls "perverseness," he mutilates his cat and drives an ax into his wife's brain. Reading Poe's tale as a temperance tract *manqué* enables us to see Karen Halttunen's point, that gothic imagery can be used to create either pietistic or secular versions of hell.[7] In this case, both are directly caused by intemperance. Like Lyman Beecher, Poe attempts to inspire fear, but whereas Beecher wants the fear to tip into religious conversion, Poe indulges in the emotion for the sensation itself. The superrational voice of Poe's psychopathic ax murderer and wife-batterer in "The Black Cat" is the occasion for an in-class discussion of the "double" in Poe's short stories and the possible link to the nineteenth-century gender ideology that posited a split between the private and the public, the domestic world of women and the public world of the marketplace. In this context Norman Clark's invocation of "the anxiety of the bourgeois interior" is a useful point of departure.

Clark argues that the new development of a private self separate from the public persona created, for the first time in history, the perception of a radically isolated self. He associates this development with an increase in binge drinking and antisocial, psychopathic behavior as the private self, cut off from community identity, drowns in a private despair (a response consistent with both delirium tremens and the violence of Poe's "The Black Cat"). In this scenario, more suggestive than my reductive summary here, Emersonian individualism leads to the bottle. He argues that this is particularly a *male* problem.

> [I]n societies where males can acknowledge their dependencies, complain of their inadequacies, or develop a sense of community rather than a drive to compete, drunkenness is seldom a solution or a problem. In early nineteenth century America, the reformation urged by Beecher and his brethren provoked a critical transformation in social sex role differentiation. We are in this historical matter much aware of the suffering of women and largely indifferent to the anguish of men: Induced to project images of extraordi-

nary strength, courage, and self-reliance (a new "masculinity"), they soon were bending to the new convention which made the measure of a man's character a measure of gender.[8]

Clark's monograph usefully engages the classic American theme of individualism—whose counterpart, fellowship, we will elaborate in the communities established through temperance groups, saloons, Alcoholics Anonymous, male bonding, and fraternities.

Like Rorabaugh, Clark ignores the questions about women that his work even more insistently raises. Where are they in this scenario of lonely individualism? What were the women doing while Deerslayer and Ichabod Crane and Nick Adams were off in the woods with their guns and bottles? What is the relationship between the wife and the black cat in Poe's tale? I supplement our discussion with a lecture on the status of women in antebellum America and what Barbara Welter has dubbed "The Cult of True Womanhood" (*American Quarterly* 18 [Summer 1966], 151–74). When the private and the public worlds split, what gender splits occurred? What splits in the psyche accompanied this ideological shift? What is the role of "reason" in Poe's tale? What is its relationship to madness? To race and culture? To crazy gender arrangements? The story raises the connection between drinking and domestic violence, which was precisely the lever with which nineteenth-century women began raising the temperance issue and women's consciousness. This leads into our discussion of women's role in the temperance movement, explored in Barbara Epstein's *The Politics of Domesticity: Women, Evangelism, and Temperance in Nineteenth Century America* (Middletown, CT: Wesleyan UP, 1981) and Ruth Bordin's *Woman and Temperance: The Quest for Power and Liberty, 1873–1900* (Philadelphia: Temple UP, 1981).

Bordin emphasizes the empowerment women gained from the temperance movement. The WCTU, ably led by Frances Willard, "represented the largest and most geographically widespread body of women to acquire political action skills in the history of the republic to that date."[9] In a complementary vein, Barbara Epstein argues that the temperance movement allowed women to engage in a symbolic politics—without betraying their socialization as women. If drinking was a ritual of masculine identity, what better way to register one's protest against patriarchy and one's exclusion from public power than to attack the barrooms and ax the barrels of liquid that, when ingested by men, led in a more or less direct spiral to loss of family wages, disruption of homes, and the continued disfranchisement of women? When women *prayed* in barrooms they were ritually reconsecrating that space to a different function, a different moral sphere, and a different sexual economy.

Rorabaugh's study of drinking in the early American republic underscores how the colonists, who had plotted sedition in the taverns of the new world, celebrated their revolution against England by downing prodigious quantities of alcohol in the belief that this was "patriotic" and "American" and "rebellious." In these symbolic and ceremonial acts, the connection between freedom (from England) and drinking was clearly articulated during this period of the early republic—to be radically inverted in the 1830s by evangelicals who campaigned against both African slavery and the slavery of drink. In either case, drinking or not drinking was directly tied to states of consciousness and ethnic and national identity. To use anthropologist Paul Antze's word, drink has a "totemic" power to confer identity.[10] Denise Herd argues persuasively that for nineteenth-century African Americans bent on self-improvement, taking the abstinence pledge was a kind of counterritual to the ritual of drinking, and established an identity separate from the "slavery" of drink.[11] The opposite connection has been observed in Native American and Irish cultures. In spite of stereotypes of drunken Indians and the deliberate use of alcohol by Euro-Americans to undermine their indigenous culture, some Native Americans have embraced drinking as a self-conscious way to embrace their ethnic identity. Many Irish-Americans have done the same. One has only to think of St. Patrick's Day cards, with their bleary-eyed leprechauns two sheets to the wind, genially grinning from the card racks of drugstores. These cards are purchased by Americans of Irish descent and sent to others of Irish descent in a celebration of their Irishness. My parents had a plaque in their kitchen that read, "An Irishman is never drunk if he can still hold on to a blade of grass and not fall off the face of the earth." In Irish culture, drink was "a good man's failing."[12]

The materials dealing with Irish drinking patterns had a particular salience for me and for many students of Irish background in the class. As I critically examined the culture I came from, I experienced some of the same wonderment and discovery that had made women's studies such a powerful experience for me in the 1970s. Like many white ethnic Americans whose families have been in this country for five generations or more, I was not really aware of having an ethnicity. I knew I was Irish and Catholic, but I didn't know *what* in my experience could be attributed to that and what was simply "American" or "universal." (To adapt phrasing from Maxine Hong Kingston's *Woman Warrior*, I didn't know what was Irish, what was Irish-American, and what was the movies.) But I did know that alcohol figured prominently in my family history. My mother's father was an alcoholic and died when I was twelve. He was a shadowy figure compared to my indomitable grandmother, who continued into her seventies to drive by herself from Illinois to California in her 1954 Chevy, "Arabella," and lived to almost ninety-eight. My mother's brother was a reformed alcoholic and a member of A.A. In a now-classic pattern, my mother married a heavy drinker, unaware that this was the case. That never changed. What changed was that my mother drank increasing quantities of beer—as a sedative to help her sleep. However, I never thought of my family as having a problem. Going to the liquor store with my father when I was a child was a weekly ritual. He would take back the cases of empty beer bottles and bring home a fresh supply. The only thing memorable about these trips was the time he left the car running and I got behind the wheel and revved the engine; he came running out of the liquor store, but didn't scold me or even observe that anything was amiss. He never brought up unpleasant subjects and would walk out of the room if anyone else did. We had an orderly household and my brother and I were not allowed to fight. But as an adult I came to see that in my family it was "normal" to have problems with alcohol.

When I read Richard Stivers's *A Hair of the Dog*, a historical analysis of Irish-American drinking patterns, I felt as if my private life were suddenly connected to history. After a chapter comparing Scottish, Irish, and English drinking patterns (heavy) in the eighteenth and early nineteenth century, Stivers observes, "Only Ireland among the three countries preserved a culturally demanded link between drinking and male identity. That industrialism missed Ireland helps explain why the Irish variant of bourgeois morality encouraged hard drinking."[13] Stivers locates changes in Irish drinking in changes in the social structure. What emerged in this poor and land-hungry country was "a pattern of few marriages, late age at marriage, and a large number of permanent celibates." In the "stem family" only one son or daughter inherited the land. The others emigrated or were celibate. The demands of a single-inheritance agrarian economy led to what Stivers calls a devotional and puritanical Catholicism that elevated celibacy above marriage and preached against sins of the flesh. In this cultural economy, the status of marriage was low; the status of bachelorhood was high. Even married men preferred to spend their time with their buddies. The male drinking group (transported to America and transformed into the immigrant saloon culture) was a substitute for heterosexual contact. "The husband's primary obligation to his wife was to provide economically for a household wherein she would wield immense power."[14] I thought of my iron-willed mother. As if admitting a family secret, she once remarked that the Irish women were strong, the men weak. While retaining some forms of patriarchal power, Irish men certainly had little within the family. I thought of the pitched battles my husband had to wage in order to stake out space on our domestic turf. I simply assumed that it all belonged to women. Although drink is conventionally associated with disorder, I learned that living with an unsedated male meant more conflict than I had experienced growing up.

In rural Ireland, alcohol functioned in the bachelor groups as a rite of passage. "According to local opinion," Stivers writes, "a young man was initiated (into the bachelor group) when he took his first drink in the public house. This was a sign that he had grown up and was acceptable to the male community" (82). The hard-drinking ethic of the bachelor group was institutionalized in the ritual of "treating" to rounds. If six men entered a pub together, each was expected to stand for a round of drinks; if the cycle began again, it had to be completed. Treating was "a norm of equality" and a "ritual of masculine renewal." In order to be a leader one had to be able to drink hard without the outward signs of intoxication. In this culture in which "bachelor-group membership and manhood were one and the same," alcoholic patterns of drinking were the norm. Much the same patterns can be observed in Jack London's drinking memoir, *John Barleycorn*. London, the son of an itinerant Irish astrologer, describes his longing for "fellowship" in the saloons, the importance of treating, the bonds of comradeship that emerged, and the alcoholic pattern that he drank in with this culture.

American popular culture reinforces these alcoholic patterns and provides opportunities for consumers of that culture to imbibe these messages uncritically. Jean Kilbourne's video lecture, *Calling the Shots* (Cambridge Documentary Films, 1991), analyzes the subliminal messages in alcohol advertising. Citing statistics indicating that something like 10 percent of drinkers consume more than half of all alcohol, she argues that advertisers consciously target the repeat drinker—the alcoholic—in their ads. Her analysis is revealing, sobering, often chilling. Through this constant bombardment of visual images, she argues, alcoholic ways of perceiving liquor are normalized. As a preparation for viewing this, I have students bring into class an alcohol ad from a magazine and provide a one-paragraph analysis of its message. For the following class they perform the same exercise, now attempting to apply Kilbourne's analysis to the ad they had selected. They loved this assignment, partly because it seemed easy and partly because it incorporated popular culture. I liked reading it because it accomplished on a small scale what sometimes seems so hard to achieve in introductory history courses: getting them to handle original evidence in original ways. And I received some truly breathtaking analyses and a wonderful assortment of visuals.

I would also recommend another short video, *Marketing Booze to Blacks* (Washington, DC: Public Interest Video Network, 1990), a hard-hitting look at the way alcohol advertising targets the inner-city black population and showing the activist response of African Americans to this threat. These materials provoked one of the best pieces of self-reflection I received. An Irish male from a working-class Boston background wrote an essay on target marketing in which he reflected on his own drinking tastes. He wrote in response to a poster in the window of a market located in a poor, Hispanic neighborhood; it showed the rapper Ice Cube promoting St. Ide's malt liquor. He observed that his own drinks of choice, malt liquor and Cisco fortified wine, were both strong and cheap.

> For example, while regular beer has an alcohol content of 3.5%, malt liquors range from 4 percent to a staggering 5.0%. Meanwhile, Cisco (at 20%) has bumped Night Train as the wine of choice on the street, because of its potency and its price. While the potency has garnered Cisco the tag, 'Liquid Crack,' the price for a sixteen ounce bottle (which reads on the label 'Suggested Serving Four Persons'), is roughly $1.75. . . . I have heard it said that a 32 ounce bottle contains the equivalent of ten shots of vodka. Perhaps that is why Cisco has been pointed at in a number of recent alcohol related deaths.

He described the powerful effect of drinking a bottle of St. Ide's or Olde English and recalled a scene he had witnessed the previous winter in Boston. "I saw two young men sitting on a subway platform. There were two empty bottles of Cisco at their feet and they were passing a third. Throughout this they were arguing. The bigger of the two wanted to play a game called 'Touch the Third Rail.'" He reflected on his own drinking patterns and "the pushing of products that are so dramatically more potent to a specific people who are already disfranchised as it is."[15] In a journal entry, he subsequently elaborated his personal reasons for drinking malt liquor and fortified wine.

> The reasons I suppose are the potency, the cost, and the cultural significance the beverages have in my type of lifestyle. To people like me, forty ounce beers like Olde English 800 and St. Ide's have become icons. Perhaps it has something to do with the odyssey many low-income and minority people have to take through urban blight. It is this urban blight which thoroughly consumes souls, which in turn consume these strong beverages to create a

different consciousness, or try to find a way to forget. It's a type of self-destruction if you look at it in one way, but in another way, it embodies the whole "larger than life" mystique about hip-hop. From the jewelry to the cars, from the clothing styles to the hair, from the music to the guns, it's all about living large, in defiance to a circumstance designed to prevent it. In a way it is conspicuous consumption at its capitalistic worst, but wearing all that gold, the crazy clothes, and drinking a forty ounce bottle of St. Ide's with 5.9% alcohol content is a way of saying, "I'm still alive, I could die at any moment, but I don't want to live long and I'm gonna live large and hard as long as I'm here. The system is not gonna reduce me to a poor old man in a project or a triple decker house like my father."

Since personal experience is the mode, and because I rarely use the first-person pronoun in my writing (in spite of my advocacy of it in women's studies pedagogy) I may as well tell you that I conceived this course in church, during the Communion service, much as Stowe claims to have conceived *Uncle Tom's Cabin.* I suppose this qualifies it as a vision or conversion experience of some kind. The circumstances were, as I later reflected on them, incredibly suggestive and overdetermined. Not only did the idea come to me during the Communion when bread and wine were being ritually consumed, but I learned later of a circumstance that I must have been aware of but had no consciousness of at the time. During the Communion service a disruption occurred when a man who was drunk, or suffering from his own personal demons, had to be led away from the altar. (I attend a downtown church that fronts onto the center of Main Street in a town that has a significant population of homeless, many of whom suffer from the disordered mental states that are both the cause and effect of homelessness, and our church has regularly been home to them.) It was only later that I heard people talking about this. As I sing in the choir, which is seated immediately behind the altar less than fifteen feet from where this occurred, it is difficult to believe that on some level it failed to register. All I was aware of, however, was a semimeditative state in which I often find myself at Communion, when open to inner states of consciousness. There, as if on a platter, was the course that I would teach.

Only in writing this essay did I come to understand how these circumstances point toward the central underpinnings of the course: the connections between alcohol, ritual, identity, and fellowship—which likewise are often important in religion and can take on ceremonial qualities in secular contexts. I had brought to the course the unexamined assumption that alcohol is a drug with specific properties that have specific (relatively predictable) effects. In *Cere-*

monial Chemistry, Thomas Szasz powerfully challenges that view, arguing that to study drugs in isolation and attempt to determine their properties is analogous to studying holy water as if it were simply H_2O.[16] Other readings suggest that people respond to alcohol in culturally determined ways, that in some cultures people exhibit drunkenness by staggering, in others, by a different set of bodily indicators.[17] Our culturally specific ideas about alcohol shape our experience of alcohol. The evidence most interesting to the students came from a balanced-placebo experiment in which four sets of college students were given either vodka and tonic or plain tonic. One group was told they were drinking vodka but were actually given plain tonic. A second was told they were drinking vodka and actually were. A third group were told they were drinking tonic but were given vodka. A fourth were told they were drinking tonic and actually were. Then these young men and women were instructed to mix with the opposite sex. Afterward they were questioned about their level of comfort. The unexpected finding was that gender was a key variable. The men who thought they were drinking vodka (whether or not they actually were) reported feeling more confident and outgoing in their social interactions. The women who thought they were drinking vodka (whether or not they actually were) reported, by contrast, that they felt *less* secure. For both men and women, the actual alcohol content imbibed was not the key indicator. Men apparently believe that alcohol increases their social prowess, whereas women apparently feel that it makes them more vulnerable and therefore less confident. These beliefs, more powerful than the substance imbibed, point toward a conclusion the experimenters did not draw: alcohol is a symbolic substance in a sexual economy.[18]

The scientific understanding of the effect of drugs on the brain is lucidly and engagingly put forth in a video called *The Mind*, which focuses on cocaine rather than alcohol but is useful in this course. I pair it with an ethnographic and historical study by Craig Reinarman on cocaine use in the United States. Both Szasz and Reinarman question the criminalization of drugs (and we read this after looking at the debacle of Prohibition). Plumbing "the conditions under which cocaine use . . . has been perceived and sanctioned as dangerous," Reinarman points out that "[i]n the late nineteenth century the proportion of addicts in the total population was about eight times what it is today, yet its status as a social problem was perhaps eight times less." He argues that what changed was a perception of who the drug users were. In the nineteenth century, most cocaine users were middle-class white women. No one perceived them as a threat. But by 1900, he argues, cocaine was constructed as a drug dangerous in black men, who were allegedly addicted, violent, and a threat to white women. (I would add that this comes at the time when the lynching of black men had peaked and was declining, in face of active resistance by Ida B. Wells and others; a new form of social control and ideology was therefore functionally necessary if black men were to be kept in their places.) In 1914 the Harrison Act criminalized possession of cocaine and opiates, and this has not changed today in spite of contrary evidence: "even U.S. Drug Enforcement Agency figures show cocaine to be 20th on a list of drugs which have caused problems for users (behind such commonplace substances as marijuana, valium, and aspirin)."[19] Szasz and Reinarman argue that drugs are scapegoats for underlying social problems and that they create categories of social deviance into which the undesirable portion of the population can be put by the more powerful. The course had come full circle, from temperance as social control to drugs as social control.

Another historical continuity is established when we look at Alcoholics Anonymous, a self-help group that in its nonhierarchical structure replicates the highly successful nineteenth-century Washingtonians, who were likewise a voluntary society. We read *Alcoholics Anonymous*, familiarly called A.A.'s "Big Book," and I have a speaker from an alcohol treatment center make a presentation on alcohol and the family. After describing the typical roles that children in alcoholic families assume as protective devices—the perfect child, the invisible child, the rebel, the clown—she taps students for family role-playing, an exercise that is both hilarious and instructive. Several students later asked for the name of the speaker and invited her to address dorm meetings. One year she brought with her a reformed alcoholic who told her story in the manner of testimony at an A.A. meeting. That many students were familiar with A.A.'s rituals was clear when she began with the catechetical "Hello, my name is Susan and I'm an alcoholic." A quarter of the class answered back, "Hello, Susan."

Inspired by an ethnographic account of Alcoholics Anonymous by an anthropologist, I encouraged my students to do fieldwork. They had the option for one of their papers of calling up the local A.A. number to determine the nearest open meeting, attending, and then writing an ethnographic description of it—taking care to respect the anonymity of the members. (I myself had never attended a meeting of A.A. and went to one before I sent my students; I found it a very moving experience.)

Founded in 1935 during the depths of the Depression, Alcoholics Anonymous poses a model strikingly at odds with the American ideal of the self-made, self-reliant man. Their well-known Twelve Steps embody the belief that self-knowledge alone cannot control alcohol; one must give over control to a Higher Power. Yet greater self-knowledge results from their emphasis on doing what they call a "moral inventory" and their stress on honesty with oneself. This dialectic between self-abnegation and self-knowledge is a familiar spiritual pattern: self-emptying is self-filling. A.A. was in the vanguard of the twentieth-century movement to proclaim alcoholism a disease—a neutral and nonjudgmental approach that lightens the moral burden on the alcoholic. "Many do not comprehend that the Alcoholic is a very sick person," A.A. proclaimed in the forward to the 1939 edition of the Big Book (xiii)—yet their understanding of the "sickness" embodies spiritual as well as physical ailments—what the nineteenth century would call "sin." As Antze summarizes, "AA's views on this point, far from being a reflection of medical knowledge, are more properly seen as elements of a folk system with a logic and coherence of its own" (155). The personal testimonies in the Big Book read like nineteenth-century conversion narratives. As Antze points out, "AA tells the alcoholic who he is, not in the dry manner of a physician or psychologist, but by situating him in a highly dramatic predicament." Poised between two powers, A.A.'s Higher Power and the "power" of alcohol, the alcoholic experiences "sudden and profound" change, a "mountaintop" experience. The founder's story of personal redemption is called "the fourth dimension of experience . . . here sat a miracle directly across the kitchen table. He shouted great tidings."[20] The Alcoholics Anonymous Big Book can be understood as a bible. It records the shaping experiences, the early history, the stories of the converted. It is subject to revision and addition as subsequent histories are incorporated into the original stories. It is read, referred to, meditated upon as a founding text by the A.A. fellowship. "Twelfth stepping," or spreading the word, as in a religion, "is a mission of intrinsic importance, a mission which only they can perform, and which thus becomes the basis for a new sense of direction and purpose."[21]

If the fellowship of A.A. is centered around total abstinence, the brotherhood of a fraternity is constructed around the regular ingestion of large quantities of alcohol. Both organizations employ ritual to create identity and belonging and both are organized around alcohol, one by avoidance and the other by the expectation of regular consumption. We read Peggy Sanday's ethnography, *Fraternity Gang Rape*, which analyzes how masculinity is constructed in a misogynist fraternity culture in which alcohol is a weapon used against women. Drawing on case studies employing informants at several colleges, she presents powerful evidence that fraternity rituals of male bonding construct a masculine identity that explicitly constructs women as degraded objects; a continuum exists from light hazing of women at parties to homo-erotic rituals like "circle dances" to "pulling train," or gang rape.

These debauches are in stark contrast to the low-key sharing of personal stories at an A.A. meeting, but both institutions describe their conversion stories in parallel ways. I ask students to reflect on these parallels in the final exam by examining the following "jaws of death" stories and placing them in the context of the course. The first is from A.A.'s *Came to Believe . . .*

> That night I was desperately ill; I should have been in the hospital. About seven o'clock I began to phone everyone I could think of, in and out of A.A. But no one could or would come to my aid. . . . I knew I was going to die. . . .
>
> I went to bed sure I would never get up again. My thinking had never been clearer. I couldn't really see any way out. I was propped up with pillows, and my heart was pounding almost out of my chest. My limbs started turning numb—first my legs above my knees, then my arms above my elbows.
>
> I thought, "This is it!" I turned to the one source I had been too smart (as I saw it) or too stupid to appeal to earlier. I cried out, "Please God, don't let me die like this!" My tormented heart and soul were in those few words. Almost instantly the numbness started going away. I felt a Presence in the room. I wasn't alone any more.
>
> God be praised I have never felt alone since. I have never had another drink and, better still, have never needed one. . . . Somehow I know that, as long as I lived the way God wanted me to live, I need never feel fear again.[22]

The second is a description of a fraternity initiation, from Sanday's *Fraternity Gang Rape*.

> One pledge stood up and began to walk out of the circle. He was immedi-ately thrown to the ground by a couple of the brothers. One placed his sword at the throat of the pledge, and the other placed his sword at the pledge's crotch. A third brother walked over to this pledge and said:
>
>> Do you want to die? Trust is the word, pledge, trust. Do you trust me not to kill you? I'm going to drop this sword across your chest. Do you trust that I won't kill you?
>
> The pledge nodded his head yes, and the sword came crashing down on his chest. As it did the pledges screamed and turned to look away. When the sword hit him, it broke into pieces, as it was made from wood. The brother continued to speak:

You see! Trust kept you alive. The only people you have to trust is us. The fraternity will never fail you. It will always be here to protect you, to feed you, to house you, it will always welcome you. You may not be able to run to your parents or to your other friends, but you will never be turned away from this house. Remember that, always. It could save your life. You, in return, must show the fraternity that it can trust you, that you are loyal to it. You must be willing to die for it.[23]

Students have no trouble recognizing where these passages are from, and most point out the inverse nature of their relationship. Whereas the "victory" in the A.A. testimony is the overcoming of fears within the self and the reliance on a Higher Power, the movement in the fraternity initiation is submission to literal tormentors who are attempting to artificially induce fear in the pledge. In the A.A. story, a lost soul is saved; Sanday argues that in the fraternity initiation, a soul is lost, that is, the individual experiences self-abnegation and the loss of self to the group. In both, a new social identity is constructed.

Watching college skits at another institution, I was struck by how often the students invoked drinking, and not just drinking, but drunkenness. Drinking to excess seemed to be a rite of passage through which one declares one's new identity as "college student." That is what defines one's social self. It also presumably melds a diverse population into one and elides the edges of difference (except that it does not; it is, as the course materials revealed, a culturally specific rite). At a school that has a sizable Irish population, drinking as a rite of passage would receive a special cultural reinforcement by virtue of its historical association with male bachelor groups. At Trinity, however, drinking as a rite of passage, for better or worse, appears to be just as *de rigeur* for college women in the mainstream, white campus culture. Alcohol probably takes on more importance at colleges and universities where there are not other institutional rituals that create a sense of group identity. I asked students to keep a "drinking journal" for two weeks to encourage observation and reflection on their own habits and culture. Excerpts from them appeared for analysis (with permission of writers) on the final exam. Here is one of them:

> My boyfriend and his fraternity brothers usually go to a strip joint every Monday where they have 'dollar days.' In other words, all drinks are a dollar. They all think this is absolutely wonderful. Guys start going to the bar as soon as they are done with classes and by dinner time most of the guys are completely inebriated and flirting with the dancers and waitresses. While they all say they would never actually take any of the girls working there out

on an actual date, they really seem to enjoy teasing the women. They seem to do a lot of bonding when they are under the influence and around women who are seen as sex objects.

Reflective students were able to make connections between this description and the masculine culture of the fraternity described by Sanday. My hope was that the "drinking histories" with which they began the course were now passed through the alembic of critical frameworks. But I'm not sure. Lyman Beecher had the fear of hell at his command. All I had was a final exam.

Conclusion

"Drink and Disorder" went beyond my expectations in terms of reaching a broad audience and introducing them to the methodologies of history, American studies, and women's studies. Many students went on to take other courses with me and other women's studies faculty. Besides recruiting a number of women's studies minors, it yielded several majors in history and American studies, one of whom became my advisee, pursued the "integrated track on women and gender" within the history major, and became an excellent TA for "Introduction to Women's Studies." He was not only male, but a fraternity brother. More men began to sign up for "Introduction to Women's Studies," understanding that it was not a male-bashing operation. Second, "Drink and Disorder" was written up in *Connecticut Magazine* (along with courses in sailing and basket weaving) as an "unusual" course in area colleges. Finally, I learned a lot about myself through the process of examining the masculine culture of drinking. I had written a book on Jack London, but not once in that process had I pondered whether my attraction to him and the particular social and psychological contradictions of masculinity he embodied could be traced to ethnic similarities in our backgrounds. I had not yet discovered my ethnicity. Nor did I understand, until I taught this course, that my ethnicity was the source of the contradiction between my feminist principles and my domestic politics. The feminist side of my consciousness argued for equality between the sexes in the household; the Irish side of it assumed that women would be in total control. My identity as "woman" was ineluctably interwoven with the Irish family culture in which I had been raised. While I had been teaching the intersection of race, class, and gender in my women's studies courses, I had been ignorant of it in my own life. To use Toni Morrison's apt phrase, I was playing in the dark, assuming that race and ethnicity were markers that other people had.

That this awareness came from a study of the male culture of drinking verifies what women's studies has taught, that masculinity and femininity are complementary constructs that cannot be understood independently from one another. In my attempt to reach out to the Other (in this case, the male, mainstream, campus fraternity culture) I discovered that the Other was myself.

Although I did not make personal revelation part of the course (being Irish and reserved), the course had deep personal meaning for me. The complex understanding of drinking behavior that I learned from the course helped me achieve some objectivity and much-needed optimism in dealing with family members who were struggling with alcohol. I know that a number of students were experiencing similar connections between their familial experience and the course materials. One woman who had done mediocre, C-level work in this and another class wrote a splendid essay in response to the presentation about children of alcoholics. She wrote that she had always been the perfect child in her alcoholic family, pushing herself to get good grades and excel in everything she did. She was now experimenting, she said, with what it meant to not *have* to succeed. Whether she knew this about herself before the class, she was able to combine the academic and the personal in a well-argued analysis that, for the moment, overcame the contradictions of her experience. This is what women's studies pedagogy does at its best.

Appendix A

History 215: Drink and Disorder in America
Joan Hedrick

GROUP HISTORY

This is an exercise designed to explore commonalities of our experience.

1. The class will divide into groups of 4–5.
2. Each group will meet once outside of class for a minimum of one and a half hours. Each individual in the group will bring to that group meeting a sheet of paper on which you will have noted the following:

   a. The *most recent* experience you have had with alcohol
   b. Your *most historically significant* experience with alcohol, i.e., an event, happening, epiphany that was for you an important milestone
   c. The *earliest* time in your childhood that you became aware of alcohol.

Be sure to begin with the present and work backwards. In each case note your approximate age.

3. At the group meeting, individuals will share their histories with the small group, explaining the meaning that each of the three historical moments had for them.

Before beginning, select a group leader whose tasks are 1) to make sure everyone has ample opportunity to tell their stories; 2) to lead the ensuing discussion; 3) to report back to the class.

Discussion: After everyone has presented their stories, explore these questions: What commonalities in our experiences have emerged? Are these commonalities great enough that we can abstract a "group history" from the individual stories?

4. Each individual will hand in two pages: one page on which the three historical events are noted and a one-page reflection on the meaning of those events (to be written *after* the small group meaning).

5. The group leader will, in consultation with her group, prepare a group history (and/or report on difficulties in arriving at same) to be presented orally to the class.

Appendix B

Joan Hedrick   Trinity College
Seabury 12–F   Fall, 1996
Office Hours: T-TR 2:40–4:00
                 or by appointment

History 215
American Studies 215, Women's Studies 215

DRINK AND DISORDER IN AMERICA

Looking at alcohol as a symbolic and culturally contested substance, this course asks questions such as: How has our understanding of drunkenness/alcoholism changed over time? What associations does drinking have with power and identity? How do gender and ethnicity enter into this? Why do people drink, and drink to excess? What cultural and psychological meanings are attached to drinking? Are there class, ethnic, and gender differences in drinking patterns and behaviors? Why does heavy drinking or temperance prevail at a given historical period? In what ways has alcohol been seen as a threat to social order? What have been the motivations of temperance reformers? What strategies have been most effective in promoting temperance and sobriety? What strategies have alcohol manufacturers used to promote their wares? What do patterns of drinking and temperance tell us about American culture?

Books

The following books are on reserve and available for purchase in the bookstore:

William Rorabaugh, *The Alcoholic Republic* (New York: Oxford UP, 1979).

Norman Clark, *Deliver Us from Evil: An Interpretation of American Prohibition* (New York: W. W. Norton, 1976).

Jack London, *John Barleycorn: Alcoholic Memoirs* (New York: Oxford UP, 1989).

Alcoholics Anonymous, 3d ed. (New York: Alcoholics Anonymous World Services, 1976).

Charles Jackson, *The Lost Weekend* (New York: Carroll and Graf, 1983).

Peggy Sanday, *Fraternity Gang Rape: Sex, Brotherhood, and Privilege on Campus* (New York: New York UP, 1990).

You will also be asked to purchase a packet of primary documents and materials.

Requirements: 1 quiz, 2 papers, 4 exercises, mid-term and final exams.

Syllabus

Sept. 5   Introduction

Sept. 10   Rorabaugh, *The Alcoholic Republic*, Preface and Chs. 1–3, 5–92.

Sept. 12   Rorabaugh, *The Alcoholic Republic*, Chs. 4–6, 95–183.

Sept. 17   Lyman Beecher, *Six Sermons on Intemperance* (Boston, 1827), 5–23, 61–73.

Denise Herd, "The Paradox of Temperance: Blacks and the Alcohol Question in Nineteenth-Century America," in Susanna Barrows and Robin Room, *Drinking, Behavior and Belief in Modern History* (Berkeley, 1991), 354–75. On reserve.

PAPER DUE FROM ⅓ OF CLASS: STUDENTS A–G.

Sept. 19   Gusfield, *Symbolic Crusade: Status Politics and the American Temperance Movement* (U. of Ill., 1963), Ch. 2, pp. 36–60. Reserve.

Rorabaugh, *Alcoholic Republic*, Ch. 7, 187–222.

Clark, *Deliver Us from Evil*, Chs. 1 and 3, 1–13, 25–44.

PAPER DUE FROM ⅓ OF CLASS: STUDENTS H–Q.

GROUP HISTORIES DUE

Sept. 24   Michael Kimmel, *Manhood in America: A Cultural History* (New York, Free Press, 1996), pp. 13–59. On Reserve.

Edgar Allan Poe, "The Black Cat."

PAPER DUE FROM ⅓ OF CLASS: STUDENTS R–Z.

Sept. 26   Jed Dannenbaum, *Drink and Disorder: Temperance Reform in Cincinnati from the Washingtonian Revival to the WCTU* (Urbana, 1984), Ch. 2, 32–68. Reserve.

Oct. 1   Barbara Epstein, *The Politics of Domesticity: Women, Evangelism and Temperance in Nineteenth Century America* (Middletown, CT, 1981), Ch. 4, 89–114. Reserve.

Elizabeth Cady Stanton, "Appeal for the Maine Law."

Clark, *Deliver Us from Evil*, Ch. 4, 45–67.

QUIZ

Oct. 3   Barbara Epstein, *The Politics of Domesticity*, Ch. 5 and "Conclusion," 115–151. Reserve.

Oct. 8   Frances Ellen Watkins Harper, "The WCTU and the Colored Woman," "The Drunkard's Child," and "The Two Offers," in Frances Foster, *A Brighter Coming Day: A Frances Ellen Watkins Harper Reader* (New York: The Feminist Press, 1990).

Oct. 10   Richard Stivers, *A Hair of the Dog: Irish Drinking and American Stereotype* (University Park, PA, 1976), 75–100, 125–131. Reserve.

Reading Week

Oct. 22   London, *John Barleycorn*, Chs. 1–21.

Oct. 24   London, *John Barleycorn*, Chs. 22–39.

Oct. 29   Mid-term Exam

Oct. 31   Clark, *Deliver Us from Evil*, Chs. 6–8, 92–180.

In-class film: "The Untouchables"

Nov. 5   Craig Reinarman, "Moral Entrepreneurs and Political Economy: Historical and Ethnographic Notes on the Construction of the Cocaine Menace," *Contemporary Crises* 3(1979), 225–334. Reserve.

Nov. 7   *Alcoholics Anonymous*, pp. xi–164.

Nov. 12   *Alcoholics Anonymous*, 171–312, and three stories each from "They Stopped in Time" and "They Lost Nearly All."
          Guest lecturer on alcohol and the family.

Nov. 14   Ernest Hemingway, "A Clean, Well Lighted Place."
          Paul Antze, "Symbolic Action in Alcoholics Anonymous," in Mary Douglas, ed. *Constructive Drinking* (Cambridge, 1987), 149–181 (handout).
          PAPER DUE FROM ½ OF THE CLASS: STUDENTS A–N, 2–3pp.

Nov. 19   Jackson, *The Lost Weekend*, Parts 1–3.

Nov. 21   Jackson, *The Lost Weekend*, Parts 4–6.
          BEGIN KEEPING JOURNAL.
          PAPER DUE, ½ OF CLASS: STUDENTS O–Z, 2–3pp.

Nov. 26   Herbert Fingarette, *Heavy Drinking: The Myth of Alcohol as a Disease* (Berkeley, 1988), Chs. 2–3, 31–69. Reserve.
          In-class film: "The Mind"

Dec. 3   Adam Paul Weisman, "I Was a Drug-Hype Junkie," *New Republic* 195 (October 6, 1986): 14–17. Hand-out.
          In-class film: Jean Kilbourne, "Advertising Alcohol: Calling the Shots."
          Exercise due.

Dec. 5   Begin reading Sanday, *Fraternity Gang Rape*
          In-class film: "Marketing Booze to Blacks."
          Exercise due.

Dec. 10   Sanday, *Fraternity Gang Rape*.
          JOURNALS DUE.

Dec. 12   Sanday, *Fraternity Gang Rape*.

Dec. 17   FINAL EXAM

Notes

1. Here the emphasis is on "mainstream." In recent years "men's studies" courses and studies of masculinity have charted a new field within gender studies. This course does not pretend to be so overtly focused on gender and masculinity.

2. Norman Clark, *Deliver Us from Evil: An Interpretation of American Prohibition* (New York: Norton, 1976), 28.

3. This in turn was adapted from an exercise that David Ruhmkorff, a consultant to troubled educational institutions, used to discover the historical fault lines of the organizations he was consultant to. I am grateful to him for introducing me to an excellent teaching tool.

4. The work of Denise Herd confirms this. See Denise Herd, "Drinking by Black and White Women: Results from a National Survey," *Social Problems* 35 (December 1988), 493–505; Denise Herd, "Subgroup Differences in Drinking Patterns Among Black and White Men: Results from a National Survey," *Journal of Studies on Alcohol* 51 (May 1990): 221–32.

5. W. J. Rorabaugh, *The Alcoholic Republic: An American Tradition* (New York: Oxford UP, 1979), appendix A1.1.

6. Joseph Gusfield, *Symbolic Crusade: Status Politics and the American Temperance Movement* (Urbana: U of Illinois P, 1963).

7. Karen Halttunen, "Gothic Imagination and Social Reform: The Haunted Houses of Lyman Beecher, Henry Ward Beecher, and Harriet Beecher Stowe," in Eric J. Sundquist, *New Essays on Uncle Tom's Cabin* (Cambridge: Cambridge UP, 1986).

8. Clark, *Deliver Us from Evil*, 34.

9. Bordin, *Woman and Temperance*, 56.

10. Paul Antze, "Symbolic Action in Alcoholics Anonymous," in Mary Douglas, ed., *Constructive Drinking* (Cambridge and New York: Cambridge UP, 1987), 150.

11. Denise Herd, "The Paradox of Temperance: Blacks and the Alcohol Question in Nineteenth-Century America," in Susanna Barrows and Robin Room, *Drinking: Behavior and Belief in Modern History* (Berkeley: U of California P, 1991), 354–75.

12. Richard Stivers, *A Hair of the Dog: Irish Drinking and American Stereotype* (University Park: Penn State UP, 1976), 94.

13. Ibid., 34.

14. Ibid., 71.

15. Paul Murphy, "Within the Cross-hairs of Target Marketing," unpublished paper, April 15, 1992.

16. Thomas Szasz, *Ceremonial Chemistry: The Ritual Persecution of Drugs, Addicts, and Pushers* (Garden City, NY: Anchor Press, 1974).

17. Craig MacAndrew and Robert B. Edgerton, *Drunken Comportment: A Social Explanation* (London, 1969); Clark, *Deliver Us from Evil.*

18. Alan R. Lang, *Alcohol: Teenage Drinking* (New York: Chelsea House, 1985), vol. 4 in *The Encyclopedia of Psychoactive Drugs*, gen. ed. Solomon H. Snyder, 66–83.

19. Craig Reinarman, "Moral Entrepreneurs and Political Economy: Historical and Ethnographic Notes on the Construction of the Cocaine Menace," *Contemporary Crises* 3(1979): 225–354. The quotations are on pp. 238 and 246.

20. Antze, "Symbolic Action in Alcoholics Anonymous," 154; Alcoholics Anonymous World Services, *Alcoholics Anonymous: The Story of How Many Thousands of Men*

and Women Have Recovered from Alcoholism, 3d ed. (New York: Alcoholics Anonymous World Services, 1976), 14, 8, 11.

21. Antze, "Symbolic Action in Alcoholics Anonymous," 167.

22. *Came to Believe* . . . (New York: A.A. World Services, 1973), 14, as quoted in Antze, "Symbolic Action in Alcoholics Anonymous," p. 161.

23. Sanday, *Fraternity Gang Rape: Sex, Brotherhood, and Privilege on Campus* (New York: New York UP, 1990), 162.

Notes on Contributors

JOHN W. CROWLEY is professor and former chair of English at Syracuse University. His books include two studies of W. D. Howells—*The Black Heart's Truth* (University of North Carolina Press, 1985), and *Masks of Fiction* (University of Massachusetts Press, 1989)—as well as *The White Logic: Alcoholism and Gender in American Modernist Fiction* (University of Massachusetts Press, 1994). Among the books he has edited are *The Haunted Dusk: American Supernatural Fiction, 1820–1920* (University of Georgia Press, 1983); *New Essays on Winesburg, Ohio* (Cambridge University Press, 1990); Roger Austen's *Genteel Pagan: The Double Life of Charles Warren Stoddard* (University of Massachusetts Press, 1991); Charles Jackson's *The Sunnier Side*; and Howell's *The Rise of Silas Lapham*. He has also published numerous essays on an array of American writers.

JOAN D. HEDRICK is professor of history and director of women's studies at Trinity College in Hartford, Connecticut. Her publications include *Solitary Comrade: Jack London and His Work* (University of North Carolina Press, 1982) and *Harriet Beecher Stowe: A Life* (Oxford University Press, 1994), which won the 1995 Pulitzer Prize for Biography.

ROBERT S. LEVINE is professor of English at the University of Maryland. He is the author of *Conspiracy and Romance: Studies in Brockden Brown, Cooper, Hawthorne, and Melville* (Cambridge University Press, 1989) and *Martin Delany, Frederick Douglass, and the Politics of Representative Identity* (Cambridge University Press, 1997). He is the editor of the forthcoming *The Cambridge Companion to Herman Melville* and *"Stand Still and See the Salvation": A Martin R. Delany Reader.* Currently he is working on a Bedford Cultural edition of William Wells Brown's *Clotel.*

EDMUND O'REILLY is an independent scholar currently living in London. He is the author of *Sobering Tales: Narratives of Alcoholism and Recovery* (University of Massachusetts Press, 1997).

DAVID S. REYNOLDS is Distinguished Professor of American Literature and American Studies at Baruch College and the Graduate School of the City University of New York. He is the author of *Walt Whitman's America: A Cultural Biography* (Knopf, 1995), winner of the Bancroft Prize and the Ambassador Book Award and a National Book Critics Circle Award finalist. His study *Beneath the American Renaissance: The Subversive Imagination in the Age of Emerson and Melville* (Knopf, 1988) won the Christian Gauss Award. His other publications include *Faith in Fiction: The Emergence of Religious Literature in America* (Harvard University Press, 1981); *George Lippard* (G.K. Hall, 1982); *George Lippard, Prophet of Protest: Writings of an American Radical* (Peter Lang, 1986); an edition of Lippard's novel *The Quaker City* (University of Massachusetts Press, 1995), as well as numerous articles and reviews.

DEBRA J. ROSENTHAL teaches in the Department of Modern Languages and Literature at Case Western Reserve University and in the English department at Kent State University.

KAREN SÁNCHEZ-EPPLER, associate professor of American studies and English at Amherst College, is the author of *Touching Liberty: Abolition, Feminism, and the Politics of the Body* (California University Press, 1993). She is currently writing a book on how the figure of the child serves to produce and enforce social norms.

DAVID S. SHIELDS, professor of American literature at The Citadel, is the author of *Oracles of Empire: Poetry, Politics, and Commerce in British America* (University of Chicago Press, 1990), and *Civil Tongues and Polite Letters in British America* (University of North Carolina Press, 1997). He is also the executive coordinator of the Society of Early Americanists.

NICHOLAS O. WARNER is professor of English and comparative literature at Claremont McKenna College. His publications include *Spirits of America: Forms of Intoxication in Antebellum American Literature* (University of Oklahoma Press, 1997).

Index